H. D. Scott

SIX MONTHS IN ITALY.

SIX MONTHS

IN

ITALY.

BY

GEORGE STILLMAN HILLARD.

IN TWO VOLUMES.

VOL. I.

Third Edition.

BOSTON:
TICKNOR, REED, AND FIELDS.
MDCCCLIV.

THURSTON, TORRY, AND EMERSON, PRINTERS.

TO

MR. AND MRS. CRAWFORD,

OF ROME,

THESE MEMORIALS OF A LAND, THE IMAGE OF

WHICH IS FOREVER ASSOCIATED WITH RECOLLECTIONS OF

THEIR KINDNESS AND HOSPITALITY,

ARE GRATEFULLY AND AFFECTIONATELY INSCRIBED

BY THE AUTHOR.

PREFACE.

THE following pages have been prepared in intervals snatched from the grasp of an engrossing profession. They contain the records of a brief and brilliant episode in my life, which filled my memory with images alike beautiful and enduring. They are printed in the belief, or at least the hope, that those who have visited the same scenes will not regret to have their impressions renewed, and that those who are looking forward to Italy, as to a land of promise, will find here some hints and suggestions which may aid them in their preparation.

G. S. H.

BOSTON, AUGUST, 1853.

TABLE OF CONTENTS.

VOL. I.

THE ROMAN NUMERALS ON THE LEFT REFER TO THE CHAPTERS.

CHAPTER I.

First Sight of Italy — The Simplon — Domo d'Ossola — The Borommean Islands — The Lake of Como — Milan — The Cathedral – The Ambrosian Library — The 'Last Supper' of Leonardo da Vinci — The Brera Gallery — Theatre of the Fantoccini — The Stelvio.

FIRST SIGHT OF ITALY.

My first sight of Italy was on the second day of September, 1847. The night — or rather a segment of it, for our journey began at three in the morning — had been passed at Brieg, a post-town on the Simplon; and the morning light played upon the sublime scenery which will be so readily recalled by those who have passed over that remarkable road. The Bernese Alps were girdled with clouds, but their snowy heads reposed in serene sunshine. The air was full of the exulting sound of mountain streams, the only voice that broke the silence of these majestic solitudes. In the highest portion of the ascent, the desolate grandeur of the scene falls upon the mind with a feeling akin to terror; and the milder aspect of the region which the descent reveals is welcomed like light after darkness.

Few scenes in Europe are more impressive than the gorge of Gondo. The dizzy plunge of the snow-white torrent, the steep dark rocks of slate crested with trees, and the thread-like stream winding away far below over its pebbly bed, derive new beauty and significance from the work of human skill which enables the traveller to observe them so safely and so completely. The emotions awakened by such elevating scenes are not disturbed by the portion of admiration claimed by the genius and the enterprise of man. God's noblest work is the human mind, and never do we feel this more forcibly than when we see its useful and magnificent efforts brought into comparison and contrast with the grandeur of nature.

At Isella, on the Sardinian frontier, the traveller's trunks are examined, one of those trifling vexations which are here more sensibly felt, because they bring down the thoughts so rudely from the serene heights into which they have been recently lifted. He who has seen the hands of a custom-house officer disembowelling his trunk can hardly help praying for another Theseus to rid the earth of this brood of monsters, the rank growth of modern civilization. However, the discipline is not without a seasoning of the ludicrous, if a sense of security permits one to enjoy it. Juvenal's line

'Cantabit vacuus coram latrone viator,'

is applicable to these chartered robbers, who hold commissions to fleece the wayfaring man. The traveller whose trunk is innocent of tobacco and Geneva trinkets may smile at the embarrassments of his neighbor, with the tranquil feeling of the philosopher in Lucretius who contemplates from the firm land the vessel tossing on the angry wave.

As the day declined, the character of the scenery underwent a gradual change. The chestnut and fig began to appear: the many-twinkling maize rustled in the breeze: the vine flung its arms along the trellis, and hung its purple clusters in the cool green shadows beneath. Little villages, with square bell-towers, dotted the distant heights: white flat-roofed houses gleamed through their sheltering walls of foliage. A softer air blew against the face, and the eye reposed on gentler outlines. All these were tokens that we were approaching Italy.

Just before sunset, the diligence reached Domo d'Ossola, and we remained there nearly an hour; our conductor having thus early caught the infection of needless delay, which is so prevalent an infirmity in Italy. Here every thing is Italian in its aspect. The houses are built with colonnades, and the shops are sheltered with awnings. The inn is constructed round a court-yard, into which the rooms open. The people are lounging, dirty, and picturesque, with brown cheeks and flashing eyes. I bought some grapes and figs of an old woman in the market-place: any where else I should have pronounced them very bad, but here they tasted of Italy and not of themselves.

For some hours our journey was continued after nightfall, and I experienced one of the small trials of the traveller, in seeing the shadows of evening steal over that living page of the landscape, of which the eye was reluctant to lose a single line. Nor was the moon, when she rose, a compensating presence, for her light, so magical when thrown over familiar scenes, becomes a bewildering and tantalizing element in connection with strange objects, since it suggests more than it reveals, and tempts the eye to efforts which end always in disappointment. It was a pleasant assurance conveyed by a broad sheet of silver, on the left, stretching away to the horizon, that we had approached the shores of the Lago Maggiore. We reached Baveno at a late hour, and it was not until after midnight that the various excitements of a long and crowded day were forgotten in repose.

THE BORROMEAN ISLANDS.

The next morning rose in unclouded beauty, and the early sun threw upon the smooth lake the dark shadows of the enclosing mountains. After breakfast, we took a boat and were rowed over to the Borromean islands. We formed quite a polyglot party. There were, besides myself, two Russians — noble-looking young men, full of the air of command, whose quiet and distinguished bearing every where exacted an unforced deference — a German student and a French savant, doubtless learned and accomplished persons, but who might have been much improved by a judicious application of cold water and clean linen — and two Englishmen, members of the legal profession, intelligent, well-bred, and well-informed, but with less susceptibility than even the generality of their countrymen to the influences of fine weather, fine scenery, and interesting localities. Our boat was of large size, manned by several men, most of whom rowed standing, with their backs to the prow. In about half an hour we reached the little landing-place at Isola Bella, and were immediately conducted over the palace by a servant who met us on the piazza.

It is not necessary to speak with any minuteness of a palace so generally visited by travellers and so often described in print. To me it was mainly interesting as being the first house I had ever seen which was southern in its character, and meant to guard against heat and not cold. The spacious rooms, the lofty ceilings, the uncarpeted floors covered with a composition like stone, and the small amount of furniture, all were suggestive of a climate in which the sun was avoided as an enemy, not wooed as a friend. Space and shade are the luxuries of warm latitudes. I saw several pictures of no great merit, none of which were so interesting to me as two fine drawings by the present Countess Borromeo, which were framed and hung in one of the rooms. Below ground, is a suite of singular apartments of rough stone or rubble work, with cases containing imitations of fruit and mushrooms, in wax. The large building in the centre, connecting the two wings, is unfinished, not being even covered with a roof.

The well known gardens attached to this palace have been the subject of conflicting opinions. I cannot but think that this must be owing, partly to the varying moods of health and feeling in which travellers have seen them, and partly to the accidents of weather. A rainy day, an ill-digested breakfast, a sleepless night, a disagreeable companion, turn every thing to gloom, and make the senses themselves unfaithful witnesses. Bathed, as I saw them, in brilliant sunshine and covered by the brightest and bluest of skies, one must have been very unreasonable not to have found something to admire. True, the artificial is every where prominent, and we need not the guide-book to tell us that the bare rock has been, with infinite pains and expense, cut, terraced, and smoothed, and thus changed into elaborate bloom and beauty. But give nature a place to stand upon, and she cannot be entirely subdued by art. An orange-tree in a box is still a tree, and even a yew cut into the shape of St. George and the dragon is more of a growth than a manufacture. Thus, in these gardens, whilst we were constantly reminded of man's intrusive hand by vases, balustrades, and statues, yet long, verdurous walls of lemon-trees starred with pearly blossoms, rich thickets of oleander crowned with spikes of pink waving in the breeze like flames of fire, clumps of laurel, cypress, and myrtle, and a wilderness of 'plebian underwood,' nameless to my uninstructed eye, suggested the creative energies of nature, mysterious alike in the mountain cliff and in the flower that grows in its shadow. The rarest and finest forms of vegetable life have been drawn from their distant and scattered homes and brought together in this harmonizing spot, a graceful and appropriate homage to the peace and beauty that seem to make an atmosphere over the island. The tea-plant, the camphor-tree, luxuriant hydrangeas, caper vines, aloes and cactuses, pines from China and Japan, and the magnolia from our own country grow fearlessly in the open air, like children of the soil. In one place, over the entrance to a sort of natural cave, there hung a long green pendulum, formed of the intertwisted leaves and fibres of the ivy, symmetrical in shape, and as large round as a delicate waist, presenting, both in its color and waving movement, a most agreeable contrast to the gray wall of rock against which it was suspended. Over the whole scene, a certain indescribable air of tropical languor and luxuriance was thrown: the spirit of Italy seemed condensed into a powerful essence and poured round the spot. The intense odor of the orange and lemon blossoms which every where pierced to the brain recalled the passionate poetry of Romeo and Juliet, and the hues and forms of the flowers and shrubs, the many-colored pages of Ariosto. When, from the highest point, all this fairy world of bloom and verdure was taken in, and when, on raising the eye, the fine forms of the mountains which enclosed the lake were seen — the distant snowy peaks of the Alps, adding an alien but not inharmonious element of sternness and sublimity to the softness of the foreground — one must have been very insensible or very fastidious, not to have dropped the defences of criticism, and yielded himself without reserve to the genius of the place.

The Isola Madre also belongs to the Borromeo family. Here is a garden, in some respects finer than that on the Isola Bella, because more natural. Oranges and lemons grow with the greatest profusion and luxuriance. The walnut, the bay, and the pine form those shady caverns of foliage, so grateful in the summer heat of a warm climate; and a tangled undergrowth of shrubbery imitates the intricacy of one of our own virgin woods. Pheasants and other birds of gay plumage are kept in spacious apartments, walled and roofed with wire.

From Lago Maggiore to Cadenabbia, on the Lake of Como, my progress left little to record. I remember with pleasure the decent inn at Luino, with its pretty garden in the rear, overshadowed with patriarchal limes, and, in front, on the edge of the lake, a row of venerable aspens, whose leaves, in a day of breathless calm, suggested the breeze which they did not feel. The situation of Lugano, on the borders of the lake of the same name, whose waters bathe the feet of steep mountains covered with vines, villas, and forest trees, leaves a picture upon the memory not easily effaced. The contrast between the dirty and comfortless inn at which I passed the night, and a very handsome town-hall recently erected and quite encrusted with Latin inscriptions, shewed that the town was Italian in character, though belonging to Switzerland. It would be difficult in New England to find so handsome a public building, or so uninviting an inn. Such are the inconsistencies of Italian civilization!

THE LAKE OF COMO.

The excellent inn at Cadenabbia is a good resting-place for one who wishes to observe at some leisure the beauties of the Lake of Como, a region so lovely that it seems the realization of a poet's dream. To the sinuous form of the lake it may be objected, that it is too much like a river and too little like a lake. But no river winds along such banks as these. Steep and precipitous in form, richly cultivated, glittering with white villas, garlanded with vines, and crowned with forest-trees, they fill the mind with images alike of beauty and grandeur. At every moment of the steamer's progress, magic combinations of scenery were revealed, which seemed like the delusions of the stage. It all appeared to be made of something finer than common earth. The crew of the little steamer, with their smart caps, nice blue shirts, striped trowsers, and rich red sashes, prolonged the illusion, and looked as if they were going upon the stage to sing a chorus in Masaniello. Under such dreamy influences, it was easy to people the wooded banks with satyrs and buskined wood-nymphs, and to listen to the sound of visionary horns.

Cadenabbia is a mere handful of houses, so close upon the waters of the lake that their soothing ripple is the musical accompaniment to all sounds and thoughts. At a short distance from the inn is the villa Somariva. A pretty fountain plays before the principal entrance. In the hall is the celebrated frieze by Thorwaldsen, representing the triumphs of Alexander, a work worthy of the best days of Grecian art; also a Palamedes and a Cupid and Psyche by Canova, which do not bear the comparison provoked by their proximity. The tendency to the meretricious observable in the latter group is rebuked by the simple and majestic genius of the great Scandinavian. There are many pictures also in the villa, but none of conspicuous merit; some very indifferent specimens being judiciously placed in what in a common house would be called the garret. One of the bedrooms had a pretty fresco on the ceiling — Narcissus viewing his face in the fountain — a pleasant object to open one's eyes upon in the morning.

In the afternoon, when fast approaching a state of

unconsciousness, my attention was roused by a storm of what seemed to me angry voices. On looking out of the window, I saw a group of men, in a half-slovenly, half-picturesque costume which every body who has seen a pictorial annual recognises as Italian, eagerly engaged in the classical game of mora. This game is played by two persons, who place themselves opposite to each other, and each, at the same moment, throws out his right hand with a certain number of fingers extended, and a certain number closed or shut upon the palm ; and each player, as the hand descends, shrieks out the number made by adding his antagonist's open fingers to his own. Each one, of course, knows how many fingers he extends himself, but those of his adversary must be caught during the lightning descent of his hand. He who names the right number makes a point in the game. When both are right or both wrong, it is a tie and no point is made. The fingers of the left hand, which is held back, serve to mark the points. This is a popular game all over Italy, suiting, as it does, the indolent habits and passionate temperament of the people. Simple as it seems, it requires great quickness of eye to play it well, and there are degrees of excellence among players, as in whist or cricket. The speaking gestures, animated movements, and flashing eyes of the players made the group an exciting picture. The life of the Italians is a prolonged childhood, and they put into their amusements all the heartiness and vivacity of children. This is rather a dangerous game, as the rapid movements of the hands lead to differences of opinion, which easily kindle the combustible temperament of the people into a blaze of strife. Among the fervid and passionate Romans, the knife is often used for the decision of such disputes.

Three days upon the Italian lakes, a period far too short, were enough however to stamp enduring impressions upon the memory. Florence and Rome exert their powerful attraction over the traveller, as soon as he puts his foot upon the soil of Italy; but let him resist their spell awhile and linger around these magic shores. He will find nothing more beautiful till he comes to Naples. Indeed, these lakes bear the same relation to the rest of Italy that Italy itself does to the rest of Europe. All that is most characteristic of the scenery of the country is here found in the highest perfection. Mountains precipitous in form and grand in outline, the foreground smoothed and softened by the richest cultivation, white villas peeping through the twinkling foliage of the vine, the maize, the olive, and the chestnut, make such combinations as the artist loves; while in the terraced gardens, the hedges of myrtle and the walls of orange and lemon plead, and not in vain, in behalf of the formal and artificial horticulture which they embellish. The people that dwell around these lakes seem of so soft and pliant mould, finding their life in agreeable sensations rather than resolute effort; roused from their repose by the flash of passion rather than the spur of enterprise. All these impressions are the more vivid from their contrast with those gleaned in Switzerland, whose snowy mountains tower in the distant background. There nature is seen in its stern, sublime, and appalling aspects. The traveller's satisfactions are associated with toil and endurance. He must earn all that he gets: he must pant up the sides of the mountain till his knees knock together and his head swims with fatigue: he must cross the slippery glacier: he must brave the cold of icy summits and sleep in lonely chalets. But a day's journey throws him at once upon the lap of the warm south, where he becomes a mere passive recipient of agreeable sensations. There is nothing to struggle for, and no price to be paid for the best part of what he receives. Reclining in a boat, sitting in the balcony of his inn, or stretched listlessly upon the grass under a spreading chestnut, an enchanting picture is ever before him. Such scenes, such influences, are not nurses of the manly virtues. Neither sturdy enterprise nor heroic valor has taken root among these vines and myrtles. They find a more congenial soil among Alpine pines and in the sands of Holland. The annals of the Italian lakes shew no names like those of Tell and Fürst, and the moral charm which exalts and dignifies the sublime shores of the Lake of Lucerne sheds no ideal gleam around the fairy waves of Como.

MILAN.

Four days in a city so large and so full of interest as Milan leave little to record and not much to remember. The attention is distracted and the mind overborne by the multitude of impressions which are crowded into so brief a space, and the memory, in looking back, is like a painter's palette — a mass of colors without form or outline.

The stranger in Milan naturally hurries to the celebrated cathedral, a structure the merits and demerits of which require an architectural eye to comprehend and interpret. I can only say that its exterior was somewhat disappointing. When we hear of a building of white marble, we expect something more overpowering and dazzling than any reality can be. Built, as the cathedral has been, at wide intervals of time, its surface presents different shades of color, which disturb the simplicity and uniformity that so large a mass requires. From the nature of a material so tempting to the chisel, there results a crowd of detail which, in like manner, impairs the general impression. It seems like a piece of jewellers' work magnified a million of times. Stone which does not attract attention to its color and surface seems best adapted to carry out the idea of Gothic architecture. Viewing the Milan cathedral from a distance, it struck me as wanting height in proportion to its breadth.

The interior, always excepting the disingenuous trick of the painted ceiling, called forth only unqualified admiration. The spirit of criticism falls prostrate and powerless before the visible sublime, embodied in such massive pillars, in a roof so airy and majestic, all shrouded in that dim, religious light which hallows every object upon which it falls. Surely, if we could bring home but one thing from Europe, that one thing should be a cathedral. It is not merely size and height, or elaborate details, or shrines blazing with gold and silver, or windows that arrest and fix all the changing hues of sunset, that give to these structures their power and significance. The impression which they make cannot be communicated by description or transferred to a picture. A spirit hangs over them which illumines what is dark, and raises and supports what is low. Their shadows are healing to the soul, as that of St. Peter was to the body. In their majestic presence, the natural language of the heart becomes thanksgiving and aspiration.

Happy are they whose faith needs no such appliances; who feel the overshadowing presence of God alike in solitude or society, upon the mountain-top, in the market-place, in the tasteless parish church, and around the domestic hearth. But with most of us the world is too much present. Its cares engross, its pleasures intoxicate, its sorrows and disappointments oppress us. Few are the moments in which our spirits lie exposed to the highest of influences, neither darkened by despair nor giddy through self-confidence nor inflamed by earth-born passions. For natures conscious of inward struggle, of wings that are often clogged and sometimes paralyzed, these glorious structures were reared. Their walls and spaces seem yet instinct with the love and faith that laid the stones and carved the saints; and transient and soon effaced as the impressions which they leave may be, they are yet aids and allies which he who is most conscious of his weakness will be the most grateful for.

The most striking part of the Milan cathedral is the outside of the roof. The great extent of the building is more justly estimated there than from any part of the interior, and the eye and mind are overpowered by the multitude of architectural details, the rich ornaments, the delicately carved flying buttresses, the wilderness of pinnacles. It is easy to understand why such buildings never are and never can be completed. The niches and spires of the exterior are already occupied by about three thousand statues in marble, which form one of the most noticeable features of the cathedral. From below, especially at any considerable distance, they look dwarfish and huddled, but when we are in the midst of this stately, silent assemblage, carved in all the attitudes of devotion, the effect is most striking, even as I saw them, by the gairish light of noonday. What must it be by the spiritualizing rays of the moon? How easy to imagine them a band of white-robed angels, newly lighted from their heavenward flight, to dedicate this majestic temple with strains of celestial music!

But the traveller must mount higher than the roof. He must climb to the octagon gallery in the tower, where he will see around and below him a wide and fine prospect; the fertile plain of Lombardy, glittering with towns and villages, closed in on the north and west by the eternal snows of the Alps.

Below the pavement of the cathedral is kept and shewn the body of St. Charles Borromeo, a saint whom the most bigoted Protestant must needs reverence, for his life was made up of the noblest Christian virtues: benevolence, humility, self-sacrifice, courage, and disinterestedness. A priest goes before, with reverent steps, holding in his hand a lighted candle. Door after door is unlocked and various passages are traversed. At last we reach a small dark room, in the midst of which stands a large case or sarcophagus, covered with a cloth. The attention of the visitor is first drawn to the bas-reliefs on the wall, eight in number, of silver gilt, and representing with much spirit some of the most memorable events in the life of the saint. The priest then removes the cloth from the sarcophagus, and on turning a windlass, the front of the wooden covering slides down, and we see through plates of rock crystal (it may be glass), set in frames of gold and gilded silver, the body of the saint, hardly more than a skeleton. A small crown of gold, said to have been wrought by Benvenuto Cellini, hangs over the head; a cross of diamonds sparkles on the breast, and a precious crozier lies at his side. It is a perversion of the feeling of reverence so justly due to that admirable man, thus to exact it for the mouldering shell from which the spirit has fled; but as the dust of Hannibal could not be common dust, so the bones of this sainted prelate do not awaken unqualified disgust. To no one, judging from his life, would such an exhibition be more distasteful than to St. Charles Borromeo himself, could he reäppear on earth. As unostentatious as he was benevolent, he would order his bones to be buried, and his jewels to be sold and given to the poor.

THE AMBROSIAN LIBRARY.

Here is a world of interesting matter, which would require and reward a week's examination, not to say a life of study. One has only time to glance at some of the most prominent objects; such as a manuscript of Virgil with annotations in the neat handwriting of

Petrarch; an early manuscript of Dante in fine preservation; a manuscript upon papyrus; several curious palimpsests; a letter written by Lucrezia Borgia, and a book of drawings by Leonardo da Vinci, showing not only great powers of hand but unmeasured patience and faithful study. In the upper part of the building are some tolerable pictures, Raphael's Cartoon for the fresco of the school of Athens, in the Vatican, precious drawings by Michael Angelo and Leonardo da Vinci; and, protected by a glass case from too curious hands, a single hair, of pale yellow, not very fine or beautiful, which we are told once belonged to Lucrezia Borgia. The burden of proof is, of course, on him that takes the negative. If the claim be true, hers was not the beauty that 'draws us with a single hair.' Through all these things one is hurried, in a most unsatisfactory manner, by an impatient conductor who is thinking of dining while you are thinking of admiring.

LEONARDO DA VINCI'S 'LAST SUPPER.'

Next to the Cathedral, this is the most interesting object in Milan. It is probably the most celebrated picture in the world; that is, the most talked of and written about. No one can approach such a work in an impartial frame of mind: we are in a flutter of expectation, prepared alike to see what is not visible and to admire what is not admirable. The picture was not painted in fresco, but in oils upon a dry wall. This was the chief cause of its decay; to which, however, the elements, the monks, (who cut a door through it,) and, worst of all, the restorers, have contributed. It occupies one end of a large, disfurnished, barn-like room; and before it is a scaffold, raised, it is to be presumed, for the benefit of the copyist and engraver, certainly not for that of the spectator. A person who had never seen Morghen's engraving, or heard of the picture, (if such a person can be supposed to exist) would be slow to recognise the greatness of the work; and on the other hand, one familiar with the engraving, especially an artist, would find in the picture something which he had not seen in the engraving. Both are necessary to a full comprehension of the artist's power. In these fading fragments of color, the trained eye of the artist can still discover Leonardo's minute beauty of finish, but I must take their judgment on trust. It is a work full of melancholy interest — a picture in ruins — and the imagination peoples the denuded walls with forms not inferior to those which time has effaced.

THE BRERA GALLERY.

Of a multitude of pictures here, few make much impression. Those which are good must be picked out from a monotonous waste of mediocrity. Lord Byron praises the Abraham and Hagar by Guercino, but it seems to me wanting both in power and refinement. Raphael's 'Sposalizio' leaves no recollections but those of unmingled pleasure. It is well known by engravings; and, as its prominent merits are in the drawing and expression, it loses little in this interpretation. It was an old friend in a richer and more becoming costume. Grace, sweetness, and delicacy triumph over defects of coloring, and that hardness of outline from which the artist did not entirely escape till a later period. The architecture, dress, and countenances are all thoroughly Italian: there is nothing that carries the spectator to Judea.

This was the first picture of Raphael I had ever seen, and such an occurrence is a red-letter day in the calendar of life. It is like the first sight of Niagara — of the dome of St. Peter's — of the summit of Mt. Blanc. It makes us, for a time, impatient of all inferior sensations. Perhaps it was this which made me so insensible to the merits of the great bulk of the collection. Of a multitude of pictures I saw very few that awakened pleasure in the seeing, or regret in the leaving. Here, and in other parts of Milan, are works, both in fresco and in oil, by Luini, an artist of feminine and delicate genius, who rarely fails to please.

A portion of the gallery was occupied by an exhibition of paintings by living artists. Most of them were very bad, extravagant in conception, feebly drawn and glaring in color. The sculpture was rather better; but more in the spirit of Bernini than of Thorwaldsen; and mediocrity in sculpture is even more common than in painting.

THEATRE OF THE FANTOCCINI.

This is a small theatre in which the performances are by puppets about three feet high; the voices being supplied by persons behind the scenes. It was very cleverly managed, and nothing could be more amusing. The plot was very tragical, darkened with love, jealousy, assassination, and suicide. There was a sentimental young lady in a pink gown, who seemed in such distress that it was really quite cruel to laugh at her; two or three young gentlemen, romantic and in love; an old gentleman very respectable and a little peremptory, as old gentlemen on the stage always are; and the gracioso or buffoon, a countryman with a red face and redder waistcoat, who was always greeted with shouts of laughter, especially from the children, who formed a considerable part of the audience, and whose riotous delight was one of the pleasantest incidents of the performance.

The afterpiece was a very pretty ballet, the scene of which was laid in our own forests, with our native Indians for performers; such Indians as are painted by Chateaubriand in his 'Atala,' but such as the West never nursed in all her boundless prairies. The curtain rises, and a little lake, not bigger than a pocket-handkerchief, is seen gleaming in the morning sun. A fairy canoe shoots from a cove and glides over its surface, and a maiden steps upon the bank and lies down to sleep. A little winged creature, a mere butterfly in human shape, flutters around her and wakes her with a touch of his arrow. And then the lover steals in, and there succeeds a series of dances, admirably managed and full of graceful movement; and all this upon a mere apron of a stage, and by a troupe of players which could be wheeled home in a wheelbarrow.

I have nothing to record of the Church of St. Ambrose, that venerable monument of the middle ages — nor of the solitary column, weary with age, which stands near it — nor of the sixteen Corinthian columns near the Church of San Lorenzo, as little in unison with any thing around them as a troop of Roman soldiers would be in Washington-street — nor of the Arch of Peace surmounted by four figures of Fame, one at each corner, showing as great a penury of invention as the work of the artist who painted the five Miss Flamboroughs, each with an orange in her hand — nor of the fine amphitheatre in which the spectator will always be sure of good air, at least; for they are all so well described in Murray's Hand-Book that no one of the 'coming men' need attempt to do it over again. Nor can I paint the gay and smiling aspect in which Milan and its environs presented themselves to my sight and still dwell in my memory. I saw its showy architecture and animated streets under a light blue sky and gilded by the most becoming sunshine, while the beautiful plain in which it is set was glowing with the exuberant life of gently declining summer. The picture I brought away is as full of light as one of Claude's sparkling sunrises. The rapid traveller cannot be too grateful for such happy accidents.

THE STELVIO.

From Milan I turned my face to the north, and in a few hours was once more gliding along the magic shores of Como, which were even more beautiful than when I had seen them before. Then I was discovering, but now I could give myself up to admiration and delight. My first resting-place was Varenna, a small village opposite Cadenabbia. The inn at this place is one of the most agreeable in Italy. The situation is fine; and its pretty garden, terraced to the water's edge, crowded with orange and lemon-trees and solemnized with here and there a monkish looking cypress, might have sat for a picture in a landscape annual. But who could have painted the sunsent I saw from it, the burnished gold of the lake, the purple mountains which slowly faded away into the gray of evening? I watched these changing colors and the glorious scenery over which they passed, as one looks upon a friendly face which he expects to see no more on earth.

The next morning my course was along the shore of the lake, on the great road which is carried over the Stelvio, and through the wonderful galleries which are cut through the solid rock for a mile in extent. At Colico, a wretched place, looking like the ancestral abode of fever and ague, the road leaves the lake and turns to the right, passing through the marshy lowlands of the Adda, over which it is carried for a considerable distance upon a raised terrace. The lower end of the valley of the Adda is a dreary morass, and the sickly appearance of the few inhabitants proclaims the poisonous influences exhaled from the rank and decaying vegetation. The parallel ranges of mountain on either hand, however, delight the traveller with their majestic forms, and as the valley narrows and the road ascends, the aspect of the nearer scenery improves, and the vine, the chestnut, and the mulberry greet the eye. But the Adda is evidently what a western boatman would call a 'wicked' river; given to sudden and angry inundations, and always of most uncertain temper. In many places, the ravages of former floods were plainly visible. At Sondrio, the junction of the Mallero, a feverish and fretful mountain stream, with the Adda, produces some striking points of scenery. Between Sondrio and Bormio is a region full of picturesque beauty and thickly peopled, in spite of malaria and the lawless river, whose overflowing leave a harvest of disease and death behind them.

At Bormio, the ascent of the mountain begins. It was rather a singular circumstance, that upon this great highway between Italy and Germany, the party of seven persons which left the inn at Bormio, in the gray morning light of September 13, 1847, comprised neither an Italian, nor a German; and more singular still, five out of the seven were Americans. The other two were a French gentleman and his wife, amiable and intelligent persons. The road is admirably constructed, and winds in such numerous and skilfully managed turns, that the pull against the carriage is steady and uniform. But it is such a dead weight upon the horses that a brisk pedestrian soon gets far ahead of them, and no man of average muscles and in good weather will condescend to be drawn up so glorious an ascent, or be content with such glimpses of the indescribable scenery as he can steal through the windows of a carriage. The day was one of rare and cloudless beauty, and even at the highest point, which is three thousand feet higher than the summit of Mount Washington, the air was that of one of our own mild days in March, and the snow was melting and running off in a thousand voiceful streams. At a short distance from the top is a custom-house where passports are examined, and an inn where a very satisfactory dinner may be obtained, if the revolutions of Europe have not displaced the smiling and good-natured German woman, who, at that time, presided over the kitchen department.

We reached the highest point of the pass about two o'clock. The descent upon the Tyrolese side of the road is steeper than the Italian, but it is so skilfully terraced, with such numerous zigzags and turns, that the horses trot down, with one of the wheels locked, as securely as upon the level roads of Lombardy. Standing upon the summit and looking down the steep mountain-side along which the descent winds and turns, the road itself is so dwarfed by the colossal scale of the objects around it, that it seems no more than a scarf thrown upon the ground. So sharp are the turns, that in many places it is quite easy — to borrow a saying of Brown, the landscape gardener — to put one foot upon zig and the other upon zag.

This astonishing road — one of the greatest triumphs of modern engineering — was built at an expense of a million and a half of dollars, and all the resources of skill and science were resorted to in aid of its construction. The names of Donegani, the engineer of the Stelvio route, and of Ceard, by whom the Simplon was planned and executed, should be recorded and preserved for the gratitude of mankind, for of the thousands who avail themselves of their admirable labors, how few remember them or mingle a sense of grateful feeling with the stirring emotions awakened by those scenes of grandeur and sublimity, which, but for them, would have been a sealed book to the mass of the travelling world. Sometimes the road over the Stelvio is led through tunnels cut in the rock; sometimes open galleries are supported by solid masonry against the upright wall of the precipice, looking, from the heights above, like a line simply chiselled on the stone: near the summit, solid roofs are extended over the road, by gigantic timbers, to break the downward plunge of the avalanche, and strong palisades are placed on its outer edge, to warn the traveller of the fearful precipice, as well as to protect him. But, in spite of all that can be accomplished by the joint efforts of capital and skill, every winter proves, by the amount of injury which is done, how powerless are the best resources of man against the destructive energies of nature. The conductor, a vigorous and athletic German, whose beard had been shaken with many a tempest, described some of the storms he had encountered; and his narratives had all the interest and excitement of shipwreck and perils by sea.

The impressive character of such scenery defies alike the powers of painting and description. The pen and the pencil may attempt, and not unsuccessfully, to reproduce the soft gradations of the beautiful or the abrupt contrasts of the picturesque, but they are alike powerless and paralyzed before the awful grandeur of Alpine heights, where there is neither life nor motion, where a stern, unsmiling sublimity has moulded every form and stamped upon the scene the frown of a perpetual winter. There is nothing in the ordinary aspect of Nature that prepares us for what we see when we have entered the region of perpetual snow. Here is no hum of insects, no rustle of foliage, no pulse of vitality. There is no provision for animal life in the pitiless granite, ice, and snow that make up the landscape. The solitary eagle, whose slow-circling form is painted on the dark sky above, seems but a momentary presence, like ourselves, and not a part of the scene. Nature is no longer a bounteous and beneficent mother, but a stern and awful power before which we bow and tremble, and the earth ceases to be man's farm and garden, and becomes only a part of the solar system.

In the passage of the Stelvio, all that is most striking and characteristic in the scenery of Switzerland may be seen — deep ravines that look as if the rocks on either hand had been convulsively torn apart, sheer precipices, huge crags worn by storms and splintered by lightning, glaciers, and mountains capped with eternal snow. Of the points visited by the ordinary traveller, I know of but one — the Jardin on Mt. Blanc — which equals the sublimity of the highest portion of the Stelvio. The presiding genius of the scene is the giant form of the Orteler Spitz, some fifteen thousand feet high, and so placed that nearly its whole height, from the summit to the base, may be embraced at a single glance. Raised far above a crowd of subordinate peaks, buttressed by enormous glaciers, crowned with a dazzling diadem of eternal snow, he towers aloft, the emperor of the monarch mountains around him. All this may be seen and enjoyed, without fatigue and without danger, in a comfortable carriage, and upon an excellent road. We hear much of the good, old times; surely, there is some reason to be thankful that we live in the good, new times.

The imposing and characteristic scenery of the Stelvio ceases at Prad, which we reached between four and five. The drive from Prad to Mals, in the deepening twilight, under the lengthening shadows of the mountains, and through a lovely pastoral region glittering with streams and fresh meadows, fell most soothingly upon the spirit after the strong excitements of the day.

The next two months were given to a rapid tour through the Tyrol and Germany.

CHAPTER II.

The Cave of Adelsberg — Trieste — Costumes at Trieste — Trieste to Venice — First Impressions of Venice — St. Mark's Place — The Church of St. Mark's — The Ducal Palace — St. Mark's Place by Night — Pigeons of St. Mark's Place — Venetian Art — Churches in Venice — The Armenian Convent — The Lido.

THE CAVE OF ADELSBERG.

My next sight of Italy was on the third day of November. The previous night had been passed at Adelsberg, and the morning had been agreeably occupied in exploring the wonders of its celebrated cavern. The entrance is through an opening in the side of a hill. In a few moments, after walking down a gentle descent, a sound of flowing water is heard, and the light of the torches borne by the guides gleams faintly upon a river which runs through these sunless chasms, and revisits the glimpses of day at Planina, some ten miles distant. The visitor now finds himself in a vast hall, walled and roofed by impenetrable darkness. Rude steps in the rock lead down to the level of the stream, which is crossed by a wooden bridge, and the ascent on the other side is made by a similar flight of steps. The bridge and the steps are marked by a double row of lights which present a most striking appearance as their tremulous lustre struggles through the night that broods over them. Such a scene recalls Milton's sublime pictures of Pandemonium, and shows directly to the eye what effects a great imaginative painter may produce with no other colors than light and darkness. Here are the 'stately height,' the 'ample spaces,' the 'arched roof,' the rows of 'starry lamps and blazing cressets' of Satan's hall of council, and by the excited fancy the dim distance is easily peopled with gigantic forms and filled with the 'rushing of congregated wings.'

After this, one is led through a variety of chambers, differing in size and form, but essentially similar in character, and the attention is invited to the innumerable multitude of striking and fantastic objects which have been formed in the lapse of ages, by the mere dropping of water. Pendants hang from the roof, stalagmites grow from the floor like petrified stumps, and pillars and buttresses are disposed as oddly as in the architecture of a dream. Here, we are told to admire a bell, and there, a throne, here, a pulpit and there, a butcher's shop; here, 'the two hearts' and there, a fountain frozen into alabaster, and in every case we assent to the resemblance in the unquestioning mood of Polonius. One of the chambers, or halls, is used every year as a ball-room, for which purpose it has every requisite except an elastic floor, even to a natural dais for the orchestra. Here, with the sort of pride with which a book collector shows a Mazarin Bible or a folio Shakespeare, the guides point out a beautiful piece of limestone which hangs from the roof in folds as delicate as a Cashmere shawl, to which the resemblance is made more exact by a well defined border of deeper color than the web. Through this translucent curtain the light shines as through a picture in porcelain, and one must be very unimpressible not to bestow the tribute of admiration which is claimed. These are the trivial details which may be remembered and described, but the general effect produced by the darkness, the silence, the vast spaces, the innumerable forms, the vaulted roofs, the pillars and galleries melting away in the gloom like the long-drawn aisles of a cathedral, may be recalled but not communicated.

To see all these marvels requires much time, and I remained under ground long enough to have a new sense of the blessing of light. The first glimpse of returning day seen through the distant entrance brought with it an exhilarating sense of release, and the blue sky and cheerful sunshine were welcomed like the faces of long absent friends.

A cave like that of Adelsberg, — for all limestone caves are doubtless essentially similar in character, — ought by all means to be seen, if it comes in one's way, because it leaves impressions upon the mind unlike those derived from any other object. Nature stamps upon most of her operations a certain character of gravity and majesty. Order and symmetry attend upon her steps, and unity in variety is the law by which her movements are guided. But, beneath the surface of the earth, she seems a frolicsome child, or a sportive Undine, who wreathes the unmanageable stone into weird and quaint forms, seemingly from no other motive than pure delight in the exercise of overflowing power. Every thing is playful, airy, and fantastic; there is no spirit of soberness; no reference to any ulterior end; nothing from which food, fuel, or raiment can be extracted. These chasms have been scooped out, and these pillars have been reared, in the spirit in which the bird sings, or the kitten plays with the falling leaves. From such scenes we may safely infer that the plan of the Creator comprehends something more than material utility, that beauty is its own vindicator and interpreter, that saw-mills were not the ultimate cause of mountain streams, nor wine-bottles of cork-trees.

TRIESTE.

The region between Adelsberg and Trieste is one of forlorn desolation; a level and monotonous waste, with neither bloom nor verdure to gladden the eye. There is no evidence of sudden change by the violent agency of fire or flood, but nature seems to have slowly wasted away and died of old age and natural decay. That 'merchant-marring' wind the Bora, so well known to every shipmaster that has dropped anchor in the harbor of Trieste, has apparently blown away the soil, and laid bare the rocky skeleton of the world. But let not the traveller's heart fail him as he drives over this gloomy desert, for a compensation is in store for him. About five miles from Trieste — that is by the road, but nearer as the bird flies — the elevated plateau over which he has been passing suddenly ends and falls off abruptly to the sea, and he finds himself, without a moment's warning, on the brow of a headland, with one of the loveliest prospects on earth before him, all the more delightful from its contrast to the dreary monotony he has just passed through. Close at hand, seemingly at his feet, lies Trieste with its mole, harbor, and shipping, a shining fringe to the green slope of a southern hill-side, which is covered with vines, fig-trees, chestnuts, and olives; beyond, is the blue Adriatic stretching away to the islands of Venice, while on the west and north-east, the prospect is closed in by the mountain chains of Istria and the Rhetian Alps. I can wish all succeeding travellers no better fortune than to see this enchanting panorama, as I saw it, gilded by the yellow light of a slow-descending sun, the waveless Adriatic as smooth as a plane of lapis lazuli, and the ships at the mole sleeping on their shadows, motionless as painted ships upon a painted ocean.* The road winds along the side of the mountain in gradual sweeps and turns, presenting at every moment most pleasing glimpses of the gardens and villas of the merchants of Trieste, by whose wealth and enterprise this mountain-side, once a rocky waste, has been converted into a smiling paradise of beauty and fertility.

Trieste is but six hours from Adelsberg, and yet in that time I had slid from the beard of winter to the lap of summer. I had left behind me the cold of one of our own November mornings, and I found open windows, a soft vernal air, and flowers in the market-

* As idle as a painted ship
Upon a painted ocean.
COLERIDGE'S *Ancient Mariner.*

place, offered for sale by women without caps or bonnets. Such is the sunny greeting which Italy gives to the traveller who approaches it from the north. The long-lingering summer and genial winter of that favored region enter largely into the agreeable impressions which it leaves upon the mind. Let no one who is sensitive to cold be found north of the Alps after October. Indeed, in the latter part of September, the Alpine winds which sweep over the table-land of Bavaria will pierce him to the bone, and chill the heart of his enterprise. Man instinctively flees from winter. From his own experience, the traveller can understand why the course of emigration and conquest has ever been from the north to the south. In the contest between the north wind and the sun, the latter always has prevailed and always will prevail, so long as man is the umpire.

COSTUMES AT TRIESTE.

There is nothing in Trieste to detain the traveller long. It is prosperous, bustling, and uninteresting, with clean streets and people that really have something to do; a bit of New England fallen upon the shores of Illyria. It has no past but only a future, which is a better tense for the inhabitants than for a casual visitor. The pleasantest thing to be seen there is the variety of costume, for Trieste is now what Venice once was, the great medium of communication between the east and west, and the 'philosophy of clothes' may be here studied through a wide range of text-books. There are really now but two nations or races, the Franks and the orientals; for civilization and intercourse have effaced all inferior distinctions; and in the matter of dress, the latter certainly have the advantage of us. Their picturesque turbans, the rich contrasts of color in which they indulge, and their full and flowing robes are in a much higher style of art than the dress of Europe, which offends the eye by its angles, its supernumerary buttons and button-holes, its curtness and stiffness. The costume of Europe, never suggests the idea of leisure or repose. It seems contrived on purpose to allow persons who are in a hurry to bustle about in a crowd without inconvenience. A party of bearded and turbaned Turks, smoking in a coffee-house, in perfect silence, is a sight which impresses an European with an uneasy sense of inferiority. In battles, says an old proverb, the eye is first overcome. So it is in all things: we are ever the dupes of sight. Such majestic persons, it seems to us, if they would condescend to speak at all, must utter sayings as wise and as rich as the proverbs of Solomon, though in point of fact there is probably more brain under the straw hat of a Yankee pedler than under three average turbans.

TRIESTE TO VENICE.

Before daylight, on the fifth day of November, I left Trieste in a steamer. How freshly does the beauty of that morning dwell in my memory! The thin sickle of the waning moon and a single star by her side shed their influences over the scene long after the day had dawned. The mountains that skirted the horizon come slowly out of the dark and put on their robes of purple and gold before our eyes. The sea was of glassy smoothness; every where dimpling into smiles, and never for a moment showing its terrors or its frowns. We have reason to be grateful for the necessity which sometimes compels us to 'prevent the day' and witness the birth of the morning light, especially if it can be seen in connection with a wide horizon of land and sea, and without the exhaustion of a sleepless night. Sunsets in themselves are generally superior to sunrises, but with the sunset we associate images drawn from departed power and faded splendor. But the morning is the infancy of the day, and is full of the beauty of hope and promise. The evening twilight is soft and melancholy, but the early twilight is pure and spiritual. We never feel the full force of the epithet 'holy' which Milton applies to light, till we see it struggling and shooting up the dark eastern horizon, and renewing to a thoughtful mind the miracle of creation.

The voyage to Venice lasted about eight hours. I am not ashamed to confess the impatience with which I watched the slowly-falling sands of time in these hours of our progress. Venice, rich with the beauty of a thousand dreams, was before me, and wings themselves would hardly have been swift enough. About noon, a faint speck — the apparition of a distant city — began to be visible, a mere stain upon the western horizon. Gradually it took the shape of spires and domes which, seen through the heated and rarefied air, seemed to quiver and pulsate with life. The vision rose slowly out of the sea and grew more distinct and individual as we approached. The whole broke into parts, and the restless and impatient gaze was at length able to select and dwell upon the domes of St. Mark's. We began to round the points of low-lying islands and to thread the mazes of the lagoons, and at about two o'clock in the afternoon, the Grand Canal opened its glittering arms to receive us, and the wonders of Venice broke upon us so suddenly, that it was not easy to separate the pictures in the memory from those which were before the eyes.

FIRST IMPRESSIONS OF VENICE.

No city exerts so strong a spell over the imagination as Venice. The book of Rome has many more pages, but no one chapter like that of Venice. The history of Venice is full of dramatic interest, and poets of all nations have found it a fruitful storehouse of plot, incident, and character. Without doubt, it had its fair proportion of prosaic tranquillity and its monotonous tracts of uneventful happiness, but these are unheeded in the splendor of its picturesque and salient points ; its conquests, its revolutions, its conspiracies, and its judicial murders. Shakespeare makes us familiar with its name, at an age when names are but sounds, and the forms with which he has peopled it are the first ever to greet the mind's eye, when we approach it. Shylock still darkens the Rialto with his frown ; the lordly form of Othello yet stalks across the piazza of St. Mark's, and every veil that flutters in the breeze shrouds the roguish black eyes of Jessica. Pictures and engravings introduce us to its peculiar architecture, and we come into its presence with an image in our thoughts, and are not unprepared for what we see. Venice never takes us by surprise. We are always forewarned and forearmed, and thus its unique character never has quite a fair chance with us.

The whole scene, under the brilliant light of a noonday sun, is full of movement and color. As soon as the steamer has dropped anchor at the entrance of the Grand Canal, a little fleet of gondolas crowds round her, and we are charmed to find them looking exactly as we expected. As they receive the passengers, they dart off in the most easy and graceful manner possible, their steel prows flashing in the sun and their keels tracing a line of pearl upon the bright green water. In time our own turn comes, and as we are borne along the Grand Canal, the attention is every moment attracted by the splendid show on either side. The long wave which the prow turns over is dashed against a wall of marble-fronted palaces, the names of which, carelessly mentioned by the gondolier, awaken trails of golden memories in the mind. The breadth of the 'silent highway' allows the sun to lie in broad, rich masses upon this imposing gallery of architectural pictures, and to produce those happy accidents of light and shade which the artist loves. High in the air arise the domes and spires of the numerous churches with which wealth and devotion have crowded the islands of Venice, the bells of which are ever filling the air with their streams of undulating music. Every thing is dreamlike and unsubstantial; a fairy pageant floating upon the waters; a city of cloudland rather than of the earth. The gondola itself, in which the traveller reclines, contributes to weave the spell in which his thoughts and senses are involved. No form of locomotion ever gratified so well the two warring tendencies of the human soul, the love of movement and the love of repose. There is no noise, no fatigue, no danger, no dust. It is managed with such skill and so little apparent effort, that it really seems to glide and turn by its own will.

So far, the picture is all in light. But it is not without its shadows. A nearer view of the palaces which seem so beautiful in the distance reveals the decaying fortunes of their possessors. An indescribable but unmistakable air of careless neglect and unresisted dilapidation is every where too plainly visible. Indeed, many of these stately structures are occupied as hotels and lodging-houses; their spacious apartments cut up by shabby wooden partitions and pervaded by an aspect of tawdry finery and mouldering splendor. On diverging from the Grand Canal, to the right or left, a change comes over the spirit of the scene. Instead of a broad highway of liquid chrysophrase, we find ourselves upon a narrow and muddy ditch. The sun is excluded by the height and proximity of the houses, and for the same reason there are no points of view for any thing to be seen to advantage. All that meets the eye speaks of discomfort, dampness, and poverty. Slime, sea-weed, and mould cling to the walls. Water in small quantities is nothing if it be not pure. A fountain in a garden is beautiful, but the same quantity of water lying stagnant in one's cellar is an eye-sore. The wave that dashes against a ship is glorious, but when it creeps into the hold through a defective seam it is a noisome intruder. Venice wants the gilding presence of sunshine. In a long rain it must be the most dispiriting of places. So when we leave the sun we part with our best friend. The black, cold shadow under which the gondola creeps falls also upon the spirit. The ideal Venice — the superb bridegroom of the sea clasped by the jewelled arms of his enamored bride — disappears, and we have only a warmer Amsterdam. The reflection, too, forces itself upon us that Venice at all times was a city for the few and not for the many. Its nobles were lodged more royally than kings, but the common people must always have been thrust into holes, close in summer, cold in winter, and damp at all times.

In external Venice there are but three things to be seen; the sea, the sky, and architecture. There are no gardens, no wide spaces over which the eye may range; no landscapes, properly so called. There are no slopes, no gradations, no blending of curved lines. What is not horizontal is perpendicular: where the plane of the sea ends, the plumb-line of the façade begins. It is only by climbing some tower or spire and looking down, that we can see things massed and grouped together. The streets are such passages as would naturally be found in a city where there were no vehicles, and where every foot of earth is precious. They are like lateral shafts cut through a quarry of stone. In walking through them, the houses on either hand can be touched. The mode of life on the first floor is easily visible, and many agreeable domestic pictures may be observed by a not too fastidious eye. These streets, intersected by the smaller canals, are joined together by bridges of stone, and frequently expand into small courts, in the middle of which is generally found a well, with a parapet or covering of stone, often curiously carved. Here, at certain seasons of the day, the people of the neighborhood collect together to draw water, gossip, and make love, and here the manners and life which are peculiar to Venice may be studied to advantage. Goethe complains of the dirt which he found in the streets. Time and the Austrians have remedied that defect, and they are now quite clean. But no where else have I heard the human voice so loud. Whether this arises from the absence of all other sounds, or whether these high and narrow streets multiply and reverberate every tone, I cannot say, but every body seems to be putting forth the utmost capacity of his lungs. I recall a sturdy seller of vegetables in Shylock's Rialto — which is not the bridge so called, but a square near it — whose voice was like the voice of three, and who seemed to take as much pleasure in his explosive cries, as a boy in beating his first drum.

ST. MARK'S PLACE.

St. Mark's Place is the heart of Venice. The life which has fled from the extremities still beats strongly here. Apart from all associations, it is one of the most imposing architectural objects in Europe. It is a noble parallelogram of nearly six hundred feet in length, and more than two hundred in breadth. Three of the sides are occupied by ranges of lofty buildings, similar but not identical in design, the façades of which, though open to criticism, disarm it by their lightness, proportion, and airy grace. These are connected together by a succession of covered walks or arcades. The church of St. Mark's closes up the square on the east.

THE CHURCH OF ST. MARK'S.

This singular edifice can neither be described nor forgotten. It is a strange jumble of architectural styles ; partly Christian and partly Saracenic — in form a Greek cross, crowned with the domes and minarets of a mosque. The façade is rich in mosaics and crowded with works of sculpture and elaborately carved pillars, which have no relation to each other and no particular adaptation to the places which they occupy. Over the central portal stand the celebrated bronze horses of which so much is conjectured and so little is known. Few horses have travelled further, for they have gone from Rome to Constantinople, from Constantinople to Venice, from Venice to Paris, and now back again to Venice. They are said not to be in the highest style of art, a point not readily settled in their present position, for there is no easily accessible place from which they can be seen to advantage. They seemed to me to be full of life and power.

The interior of St. Mark's has two obvious defects. It is too crowded and too dark. The attention is distracted by the vast mass and crowd of gilding, mosaics, and columns, of which last there are more than five hundred — all of marble and some very rare and costly ; but huddled together with tasteless profusion, and many of them, architecturally speaking, with nothing to do.

There is no unity, no simplicity, and no grandeur. The general effect is poor, in spite of the wealth of materials. The first impression, which is so important in architecture, is bewildering and not imposing. Every thing needs interpretation and explanation. The separate parts must be put together and a new whole formed.

And yet, in spite of architectural defects, the church is one of the most interesting buildings in the world. It is a vast museum, filled with curious objects collected with religious zeal and preserved with religious care. It is the open lap of Venice, into which the spoils of the East have been poured. Here the progress of art may be studied in a long succession of mosaics, from the stiff and staring scarecrows of early Byzantine art to the figure of St. Mark over the entrance, which was executed from the designs of Titian. Of all the numberless details that crowd upon the attention, the statues, columns, bas-reliefs, the rare marbles which line the walls or cover the pavement, there is not one that has not its value and significance, either in itself or in its past history. Such a church cannot be conquered without time. It must be visited again and again, and slowly and patiently studied. To despatch such an edifice in an hour or two is like trying to read through Gibbon at a sitting. Long before the task is completed, the eye refuses to look, and the wearied brain to receive impressions, and we find that in attempting to grasp every thing we retain nothing.

But in a building of such unique character and interest as the church of St. Mark's, it is as impossible to divorce the pictures of the eye from the associations of the mind, as it would be to look down the pass of Thermopylæ and think only of the landscape. It links the east to the west, as well as the past to the present. It is at once a mosque and a temple, and stands as a type of Christianity, as shaped and colored by the oriental mind. It has little in common with our bustling, western civilization, but belongs rather to the distant and the past. Its solitudes are populous and its silence is vocal. It is the symbol of the Venice of which we read, and not that which we see. The shadows of time which brood over it are deeper than those which shroud its dim vaults and secluded aisles. The faces and costumes of the persons we meet there seem incongruous elements, like actors playing at night in the dresses they wore at rehearsal. The aspect of the place demands the flowing robes and bearded majesty of Faliero and Dandolo. To a Venetian of reflection and sensibility — if there be any such left — this church must be what their temple would have been to the Jews, if they could have carried it into the land of their captivity — a source of exultation and of sorrow — the proudest of trophies, and yet the saddest of memorials.

THE DUCAL PALACE.

The Ducal Palace is so extensive a structure that the church of St. Mark's seems nothing more than a chapel appurtenant to it. Its vast and desolate apartments, through which the visitor is carried, serve as a standard by which the ancient greatness of Venice itself may be measured. Men who could build on so gigantic a scale, could have had no thought of decaying fortune or declining power. It is crowded with pictures, some of which have suffered from time and neglect, while many are so hung as to be examined with difficulty. They are all instinct with power and truth. They are mostly descriptive of striking scenes in the history of Venice, and, unlike most pictures in Italy, owe their birth to the inspiration of patriotism, and not of religion. But, like the religious pictures of Italy, they prove that high excellence in art cannot be attained without deep and self-absorbing feeling. An age without faith and love, will produce no great painters. With the Venetians, patriotism was a devotion. It glows and burns all along these speaking walls. Their artists painted as if the glory of their country hung upon their pencils, and they recorded victories in the same spirit in which they were won.

In these rooms, admiration is especially claimed for the colossal genius of Tintorretto, who grapples with whole acres of canvas. What lavish and exuberant energies were put into the brain and arm of this extraordinary man! If the amount of what a man does, no less than its quality, is to be taken into account in forming an estimate of him, as surely should be done, he must stand very high upon the list of artists. I imagine him to have been one of those men in whom activity and endurance were so blended, as to produce a combination which appears hardly less than supernatural to those who are doomed to struggle against frequent invasions of weariness and exhaustion. I suppose him to have been content, like Napoleon and Humboldt, with four hours' sleep in the twenty-four. From the crown of his head to the sole of his foot, he seems to have been filled, pressed down, and running over with condensed and concentrated power. The canvas which weighed so long and so heavily upon the sensitive and delicate genius of Allston would have been but a plaything in the Titanic grasp of Tintoretto.

In traversing these immense halls, the traveller from England or America feels the spiritual presence of a great writer who was foreign to the soil and the language of Venice. The name of Chaucer is not more identified with the Tabard Inn at Southwark, nor Scott's with the Trosachs and Loch Katrine, nor Rosseau's with Clarens and the rocks of Meillerie, than is that of Byron with the ducal palace. He is to us the presiding genius of the place. We hurry by Titian and Paul Veronese, with half a glance, in our impatience to gaze upon the black panel which denotes the place which should have been occupied by the portrait of Marino Faliero. Poets are benefactors of the race, and we owe them gratitude as well as admiration. Poetry gives to history a charm like that which sunlight bestows upon nature, animating the dead facts of the chronicler with the vital warmth of human passions and human affections. Were Venice an independent state, it should set up statues of Shakespeare and Byron, and busts of Otway, Schiller, Cooper, and that mysterious epicene, George Sand; for they deserve such honors at her hands.

ST. MARK'S PLACE BY NIGHT.

Venice, like all beauties that have passed their prime, shows best by candle-light. The day reveals too plainly what the defacing fingers of Time have been doing during the last two or three centuries. It was my custom to go down to St. Mark's Place in the evening, in a gondola, and afterwards to walk home through the silent and solitary streets. It was not my good fortune to have the companionship of the moon in these nocturnal wanderings, but the stars were bright in the heavens above, and, till blotted out by the gondola's keel, nearly as bright in the reflected heavens below. From the windows of the palaces, lines of yellow and tremulous light fell upon the dark waters of the Grand Canal, and the lanterns of the gondoliers shot across each other like fire-flies on a summer's night. St. Mark's Place, brilliantly lighted with gas and filled with groups of well-dressed persons, walking, chatting, eating ices, sipping coffee or listening to music, was like a ball-room in the open air. A few moments were enough to show that it was occupied by a good-natured and gregarious people, easily pleased, and with whom time was of very little value. I fear that a society for the diffusion of useful knowledge would have found few supporters, and that a lecturer upon the application of science to the arts of life would have gathered a thin audience around him. Chemistry enough to make a cup of coffee or freeze an ice suffices these grown-up children. I always found there one of those musical and itinerant families, so common in Europe; the father playing the violin, the mother the harp, and the daughter accompanying a guitar with the voice; their countenances all wearing that anxious and doubtful expression, so saddening from its contrast with their airy strains, and the exhilarating effect they produce on others. The mechanical and melancholy smile of the young maiden still lingers in my memory. In a run of ill luck, how they must hate the sound of their instruments, and with what sad associations of struggle and disappointment their gayest airs must be darkened. Few persons are more to be pitied than those who are doomed to earn their bread by the exercise of this beautiful art, and yet never to attain to excellence in it.

One of the numerous coffee-houses of St. Mark's is resorted to by Greeks. I never failed to look in upon them. Their regular features, smooth brows, and large liquid eyes, vindicated their claim to be the countrymen of Pericles.

All this is but little in the telling. Bright lights, an ice, and indifferent music seem hardly worth going to Venice for. What a waste of time ! says the moralist. What an unprofitable evening! says the schoolmaster. Certainly, not profitable, taking life through, but a week of such evenings leaves very pleasant recollections behind. It was agreeable to one coming from our restless country, to breathe for a while the soothing atmosphere of repose — to see men sitting quietly in their chairs, and evidently not struggling against an impulse to whittle at the arms by way of safety-valve to their nervous unrest. And then, too, it was a refreshment to see so many happy faces. Content, when it is the result of discipline and struggle, is a great virtue ; when it is the natural birth of a tranquil mind and a healthy body, it is a great blessing ; in any event, the picture it paints upon the countenance is alway exhilarating ; and St. Mark's Place, on a fine evening, is a gallery of such pictures. The Italians want many things, especially political freedom, and the manly energy to vindicate and sustain it; but they have a delicious climate and a pleasurable organization, and from such life as is bestowed upon them they extract many satisfactions. That unconscious enjoyment of the mere sense of existence, which, as strongly marked in the young of all the animated creation, was to the benevolent mind of Paley the most convincing proof of the goodness of God, is stamped in expressive and unmistakable lines upon the general Italian face.

PIGEONS OF ST. MARK'S PLACE.

Before taking leave of St. Mark's Place, let me not forget one of its pleasant appendages, the flocks of pigeons that haunt it, wheeling about in graceful and lazy flights, or sunning themselves in long, architectural rows, with an air of being perfectly at home, and entirely secure of their position. And so indeed they are. They are cherished with a sort of superstitious fondness by the Venetians. Their origin goes back so far into the dim, middle ages, as to be quite out of sight. It is well for a people when any circumstance guides into the channels of tenderness and humanity that veneration for the past, which is so often blind and mistaken in its worship. We respect that 'backward-looking' sentiment which shelters the stork in Holland, and the rook in England. Every boy in Holland and in England is the better for the lesson of forbearance and compassion thus taught him. On Sundays, at noon, the pigeons of St. Mark's are fed, and let not the traveller who has a taste for innocent pleasures fail to be present. As the hour approaches, flock after flock of hungry expectants comes wheeling in, and the air is filled with the rustling of innumerable wings, from which the sunshine is flung in dazzling gleams. And then ensue such quick glancing of eager bills, such mellow cooings of satisfaction, such expressive throbbings of mottled throats, such tokens of pleasure in being alive and in each other's company, that one is tempted to record on the spot a life-long vow against pigeon-pies. All good papas make it a point to carry their little boys and girls to see the sight, and, with their happy faces and animated gestures, they adorn the show which they enjoy.

VENETIAN ART.

The cynical Forsyth remarks of the Venetian school of painting, that 'with all its coloring and fidelity to nature, it seems deplorably vacant of interest, drama, mind, and historical truth.' A stranger judgment in art was never spoken. No 'mind,' no 'interest' in Titian; no 'drama,' that is, 'dramatic power' in Paul Veronese; no 'historical truth' in Tintoretto and Bellini! In Venice, especially, Titian is in his glory, revelling in his amber and crimson splendors, and filling his canvas with light and power. In technical merit, in the excellences which are peculiar to painting, and not shared with it in common with the other fine arts, this great painter seems to me to have no superior, hardly a rival. From the evidence furnished by his pictures, we may safely infer that he was a man of a gay and joyous temperament, free from any thing morbid or ascetic; enjoying the world, but not subdued by it; enamored of his profession, and with the manners and sentiments of a gentleman. The dignity of his men, and the imperial splendor of his women, are full of the air of high breeding, of a courtesy at once lofty and gentle. We may be assured that no man who ever sat to Titian, however high his rank, ventured to take a liberty with him. He is usually esteemed the first of portrait painters, and if I do not confirm the judgment, it is because as between him and Vandyke I am not competent to hold the scales. It is true, that he who values art solely as the expression of spiritual sentiment will turn away with coldness from the splendid canvas of Titian. He was evidently well content with the earth on which he lived, and with the forms and faces he found there. His men are not rapt enthusiasts, pining for ideal worlds, but beings full of physical and intellectual life, whose passionate and exuberant energies accident might direct into the channels of glory or of crime. His old men are full of the dignity of success, and his young men shine in the light of hope and of courage. The beauty of his women is of the earth, but compounded of the finest elements that earth can furnish, and flowing from that warm life which waves in the golden locks, beams in the impassioned glances, glows through the sunny cheek, and floats around the luxurious form. His paintings never give the impression of effort, but refresh the eye and the spirit with a sense of repose. They bear the inevitable stamp of easy and unconscious power. It was as natural, as little difficult for him to paint, as for a beautiful person to look beautiful. Every book upon art praises the coloring of Titian, but they who have never seen his pictures are hardly aware of the extent to which the coloring of Titian comes from and speaks to the mind. Between him and Rubens, in this respect, the difference is like that between autumn and spring. The pictures of Rubens remind one of a flower garden, glittering with dew, in a June morning; those of Titian are like one of our own golden sunsets in autumn, seen through a thick screen of scarlet maples. In Rubens, coloring is more of an external charm; in Titian, more of an essential quality.

It is a compliment to a picture to say of it, that it produces the impression of the actual scene. In Venice, the paintings of Titian and of the Venetian artists generally, exact from the traveller a yet higher tribute, for the hues and forms around him constantly remind him of their works. It is curious and instructive to trace the natural relation of cause and effect between the atmosphere and scenery of Venice, and the peculiar characteristics of the Venetian school. Under the circumstances in which we usually see the landscape, the earth absorbs a considerable portion of the light which falls from the heavens; but in Venice every thing multiplies and increases it. The sea is a wide and glittering mirror, and every ripple and wave and oar-blade, like the facets of a gem, breaks and scatters the incident ray. The rich marble fronts of the palaces lend themselves to the same results. Thus, the air in Venice seems saturated with sunbeams, and the shadows themselves are only veiled and softened lights. Such an atmosphere seems to demand a corresponding style of dress, decoration, and architecture. Gilding and polished marble, which under the gray sky and in the watery light of England, would seem tawdry, are here necessary embellishments. The richest and brightest colors, red, yellow, and purple, content the eye from their being so in unison with the dazzling and luminous medium through which every thing is seen. The Venetian painters were evidently diligent students of the nature that was around them. They have transferred to their canvas all the magic effects produced by the combination of air, light, and water. There are pictures by Titian so steeped in golden splendors, that they look as if they would light up a dark room like a solar lamp.

The pictures which are to be seen in the Academy are a tempting theme, but I will not descant upon them. It is very easy to transcribe the emotions which paintings awaken, but it is no easy matter to say why a picture is so painted, as that it must awaken certain emotions. Many persons feel art; some understand it; but few both feel and understand it. But there is an element of compensation in all things. The want of a nicely critical skill in art is not on all accounts to be regretted. When I stood before Titian's 'Assumption of the Virgin,' and felt as if lifted off my feet by the power and beauty of that incomparable picture, I could not lament that I did not see the slight imperfections in drawing and design, which more trained and more fastidious eyes detect in it.

The works of Paul Veronese are not of the highest merit by any means, but they are valuable as illustrations of Venetian life and manners. There is a large picture of his, occupying one end of a room in the academy, the 'Supper at the house of Levi,' which is a fair specimen of his excellences and defects. It wants imagination, depth of feeling, and spiritual beauty, and there is a touch of the upholsterer in its conception and treatment. It is, moreover, historically untrue, with no Jewish or oriental features in it, but is really a splendid entertainment in Venice, with Venetian noble men and women for guests. But though other pictures are more admirable, few are more fascinating than this. Its power over the spectator is quite magnetic. There is such brilliant coloring, such admirable perspective, such depth and transparency of atmosphere, such life and movement, that the longer we look upon it, the more it seems like a real scene. We begin to wonder that the servants linger so long upon the stairs, and that the impatient master, who seems to be quickening their steps, does not rejoin his guests. Even its anachronisms have now a value of their own, since the time of the event and the time of the picture are to us equally in the remote past. It is true that it is not Judea, but it is a most living Venice. These were the men, the politic sages, the accomplished noblemen, the gallant soldiers, that upheld so long the state of Venice, and bore her winged lion over so many lands and seas. These were the superb and impassioned women, to whom their vows were breathed, and at whose feet their laurels were laid. Such pictures are historical in more senses than one. They have an authentic value as records, and are silent contemporary witnesses to the splendor and glory of Venice.

CHURCHES IN VENICE.

The churches in Venice are numerous and full of interest, but, in a short stay, only a few could be visited, and they imperfectly seen. The church of San Giovanni and Paolo, besides the magnificent monument of the Doge Andrea Vendramin, and a fine window of painted glass, possesses one of the most celebrated pictures in Europe — 'The Martyrdom of St. Peter' by Titian, generally deemed to combine the highest excellences, both of history and landscape. In the open space in front of the church is a bronze equestrian statue of Colleoni, designed and modelled by Andrea Verrochio, and after his death cast by Alessandro Leopardo.

Bartolomeo Colleoni, to whom this statue is erected, lived in the fifteenth century, and is called one of the founders of the modern art of war. He is said to have been the first to use cannon in the field, they having before his time been employed exclusively in batteries. He was one of the most famous of those hireling soldiers with whom mediæval Italy was so cursed, selling their swords to the highest bidder, engaging in war without any of those motives or sentiments which can soften or ennoble its atrocities, and whose constant object it was to keep that unhappy country in a state of strife, without which their ruffian trade could not have been exercised. It is a comfort to find the name of such a man slipped out of the records of history, and only preserved from entire oblivion by the labors of an humble artist.

The church of the Jesuits, built a little more than a

hundred years ago, which is but yesterday in Venice, glitters with theatrical and meretricious elegance. The columns are of white marble, so inlaid with verd antique as to represent a climbing vine — an intrusion of painting into the region of architecture, in very questionable taste, to say the least. The altar rests on twisted columns, of verd antique, a material, the rarity and costliness of which must always be proclaimed, in order to win the admiration which it seems to challenge. The pulpit is of verd antique and Carrara marble, so wrought as to produce the effect of drapery hanging in folds, a trick which we should pardon more readily any where else than in a church.

The church of Santa Maria dei Frari is hallowed by the dust of Titian. His grave could only be seen through the chinks of a deal partition, which concealed the preparation of a monument to his honor. In the body of the church is the monument to the unfortunate Doge Foscari, to whom the genius of Byron has erected so much more enduring a memorial. Opposite, is one to a more fortunate magistrate, the Doge Nicolo Tron; a magnificent work of art, adorned with bas-reliefs and colossal statues. But sorrow and suffering have their rights, as well as wealth and success. Nicolo Tron was a princely merchant, who had gained an immense fortune by commerce; and during his reign, Venice acquired the island of Cyprus. He might have been present, with a countenance of pity, when Foscari, with feeble and tottering steps, descended the Giant's staircase, and fainted at the sound of the bell which announced the election of a successor. But the whirligig of time has brought in his revenges. The name of Nicolo Tron has passed away as effectually as that of the gondolier who wore his livery and badge, while love and grief have made that of Foscari immortal. The monument to Foscari was erected by his grandson, a son of the unhappy Giácomo, and is a work of great simplicity and expression. Within a hollowed niche lies a recumbent figure, with clasped and upraised hands, stretched upon a sarcophagus, and two armed soldiers sit at the head and feet, as if watching the old man's sleep. No inappropriate ornaments offend the taste; no crowd of details distracts the attention; no cold allegory jars upon the mind.

In this church is a most extraordinary combination of expensiveness and bad taste; the monument to the Doge Giovanni Pesaro. It is an immense structure, some eighty feet high, like the façade of a palace. The most prominent objects are four enormous negroes, or Moors, of black marble, but dressed in jackets and trowsers of white marble, and, oddest of all, the artist has represented them with their knees and elbows protruding through rents in their garments. Never was there a greater perversion of art, or a greater waste of good material. Nor is this all. There are two bronze skeletons supporting sepulchral scrolls, and a sarcophagus resting upon dragons. And, in the centre, not at all frightened by the monsters around him, sits the doge himself. In grotesqueness and bad taste this monument has no rival in all Europe, to my recollection. It is so extraordinary a spectacle, that, as we stand before it, we shut our eyes and open them again, to satisfy ourselves that it is not an optical delusion. It is like the monstrous architecture of a feverish dream, and there is matter enough in it for a whole stud of nightmares.

Next to this caricature in marble is a monument to Canova. It is his own design, originally intended for Titian, and subsequently applied to the Archduchess Christina at Vienna. It is a pyramid of marble, with an opening in the centre, into which various allegorical mourners are seen walking in funeral procession. The uniform practice of many ages has sanctioned the use of allegory in marble, but, in spite of precedent, it may well be asked if there is not an insuperable objection to its essential character? Is not allegory a purely mental notion? Can there be such a thing as an allegory to the eye? Does a young female become Charity because she supports the feeble steps of an old man, and another Virtue, because she looks upwards? The design itself, allegory apart, is very good.

In one of the chapels of this church is an admirable picture by Titian, and scattered through it are statues, pictures, bas-reliefs, and inlaid wood-work, in the greatest profusion and of high merit. The traveller in Italy is constantly forced to compare the amazing fertility in art of a former age with the barrenness of our own times. How does this happen? Is the progress of society, which is so favorable to the useful arts, necessarily unfavorable to those which are addressed to the sense of beauty alone? Are gas lamps, cheap calicoes, and railways inconsistent with Titians and Sansovinos?

The conventual buildings attached to this church have been converted into a depository for the archives of the Venetian state. These are among the most curious things to be seen in Venice. Nothing gives a stronger impression of the power which Venice once possessed, and of the length of time she continued to enjoy it, than the amazing bulk of these archives. They are contained in two hundred and ninety-five rooms. Besides the state documents, the collection includes manuscripts from the archives of nearly two thousand families, convents, and monasteries, making up the number (it is said) of ten million *fasciculi* of documents. Of course, when we once get into the millions, all numbers are conjectural, but from what the visitor sees there is nothing improbable in this estimate. It is a vast and enormous labyrinth of books, in which it would be quite easy to lose one's self. We are led through a succession of halls and passages, all closely piled and packed with books, with only space enough left to pass through from one to the other. And this extent is not to be wondered at. Here are the records of many centuries of the most watchful, observant, and suspicious government that ever existed, in which every thing was written down and nothing spoken out. What a world of curious and interesting matter there must be hidden within these mysterious leaves; what tragedies must be there recorded; what passages of crime and suffering set down! As I walked through these interminable walls of books, I could not help thinking of the long procession of Waverley novels which a man of Scott's romantic genius and historical insight might extract from them. The attendant showed me the letter from the Venetian ambassador which announced the assassination of Henry IV., written in a delicate,

Italian hand, the ink and paper alike untouched by time. One of the oldest volumes in the collection is a manuscript of the ninth century, containing, among other things, descriptions by metes and bounds of some of the then recently acquired possessions of the republic.

Paul Veronese is buried in the church of St. Sebastian, and from his tomb the visitor can turn and look at some of the best of his productions, with new wonder and delight at their glowing and exuberant life. How appropriate and becoming it is thus to make the works of an artist his monument, and to lift up the thoughts from the dust, and the funeral urn, to the undying mind, yet speaking to us through the canvas or the marble!

THE ARMENIAN CONVENT.

One of the things to be seen in Venice is the Armenian Convent, which is upon an island of its own, a short distance from the city. Here Lord Byron was in the habit of coming to diversify his degrading life in Venice, by the study of the Armenian language. In going to the convent, the mad-house mentioned in Shelley's 'Julian and Maddalo,' is passed. We were received by one of the monks, a handsome man, dressed in a becoming robe of black, with a fine flowing beard, and of very pleasing manners and speech. The library is a modest collection of books contained in two good-sized rooms. The garden attached to the convent commands a beautiful view of Venice and the sea, and is tastefully laid out and neatly kept. The most intolerant enemy of monastic institutions must feel his rigor relent in the presence of these excellent Armenian monks, whose lives are most industrious and most useful. They are instructors of youth, and printers of books in the Armenian language, and their convent is both a school and a printing-office. They were striking off, at the time of my visit, an edition of the Penny Magazine. It was curious to see the familiar plates of that work in company with so unfamiliar a text. I believe this is the only Armenian press now at work in the world, and its publications circulate all over the east. I could not look without veneration upon the spot to which all the people of one language turn for intellectual light; nor without respect upon the self-sacrificing men who, without hope of fame or wealth, are toiling patiently for the diffusion of knowledge among their scattered brethren. Nowhere have I ever seen the monastic life so respectable or so attractive. There must be some chord in the heart of man that responds to such a life, otherwise we should not see monks and friars swarming as they do in the streets of all Catholic cities. Every one has moments of weariness or disgust, in which he longs for profound retirement and entire repose; and then there glides before his eyes a vision of a monastery, with books to read, a garden to till, a grand prospect to look at, and a few congenial friends to talk with. All these the good monks at San Lazaro enjoy, and it is to be hoped that they do not despise what they have, or sigh for what they have not.

THE LIDO.

From the Armenian convent we were rowed to the Lido, the shore of a long, low island, lying south-east of Venice. The shade of Byron attended us, for he was accustomed to come here and ride upon the beach, keeping his horses in a stable put up for the purpose. A portion of the island was, and perhaps still is used as a burial-place for the Jews, and the old tombs, grass-grown and carved with mouldering inscriptions in Hebrew, gave a mournful aspect to a scene which had few cheerful features at best. There were certainly nothing remarkable in what we saw; a long, monotonous beach — a mere selvage to a flat, uninteresting island — not unlike Nantasket beach at Cohasset, except that it was not so long or so curved. But there is more in such a spot than meets the eye. The bright blue sea which broke in lazy waves upon the shore was the Adriatic, and memories and traditions mingled with its swell, and lent their voices to the dash of its waters. The sky and the sun of Italy were above us, and the breeze blew from the land of the past. Every shell, every stone, every bit of sea-weed, had an historical significance, and a visionary gleam played along the shore, brighter than the sparkling foam of its sea.

Let the visitor to the Lido so arrange his hours as to return to Venice at sunset, and may it be his good fortune to see its domes and spires bathed in such hues of 'vaporous amethyst' as I saw them, and the same golden light upon its waters. He will not fail to wish that he had the power to hold fast the 'fleet angel' of the moment, that he might stamp more deeply upon his memory the hues and forms of a picture of such rare and unearthly beauty, looking as if the gates of heaven had been unbarred, and the vision of some celestial city for a moment vouchsafed to mortal eyes.

CHAPTER III.

The Arsenal at Venice — Gondolas and Gondoliers — Origin and History of Venice — Science and Literature in Venice — The Archduchess Maria Louisa.

THE ARSENAL AT VENICE.

No reader of Dante will fail to pay a visit to the Arsenal, from which, in order to illustrate the terrors of his 'Inferno,' the great poet drew one of those striking and picturesque images, characteristic alike of the boldness and the power of his genius, which never hesitated to look for its materials among the homely details and familiar incidents of life. In his hands, the boiling of pitch and the caulking of seams ascend to the dignity of poetry. Besides, it is the most impressive and characteristic spot in Venice. The Ducal Palace and the church of St. Mark's are symbols of pride and pomp, but the strength of Venice resided here. Her whole history, for six hundred years, was here epitomized, and as she rose and sunk, the hum of labor here swelled and subsided. Here was the index-hand which marked the culmination and decline of her greatness.

Built upon several small islands, which are united by a wall of two miles in circuit, its extent and completeness, decayed as it is, show what the naval power of Venice once was, as the disused armor of a giant enables us to measure his stature and strength. Near the entrance are four marble lions, brought by Morosini from the Peloponnesus in 1685, two of which are striking works of art. Of these two, one is by far the oldest thing in Venice, being not much younger than the battle of Marathon; and is thus, from the height of twenty-three centuries, entitled to look down upon St. Mark's as the growth of yesterday. The other two are non-descript animals, of the class commonly called heraldic, and can be styled lions only by courtesy. In the armory are some very interesting objects, and none more so than the great standard of the Turkish admiral, made of crimson silk, taken at the battle of Lepanto, and which Cervantes may have grasped with his unwounded hand. A few fragments of some of the very galleys that were engaged in that memorable fight are also preserved here.

Of weapons and armor there is an extensive and curious collection; helmets, shields, and cuirasses, rough with elaborate workmanship; leathern quivers full of arrows, such as were used before the fifteenth century; the cross-bows of a later period, something between a long bow and a musket; many of the swords sent by the popes to the newly-elected doges; and, most interesting of all, the full suit of armor presented to the republic by Henry IV. of France, when he desired to be enrolled among the patricians of Venice. The sword, which formed part of the original gift and was worn by the monarch at the battle of Ivry, has disappeared.*

In the model room, an apartment of large size, are miniature representations of all forms of navigable craft, from ancient galleys down to modern frigates. There is also a model of the Bucentaur,† made from

* Henry IV., in his early struggles to maintain his throne, while yet a Protestant, and languishing under the excommunication of the pope, had been recognised by the Venetians, never bigoted Catholics. Many citizens of the republic entered into his service and fought in his ranks, and it aided him with considerable loans of money, the evidences of which their ambassador at Paris was afterwards ordered to burn in the king's presence. It was in gratitude for these services that Henry IV., upon his marriage with Mary de Medici, sent the suit of armor to Venice, and desired his name to be entered upon the Golden Book in which the names of their nobles were enrolled. The republic gratefully acknowledged the honor, and the King of France and his decendants were received among the patricians of Venice.

In 1795, Louis XVIII. was living at Verona, then forming a part of the territory of Venice. The Directory of France required the Senate to expel him from their state, and they had the weakness to consent. The king told them that he should depart, but desired that they would allow him to erase with his own hand the names of his ancestors from their Golden Book, and that they would restore to him the sword of Henry IV. The Senate replied, that they would erase the names themselves, and would return the sword when the debts contracted by Henry IV. had been discharged. With this interchange of compliments the matter ended, and the king took his departure. He did not often show so much spirit as on this occasion. The sword, if he had obtained it, would have done him no good, and nobody else any harm.

† The Bucentaur was the state galley, in which the doge went out every year to espouse the Adriatic. The name is

drawings and recollections after the original had been destroyed. This must have been a gorgeous toy, but very unseaworthy. A bit of the mast of the original structure is still preserved.

Here is also an early and beautiful work of Canova's, a monument to the Admiral Angelo Emo. It is a rostral column surmounted by a bust. Emo was the last of the great men of Venice, and worthy of her best days. He behaved with equal courage and naval skill in the wars carried on by the republic against the Barbary powers, which were the last gleams of energy shown by the dying state. In the civil functions which he discharged, he manifested distinguished ability, and the virtue, less common at Venice, of humanity. He was probably the first member of the terrible Council of Ten who ever lifted up a voice in favor of condemned criminals, to plead for mitigation of punishment, and that their destitute families should be aided from the public treasury. As superintendent of the Arsenal, he infused new life into its administration, and caused the most approved models of naval architecture to be procured from England. He devised a scheme for improving the harbor, and suggested a plan by which the levying of taxes might be simplified, and their amount increased.

supposed to be a corruption of Ducentorum, a ship of two hundred oars. There have never been but three Bucentaurs. The first, built in 1520, lasted till 1600. The second, more magnificent, continued till 1725, when the third was constructed, which was destroyed in 1797. Of this last, the gilding alone cost more than forty thousand dollars. The ceremony of the espousal of the Adriatic goes back to a much earlier period than the date of the first Bucentaur.

In spite of his great services, the Senate had the meanness and ingratitude to assess upon his own property the cost of two frigates which had been lost by shipwreck, while under his orders. He died in 1792. Had he lived, the cowardly and disgraceful scenes of 1797 might not have taken place. Canova refused any remuneration for this monument, but the Senate insisted upon his receiving a pension for life of a hundred ducats a year; and they also testified their sense of his services and his disinterestedness, by having a medal struck, of which an impression in gold was sent to him. This pension was assumed by Bonaparte, and subsequently by Austria, so that the amiable artist enjoyed it to the last.

The French dealt with the Arsenal and its treasures in a wanton spirit of destruction, which seems inconceivable when we consider how easily they got possession of the place. They destroyed the Bucentaur, and also a curious model of a Roman quinquireme, of beautiful workmanship, made by Victor Fausto in 1529. An interesting and unique collection of cannons, from the earliest invention of this weapon, some of them wrought into strange forms, and others ornamented with elaborate work, was dispersed and melted by their worse than Vandal hands.

The Arsenal dates from the beginning of the twelfth century, and within a hundred years from its foundation it had attained its present dimensions. For a long period, it was the most perfect and extensive establishment of the kind in the world. The ropewalk, built in the early part of the last century, is still the largest in Europe, with the exception of that in Toulon. There are eight wet docks, and about a hundred dry docks, or slips, where vessels were repaired or built under cover, an improvement first introduced here, and now adopted by all maritime countries.

In the height of the power and prosperity of Venice, the number of laborers employed in the Arsenal is said to have been no less than sixteen thousand. The male population being hardly sufficient for all the exigencies of the state, the sails were cut and sewed by women. On one occasion, the republic received with gratitude the singular present of a large number of galley slaves from the Emperor of Germany. Before the discovery of the passage round the Cape of Good Hope, the naval force of Venice amounted to three hundred and thirty large vessels, manned by forty thousand sailors. This was in addition to an immense commercial marine. For a long period, the whole carrying trade of Europe, and between Europe and the East, was in their hands, and even in the thirteenth century, there were more than three thousand vessels, of all sizes, sailing under their flag.

The Venetians, at an early date, constructed vessels of a great size, which, besides their complement of rowers and sailors, carried two hundred soldiers. Their transport galleys were upwards of two hundred feet in length, and the largest would accommodate a thousand men. By a treaty with St. Louis of France, preparatory to his African expedition, the republic engaged to furnish him with the means of transporting four thousand horsemen and ten thousand foot soldiers, and this was accomplished by fifteen of these transport galleys. They had but two sails, and were mainly propelled by oars. The war galleys were of smaller size and lighter build, but they had three sails. The soldiers who were on board these galleys were armed with helmet, cuirass, and buckler, sword, and lance. Naval engagements in those days differed much less from land battles than they do now. There was no manœuvring and no distant cannonading, but each galley laid itself by the side of an enemy, and the men fought hand to hand as on shore.*

The commercial supremacy of Venice made the navy the favorite service of the republic, as it now is in England. The policy of the state entrusted the command of their armies to foreigners, but their ships were always officered by natives. In time of peace, a fleet of national vessels was employed in commerce, but not on account of the state. They were chartered by individuals or companies, and, by special privilege, some of the most important and lucrative branches of traffic were exclusively in their hands. In the best days of the republic there were twenty or thirty national vessels of the largest size, engaged in commerce,

* It is only within a comparatively recent period that a naval education has been thought a condition precedent to the command of a naval expedition. Don John of Austria, the admiral of the Christian fleet which fought at Lepanto, was chosen to that post on account of the military reputation he had acquired in his campaigns against the Moors, in the mountains of Granada. Even so late as the time of the English Commonwealth, the great naval hero, Blake, was trained in the army, and did not enter the naval service till he was fifty years old. What would be the scorn and wrath of the sailors of an English squadron, at this day, if a soldier were set over them !

the cargo of each of which was valued at upwards of three hundred thousand dollars.

Among the laborers of the Arsenal was a select body of about three thousand men called Arsenalotti, who were regarded with peculiar favor by the state, and formed a sort of guild or corporation. Their sons had the privilege of succeeding to the places of their fathers. They attended the doge on all public occasions, and when a new magistrate was chosen, he was borne by them in triumph, in a chair around the Place of St. Mark's.* They guarded the bank, the treasury of St. Mark, and the mint. They also formed the fire department of Venice. They rowed the Bucentaur on the day of the espousal of the Adriatic, and afterwards dined together at the public charge, when each one received a present from the doge; and they enjoyed the singular privilege of carrying off every thing on the table, including linen, plates, and drinking vessels, a right which must have abridged the length, and disturbed the harmony of their repast. Their patriotism was of that rampant kind now exhibited by the shilling gallery of a theatre in an English naval station, and in emergencies the state relied upon them as an arm of offence or defence, often tried and never found wanting.

The Arsenal is still kept up by the Austrians, but

* The doge, while undergoing this ceremony, was in the habit of distributing money among the crowd from a vase by his side. All that remained in the vase, on arriving at the ducal palace, was the perquisite of the bearers, and the consequence was, that the newly-chosen ruler was hurried through the course in an undignified and even dangerous manner.

the few laborers they employ are like the snail in the lobster's shell, and force a comparison of the past with the present upon the mind, even more vividly than absolute solitude would do.*

GONDOLAS.

Gondolas are as inseparable from our idea of Venice as flowers are from that of a garden. They are the most gliding, delicate, and feminine of all the forms of transport that ever floated upon the waves. A clever French writer † compares a gondola to a palm-leaf dropped upon the water, for it rests upon the water and not in it. The draught is so light that they seem able to go — as a western captain said of his steamer — wherever there is a heavy dew. A row-boat walks through the water, like a man of business tramping through the mud, but a gondola trips over it, like a maiden over a ball-room floor.

They are from twenty-five to thirty feet long, and sharply curved at the stern and prow. The centre, which rests upon the water, is occupied by a sort of small cabin, or tent, able to accommodate from two to four persons, covered by an awning which may be entirely removed, or so arranged by blinds and curtains as wholly to conceal the persons within. Every thing — the gondola, the awning, the morocco cushions of the cabin — is of solemn black ; the result

* My authorities for most of the above statements respecting the Arsenal, are Daru, Histoire de Venise, and Venise, par Jules Lecomte.

† M. Jules Lecomte.

of a sumptuary law of the republic passed to restrain the emulous extravagance of the nobles. Only the foreign ambassadors were allowed to flaunt in gay colors, a distinction which made them more easily watched by the jealous eyes of the state. This funeral livery, in combination with the noiseless and gliding movement, and in contrast with the gay hues around, adds to the effect produced upon the imagination. The gondola seems to have assumed that sable shroud in order to escape the glances of a suspicious and prying police, as the cuttle-fish darkens the water to baffle its pursuer. It is a figure in a mask and black domino which quickens the curiosity and stirs the fancy. It is moving probably on the most common-place of errands — taking a traveller to his banker, or a lady to make a morning call — and yet it seems to be stealing towards some mysterious end, prompted by love, treason, or revenge. The prow is fitted with a piece of glittering steel, which flashes in the sun like a diamond relieved upon black velvet.

The smaller gondolas have one rower, and the larger two. From the narrowness and intricacy of the canals, their many sudden turns, and the number of gondolas that navigate them, the rower must keep a sharp look-out in the direction in which his craft is moving. He thus stands up in rowing, and propels the gondola by pushing the oar from him instead of drawing it towards him. Where there is but one rower, his position is near the stern and so elevated that he can look over the top of the awning. The upright stem against which the oar plays has two or three row-locks, one above another, to accommodate the varying stature of different gondoliers, and to meet the necessity of using a longer or shorter lever which so winding and changing a navigation demands. To ship the oar from one to another of these, while in rapid movement, requires a quick eye and a quick hand. Where there are two rowers, the stronger arm takes the stern oar. In the living days of the republic, the rivalry of the patricians, limited to uniformity in the style and decorations of the gondola, displayed itself in the stature and beauty of the gondoliers. One was chosen for strength and vigor, and in the other, who stood gaily dressed upon the prow, youth and grace were the chief requisites. The rowing of a gondola brings every muscle into play, and is highly favorable to physical development; and among the gondoliers, figures are frequently to be met with, which present the finest combination of strength and grace. Their forms, rapidly darting along, and relieved against the sky, often reminded me of a statue of Mercury waked to life.

The gondoliers are, or were, divided into two parties or factions, the Castellani and the Nicolotti; the former wearing red bonnets, and the latter black. It was a division founded upon locality, the Castellani occupying the eastern part of the city, including St. Mark's, and the Nicolotti the western; the Grand Canal being the separating line. The Castellani formed the aristocratic faction, and the Nicolotti the democratic. The doge, from his residence in St. Mark's Place, was held to belong to the Castellani, and the Nicolotti, by way of equivalent, always elected with great solemnity a mock doge of their own, who was called Gastaldo dei Nicolotti. He was usually an old and experienced gondolier, and on all state ceremonies appeared in gala costume, and had a conspicuous place assigned to him; but, on ordinary occasions, he plied his calling among his subjects. These divisions never led to any thing more serious than a constant interchange of rough wit, and, occasionally, a general fight with fists. Venice, singular in so many other points, is also singular in never having been scourged by a civil war. The government, confident of its own immense power and always indulgent to the lower orders, encouraged this spirit of rivalry among the gondoliers, in order that, by the emulation it awakened, the moral and physical energy of both parties might be kept up

The gondoliers do not now sing the stanzas of Tasso, though the echoing canals of Venice seem made for vocal music.* That it was ever any thing like a general habit may be well doubted. There has been, probably, a good deal of exaggeration on this point by poets and poetical travellers. The constant shouting of the gondoliers is sure to destroy the musical powers of the voice.

ORIGIN AND HISTORY OF VENICE.

The existence of Venice is a curious chapter in the general history of the relation of man to the globe. Between the Piave and the Adige, a succession of rapid

* Bernardo Tasso, the father of Torquato, was a Venetian subject, having been born at Bergamo. Torquato, though born at Sorrento, came to Venice when ten years old, and was educated there and at Padua, then a Venetian city. The Venetians thus claimed the illustrious poet as in some measure a countryman.

mountain streams, flowing from the spurs of the Alps, have for innumerable ages been bringing down to the sea the tribute of the land. Each grain of earth that was taken up was whirled along till the force of the stream was spent, and then silently deposited; and thus has been gradually formed that natural breakwater of islands, of which the Lido is the chief, by which a portion of the Adriatic, a side-closet, as it has been happily termed, has been shut off.* But the same agencies which created the breakwater were modified by it after it had come into existence. The resistance or back-water force was increased. The onward impulse of the streams was sooner checked, and their earthy particles earlier deposited. The whole space shut off began to shoal, and a number of spongy islands gradually to lift their heads above the surrounding waters. A few fugitives, fleeing in the fifth century from the terrible presence of Attila, settled, like a flock of sea-birds scared by the sportsman's gun, upon these islets, and, being left to themselves, began to increase and flourish. Such was the beginning of Venice. The desolating ravages of a conqueror gave a population to a spot which a long struggle between the land and the sea had made habitable for man. It was fitting that a state that began with Attila should close with Bonaparte.

* The long, narrow form of this outwork of islands is owing to their position at the point of meeting of two opposing forces. The stream of the rapid rivers is encountered not only by sea currents, but by the south wind, which constantly blows up the trough of the Adriatic, shut in by mountain ranges on either hand. When the sand and mud, brought down by a river, meet no resisting force or current, the deposits assume a rounded form, as at Grado, near Trieste.

Between these two destroyers are thirteen hundred years of growth, maturity, and decline; a good old age for a nation to reach.

The history of Venice, and especially of its commerce, to which it owed every thing, is a striking exemplification of the triumph of energy and industry over difficulties, or rather of the manner in which energy and industry are created by difficulties. It equally illustrates the great moral truth, that Providence is often most generous when it denies, and most bountiful when it withholds. The early Venetians drew their Roman strength and vigor from the wolf's milk of poverty and struggle. Huddled together on a cluster of islands, the necessity of obtaining all the articles of consumption from the mainland made them sailors and boatmen. It has been said with more point than truth, that the only natural products of Massachusetts are granite and ice; but it is strictly true of the Venetians, that the only exchangeable commodities they had to start with were fish and salt. On this slender capital they began business. From this minute seed there grew a tree of commerce, whose branches overshadowed the earth.

The struggle with difficulties, which began in their cradle, was never intermitted. At all times they were obliged to maintain a vigorous contest against the hostile energies of nature. The advantages which they derived from their geographical position were counteracted, or at least impaired, by the imperfection of their harbor. Its excellence, and indeed its very existence, depended upon the channels, which were the deep cuts formed by the streams which flowed into the lagoons, and scoured a passage by the rapidity of their course. The tendency in these was constantly to shoal by the accumulation of deposit, and in the prosperous days of the republic they were kept at their primitive depth by much labor and expense. From an early period, the peculiarities of their harbor awakened the attention of the government, and there exist many reports and essays upon the subject, both in print and in manuscript. Different views have prevailed at different times, as to the most judicious course to be pursued. As early as the fifteenth century, the channels of the Brenta and other streams were diverted, so as to discharge their waters into the open sea outside of the lagoons, but subsequently this expedient was abandoned. The Austrians have no motive to keep the harbor of Venice unimpaired, for the rival port of Trieste is their favorite. The most stupid and unintellectual government in Europe sees with unconcern the decline of Venice, and is as insensible to the magic associations which belong to its name, as were the keepers of the baths in Alexandria, after its capture by Omar, to the eloquence, poetry, and science contained in the manuscripts with which they heated their furnaces.

It seems as if Venice must, at some remote period, yield to that process of encroachment of the land upon the sea, which has so changed the geography of the whole northern part of the Adriatic. The town of Adria, which gave its name to the gulf and was a seaport in the time of Augustus, is now about twenty Italian miles inland. Ravenna, once a seaport, is now about four miles from the sea. The lagoons are slowly but surely filling up. In the contest between the land and the sea, the former power must ultimately prevail, and the Palmyra of the ocean, as Venice has happily been called, must lose every thing, in losing its canals and its gondolas.*

SCIENCE AND LITERATURE IN VENICE.

The history of Venice has been rather a favorite study of late years, and the merits and defects of its administration are generally understood. Montesquieu has stated, that virtue is the principle of a democracy and honor of a monarchy. Of the Venetian aristocracy, fear was the principle which, wielded and guided ably and unscrupulously, maintained for centuries a system essentially false and bad, and which did not rest on either of the natural supports of political power, property or numbers. Hallam,† in a few admirable paragraphs, has exposed the character of a government which, even more than that of Sparta, sacrificed the individual to the state ; and his wise and generous judgment will command the assent of every candid mind. The influence of the constitution of Venice upon the intellectual development of its people presents some interesting points of inquiry. To state this

* This view is not inconsistent with the well known fact, that the level of the sea rises at Venice at the rate of about three inches in a century. This phenomenon would seem to be dependent upon a gradual subsidence of the crust of the earth. See Cuvier, Recherchés sur les Fossiles, quoted in Daru, Histoire de Venise, chap. I. § 2 ; D'Archiac, Histoire des Progres de la Geologie, vol. I. p. 659.

† Middle Ages, vol. I. p. 323.

influence broadly and unqualifiedly, the government encouraged all forms of intellectual activity which aided in the growth of Venice, increased its wealth and extended its power, as well as those arts which decorated and embellished the capital, but discouraged all inquiries which might create a freedom of opinion dangerous to the security of their institutions. Science, especially in its application to the arts of life, was pursued zealously and successfully under the fostering smiles of the state. Their early developed commercial enterprise enabled them to make important contributions to geographical knowledge, and the travels of Marco Polo and the map of Fra Mauro are honorable monuments of what was accomplished by them in this direction. John Cabot, the father of Sebastian, was a native of Venice, as was Ramusio, whose learned and laborious collection of voyages is so creditable to his zeal and industry. In civil and military engineering, in astronomy, in mechanics, in natural history, botany and chemistry, and in medicine, they show many respectable, but no very eminent names. In mathematics, Tartaglia enjoyed an European reputation ; and many other persons obtained an honorable, though less extended distinction in the same department. Fracastorius, better known as the author of perhaps the finest Latin poem that has been written since the language ceased to be a vernacular tongue, was also distinguished as a physician and an astronomer. Classical literature and philology were also studied with zeal and success in Venice, at the time of the revival of learning. In these departments there is no more honorable name than that of Aldus Manutius, a printer, but also an admirable scholar, who pursued his art as a liberal profession, and not a lucrative trade, and, by his correct, beautiful, and convenient editions of the Greek and Latin classics, diffused the fame of his press at Venice all over Europe. His son and grandson followed in his steps, and continued their labors in the same spirit.*

But, on the other hand, the annals of Venice show no eminent name in theology, jurisprudence, or mental philosophy. All original speculation was frowned upon by a government, whose first care was to secure its own continuance, and to allow no existing institution to be called in question. They had learned professors in the canon and civil law, but these sciences were pursued rather in a polemic than an inquiring or creative spirit, and mainly to furnish arguments and authorities in the long and successful contest which the republic waged against the aggressions of the pope. In these directions the movements of the human mind at Venice were like the flight of a bird tied by a string to the earth: sooner or later the limit of the tether was reached and the check felt. Of eloquence, whether of the pulpit, the bar, or the popular assembly, there is absolutely none to show in the whole career of Venice; and this was but the natural result of that universal pressure, exerted by so powerful and suspicious a government, preventing all expansion or expression of popular feeling. In history, they can point to Father Paul Sarpi and Cardinal Bembo, the former an eminent, and the latter a distin-

* Printing has always been, and still is carried on to a considerable extent in Venice; and, in its reduced condition, the trade in books is an important part of its manufacturing industry.

guished name; besides a succession of annalists whose merits have hardly travelled beyond the lagoons. Tiraboschi was also a native of the Venetian territory, though most of his life was passed out of it.

But in creative or imaginative literature, the poverty of Venice is most conspicuous, especially when contrasted with her eminence in painting and architecture. Bernardo Tasso, born at Bergamo, and Trissino, at Vicenza, were Venetians only in the accident of their birth; and they are but lesser lights in the glittering constellation of Italian genius. In the fourteen hundred years of the life of Venice, we find no great original writer whose mind, trained by the influences around it, reproduces the spirit of its age and country. The patriotism of Venice expended itself in action, and not in thinking or writing. There is no state whose annals are more rich in materials for poetry and romance, and no history more animating or inspiring to genius. Her long and brilliant wars against the Turks, especially, were calculated to bring the two powerful impulses of religion and patriotism to bear upon literature; but poetry neither celebrates her victories nor mourns her defeats. The Spanish Herrera sung of the battle of Lepanto in strains which rang all over Europe like the sound of a trumpet, but not a voice of triumph was heard from Venice, which had contributed so much to the glory of that day. Writers from every other country — Shakespeare, Otway, Byron, Schiller, Casimir Delavigne, George Sand, Cooper — have found in her annals the themes and inspiration, which her sons have missed. The mystery and terror of the government, the plots, assassinations, and judicial murders which darken her history, the spies and informers, the lidless eyes of a secret police, the blows from a bodiless hand, the universal atmosphere of suspicion and distrust — all that made and still makes Venice so fruitful in subjects for poetry and romance to strangers — must have had a repressing and paralyzing effect upon native writers themselves. Who would venture to write a domestic novel, or a national tragedy, when the incidents and machinery must be sought in regions guarded by the flaming sword of despotism and jealousy, and the danger incurred would be in exact proportion to the merit of the result? A Venetian would no more have dared to publish such a play as 'Marino Faliero,' than to pull the doge by the beard.

We may form a strong sense of the paralyzing influence of the institutions of Venice upon the minds of her people, by reflecting upon the impossibility of such an intellectual phenomenon as Dante having been reared there. His mind was formed and braced by the mountain air of freedom and struggle, and every line of his great poem breathes the spirit of a man accustomed to examine, to dissent, to assail, to praise, and to denounce. In the exhausted receiver of Venice, a genius like his would have perished of inanition. Florence and Venice, indeed, present striking illustrations of the respective influences exerted by liberty and despotism upon intellectual development. The history of Florence is disorderly and tumultuous, and ringing with the clash of civil warfare. Her citizens fought in the streets; revolution succeeded revolution; and constitutions were changed more rapidly than the fashions of garments. But every where, and at all times, there was rich, crowded, and animated life. There was free thought, free action, and free speech; and the human mind, under the powerful excitements by which it was acted upon, left no path untried and no triumphs ungathered. In Venice there was long and unbroken calm — no convulsion — no civil strife — no whirl of revolution. But it was the repose of death, and the mind of man slept from age to age, like a mummy in its sarcophagus. It is far better to suffer from the occasional excesses of freedom, than to have every energy sealed by the arctic frost of despotism.

It is a curious fact, that the two most original names in the literature of Venice, Goldoni and Gozzi, arose after the eleventh hour of her day had struck, and her once-dreaded oligarchy had become as little formidable as a painted dragon.

Father Paul Sarpi, who has been already mentioned among the historians of Venice, was perhaps the greaters of all her writers and men of letters. His capacity was universal, and his activity boundless. He was trained to theology and philosophy, but he also made extensive researches into mathematics, astronomy, and anatomy. He was the champion of Venice in her long struggle with the see of Rome, and had an appointment — a sort of theological attorney-generalship — with a liberal salary attached to it; and, in that capacity, wrote book after book against the pretensions of the pope. His services were so highly valued, that when he had been attacked and severely wounded by assassins, the senate immediately adjourned on hearing the news, and went, as one man, to inquire into his condition. The most eminent surgeon in Italy was summoned to his aid from Padua, the expenses of his illness were borne by the state, and, on his recovery, his salary was doubled. Upon his death, many years later, the republic directed its ambassadors to communicate officially the fact to all the crowned heads in Europe, as a public calamity.

A highly honorable name in the literature of Venice is that of the Abbé Morelli, a man of great learning and immense industry, for many years librarian of St. Mark's, and the writer and editor of books enough to form of themselves a moderate library.

There is still a considerable amount of intellectual activity at Venice. Adrien Balbi, the great geographer, who died in 1848, was a native of Venice. Madame Albrizzi, well-known by a sketch of the works of Canova, though a native of Corfu, passed the greater part of her life at Venice, and was a Venetian in every thing but birth. M. Lecomte, in his interesting work on Venice, from which I have already more than once quoted, records a list of the living men of science and letters in Venice, with a brief account of their labors, which gives honorable proof of scientific and literary industry, under circumstances little calculated to encourage it.

THE ARCHDUCHESS MARIA LOUISA.

My last day in Venice was marked by the arrival of the Archduchess Maria Louisa, of Parma, at the hotel where I lodged.* She came in the steamer

* My lodgings were in the Palazzo Grassi, degraded into a hotel called the Emperor of Austria. It is on the Grand Canal near the first turn. It is an imposing building, with a

from Trieste, which in honor of her, instead of stopping at the entrance of the Grand Canal, proceeded a considerable distance upon it, and landed her distinguished passenger from a point opposite the hotel. The dignitaries of Venice, civil and military, were assembled there to receive her; among them an old officer, very short and very fat, dressed in a rich, scarlet, hussar uniform, which was very ill suited to his style of beauty, and made him look like an Easter egg dyed red. The suite of the Archduchess consisted of twenty-eight persons and five dogs. She closed the procession, leaning on the arm of one of her attendants. Her figure and countenance were commonplace and unexpressive. The most curious part of the whole thing was to see the steamer so far up the Grand Canal. In comparison with the gondolas that skimmed around it, it looked like an elephant in a menagerie. It gave one the impression of a giddy young steamer that had strayed away on a frolic and lost its way — an impression confirmed by the clumsy way in which it was managed, and the great length of time it took to get her out again. There was much food for reflection in the mere fact of a steamer's puffing and hissing in the shadow of the Foscari palace, and no barren theme for a poet to meditate upon.

front of rustic, Doric, and Corinthian architecture. The court, or vestibule, is of noble proportions, supported by granite pillars, among which were three or four large orange-trees in tubs, making a fine picture as one entered. The spacious rooms were cut up by shabby partitions, in a way to make the bones of the founder stir in his grave. M. Lecomte says, that this palace was sold a few years since for a hundred thousand francs, and that it must have cost six times that sum.

CHAPTER IV.

Departure from Venice — Railway over the Lagoon — Verona — The Amphitheatre — Veils — Romeo and Juliet — Austrian bands — Verona to Mantua — The Po — Parma — Pictures of Correggio — The Archduchess Maria Louisa — Bologna — Picture-Gallery — Fountain and Leaning Towers — The University — Palaces — Snow-Storm on the Apennines.

DEPARTURE FROM VENICE — RAILWAY OVER THE LAGOON.

On the morning of November the thirteenth, I left Venice for Verona, crossing the lagoon, and proceeding as far as Vicenza, by the railway. This railway is usually regarded as a most incongruous element in the scenery and associations of Venice, and much sentimental regret is expressed at the necessity of entering or leaving it in this way. But I cannot join in such lamentations. They seem to me to flow from an essentially superficial theory as to the source of that class of emotions which a place like Venice gives birth to. Setting aside the merely practical element — the fact that by multiplying the means of communication, the benefits and the pleasures of travel are extended to a continually increasing class — have not the great results and achievements of modern civilization a certain feeling of their own, all the more impressive when brought into comparison with what is purely sentimental, romantic, and imaginative? I confess, that as I saw this noble railway, spanning the lagoon with its two hundred and twenty-two arches, it seemed to me all the grander from its very incongruity. It was an artery by which the living blood of to-day is poured into the exhausted frame of Venice. Venice is the beautiful legacy of a past age; an age of pictures, palaces, and cathedrals, when life, like a flower-garden, ran more to ornament than to use, and was more made up of exhilarating sensations than of homely duties. The railroad is one of the symbols of a new civilization, in which wealth and genius are spent in lightening the burdens of common life; the growth of an age of schools, hospitals, and alms-houses, in which the privileges of the few are giving ground before the rights of the many. Here these two forms of civilization meet and blend, like day-light and evening in the western sky. Old memories are twined with fresh and budding hopes. The railway not only connects Venice with the mainland. but the past with the future. It is an ennobling thought, that the spirit of man is ever young, and that if it has ceased to speak in cathedrals and campaniles, it is yet vocal in railways, tubular bridges, and magnetic telegraphs. The productive power of nature, as it is differenced by space, shows itself in pine-trees or in palms; and from the teeming brain of man there springs in one age a gondola, in another, a steamer; at one period, a Cologne Cathedral, at another, a Menai Bridge. Let us be thankful that we, who are now alive, have both the 'old fields' and the 'new corn.'

VERONA — THE AMPHITHEATRE.

In Verona there are two things to be seen; one by the eye, and one by the mind; the former is the amphitheatre, and the latter, Romeo and Juliet. The amphitheatre is interesting from the excellent preservation in which the interior still continues, thanks to the assiduous care with which it has been watched and repaired. There is little in such a structure to gratify the sense of the beautiful, but it satisfies the perception of fitness most completely. We see here that root of utility, out of which the flower, architecture, springs. The idea of an amphitheatre is simply that of a building in which he who is the most distant, in a horizontal line, shall have the highest place. This is the way in which a crowd, on any occasion of interest, dispose themselves. Those who are nearest sit or lie down; those who are less near stand; and those who are most distant climb upon trees or fences. Such an arrangement is favorable to the ear as well as to the eye. A speaker should never be above his audience. The best model for a building to speak in is that furnished by a cup or bowl, in which the speaker shall stand in the bottom, and the hearers be disposed around the sides and the rim. A New England church, with the pulpit at one end stuck half way up the wall, is the worst of all arrangements for the voice. The amphitheatre is still used for public exhibitions. I hope no lover of the past will be shocked when I confess, that I could not help thinking what a capital place it would be for a political caucus or a mass meeting. It will hold twenty-two thousand spectators.

Verona is full of curious and interesting objects, but in a half day, which was all I had to give to it, little can be conscientiously seen. A hurried visit to the church of San Zeno left no impressions worthy of being recorded. The tombs of the Scaligers are elaborate structures, but they did not seem to me to be of a high style in art, and they are badly placed, in a narrow court, where they can be seen to no advantage. The best rose in the chaplet of that family is the generous protection which Cangrande afforded to Dante, and which he has more than repaid by his well-known lines in the seventeenth canto of the Paradiso.

VEILS.

I was in Verona on Sunday. The weather was fine, and the streets were filled with well-dressed persons of both sexes. Of the women, the majority wore veils, but a portion, apparently the higher classes, were in bonnets. In the comparison, the former had greatly the advantage. A veil seems the natural covering of the female head, because in its flow and folds it resembles the waving and floating of the hair, and it crowns and shades the face in the same manner. Its lines blend with the rest of the dress gracefully, and without abrupt transitions; and it can be so disposed as to suit every style of face and head. We are accustomed to bonnets, and do not recognise their essential ugliness, just as people, a hundred years ago, found beauty and becomingness in the powder, pomatum, wire, and crape with which the hair was tortured and deformed; but no one, whose eye has rested for any time upon the beautiful head-dresses so common in Italy, will ever be reconciled to the bold staring front and incongruous ornaments of a bonnet. A veil is not only a beautiful piece of dress, but it is the most expressive and symbolical of all forms of costume. It is the representative of purity, gentleness, and modesty. It is hallowed by a thousand associations and traditions, and graced by a thousand poetical fancies. Its folds come floating to us from the distant East, and the dim past. Art, in all it forms, welcomes and adopts it; but, before a bonnet, the poet drops his pen, the sculptor his chisel, and the painter his brush.

ROMEO AND JULIET.

Verona is beautifully situated, with a boldly diversified surface, divided into two parts by the Adige, which is here a swift and turbid stream, full of an untamed mountain youth, and sometimes doing much mischief in its boyish frolics. Over the whole town the spirit of Shakespeare broods. He is its spiritual lord. His immortal lovers have touched its towers with light, and mingled the breath of passion with its breezes. I believe there are no authentic memorials left on which the most credulous fancy can repose. The moon still shines as when Romeo talked with Juliet in her father's garden, but the walls which the lover 'o'er-perched,' and the 'fruit-tree tops,' have long since disappeared. That which is shown as Juliet's tomb has about as much claim to the honor as the barber's basin in Don Quixote had to be Mambrino's helmet. But as a man thinks, so it is. A porcelain nest-egg is to the eye as good as any other, and an old wash-trough serves well enough to call forth that unimaginative enthusiasm which is only aroused by some object addressed to the senses. The tomb which Shakespeare has built will outlast the amphitheatre, and endure as long as love and grief twine the rose and the cypress in the garland of life.

AUSTRIAN BANDS.

As I drove out of Verona, the band of the Austrian garrison was playing in the public square. It was difficult to believe that such delicious strains could proceed from figures so coarse and countenances so stolid. In Lockhart's novel of 'Valerius,' there is an old Roman soldier who had been at the siege of Jerusalem, and, in recalling its incidents, he says; that when the Jews came out to battle, their trumpets sounded so gloriously that he wondered how they ever could be driven back. Under the influence of music we are all deluded in the same way. We imagine that the performers must dwell in the regions to which they lift their hearers. We are reluctant to admit that a man may blow the most soul animating sounds from his trumpet, and yet be a coward; or melt an audience to tears with his violin, and yet be a heartless profligate. A blind man would have said of these Austrian bands, that none but heroes and patriots could breathe such strains. Perhaps, however, these poor fellows were possible heroes and patriots. If lower than their music, they were higher than their faces. A German without a heart is not often to be found. The feeling which these coarse men put into their playing was the voice of the soul striving to break out of its rude prison. It was Ariel singing from the knotted pine. They were thinking of the homes from which they had been torn; and the voices of their children mingled with the pathetic tones they drew from their instruments.

VERONA TO MANTUA.

The country between Verona and Mantua is flat and uninteresting. I reached the latter place at about six, crossing the 'smooth sliding Mincius crowned with vocal reeds.' It was entering the place in good company to have such shadows as Virgil and Milton at one's side.

As I reached Mantua at six in the evening, and left it at six the next morning for Parma, my journal, so far as that city is concerned, is a blank. The diligence was in form a lumbering omnibus, so rickety and infirm with age that it might have passed for the father of all omnibuses. It was drawn by three wretched horses, who were changed but once in the day. The distance was but forty miles, but it occupied nearly ten hours. The weather was hot, the carriage uncomfortable, the road dusty, and the country uninteresting; but more exhausting than all was the silent and suppressed rage in which I was kept by the brutal cruelty with which the driver beat his poor horses. My Italian was far too limited for me to remonstrate with any effect, for nothing is more ludicrous and ineffectual than the anger of a man who cannot make the object of his wrath understand him. I contented myself with wishing that his punishment in purgatory might be to be driven in a carriage by one of his horses on the box. This ill-treatment of the horses made the more impression upon me, because it is by no means common in Italy.

THE PO.

The Po was crossed in the course of the day in a most clumsy ferry-boat — a tedious operation, and not without danger. This day's experience was a curious exemplification of the truth of the remark, that extremes are ever meeting. The infancy and the second childhood of a country have their points of resemblance as in man. Here, in this time-honored and historical land, there was the same low ebb of material civilization — the same necessity for 'roughing it,' so far as the vehicle, the horses, the inns, and the ferry were concerned — that there is in one of our remote Western States. The Po here is a broad stream, with flat banks, and, as the water was low, with many gravelly islands in its bed. I did not like its looks at all. Indeed, a river of a more forbidding countenance I have never seen. It had a dark and sullen aspect, as if it enjoyed the mischief which it is so constantly doing. The latter part of the journey was much enlivened by the conversation of an amiable and intelligent young Italian, a composer of music, who told many amusing stories of Rossini, whose riotous and reckless humor is as marked as his musical genius.

PARMA — PICTURES OF CORREGGIO.

To Parma I devoted a day. The chief, and indeed only attraction of this city is in the works of Correggio. It is only here and at Dresden that the peculiar merits of this fascinating painter can be appreciated. His frescoes in the cathedral, from their great height and their injured condition, must be taken on trust, at least by an untrained eye. In the 'Camera di Correggio,' a small room once belonging to a convent of Benedictine nuns, his airy and graceful genius disports itself in a charming series of compositions, in which the smiling faces of children are happily blended with flowers and foliage; and over a projecting chimney is a fine figure of Diana mounting a car drawn by stags. The colors are much faded, but the admirable design is distinctly visible. In their fresh prime, these frescoes must have filled the room with the light and bloom of spring. No painter has caught the frolicsome grace of childhood more completely than Correggio. His children are not cherubs that have lost their way, in whose looks we trace a softened remembrance of their celestial home, but they are the most engaging creatures that ever romped upon a nursery floor — with dimpled cheeks, and roguish eyes that seem equally loving and mischievous.

In the gallery are some of Correggio's finest easel pictures. Of these, the most celebrated is a Holy Family, commonly called the St. Jerome, as the figure of this saint is a conspicuous object. This picture is open to the criticism, that its highest excellence is not found in its central and prominent parts. The Virgin is lovely but not divine, and there is a want of simplicity and repose in the child. But the Magdalen, who bends forward in an attitude full of tenderness and devotion, is one of the highest triumphs of art.

It is curious that almost nothing is known with certainty of the life and fortunes of Correggio. After all the researches of modern zeal and curiosity, it seems yet an unsettled point whether he was rich or poor; sprung from an honorable or an obscure family. He is a mannerist in his style, and perhaps it is well for his fame that he has not left a greater number of works. The charm of his pictures, like the flavor of certain tropical fruits, might be impaired by frequency and repetition. No artist was ever born with a more exquisite organization, or a spirit more sensitive to the touch of beauty, but he wants dignity of sentiment and severity of taste. The same tendency to voluptuous excess which marks the poetry of Moore is perceptible in his finest works. He rarely falls into affectation, but he sometimes hovers very near the verge of it. His pictures charm and fascinate, but they do not lift us above the earth. He reproduces the light of female loveliness, the graceful movements of childhood, and the dewy freshness of foliage and flowers; but that mysterious depth of expression which plays around the brow, and looks through the eyes of Raphael's cherubs, did not wait upon his pencil.

One of the most interesting places in Parma is the studio of the Cavaliere Toschi, one of the first engravers of the age. He has long been engaged in the important enterprise of engraving the frescoes of Correggio, on a large scale, and in the highest style of art. This work, when completed, will make the merits of this great painter known as they never have before been known, and will mitigate the regret which one feels in seeing how fast the originals are disappearing.

THE ARCHDUCHESS MARIA LOUISA.

At Parma I crossed a second time the path of the Archduchess Maria Louisa, for on the day that I was there she made her entrance, and was received by her subjects. The military were all paraded, and the weather was most propitious, but there was a sad lack of interest and enthusiasm. A colder reception could not be. It was like a theatrical pageant in which the actors performed what was set down for them, and nothing more. No man cried, 'God save her,' and even the children seemed to put on a perverse and most unnatural staidness. Her own bearing and expression were equally cold and indifferent. The Archduchess has since died. A life like hers, unless it were elevated by a sense of duty, or sweetened by the gratitude and affection of her people, could have had but few satisfactions. A petty sovereignty, like that of Parma or Lucca, without any substantial power, must be the most stupid of burdens. To manœuvre a little plaything of an army, to regulate the duties upon a cask of wine or a cart-load of cheeses, to eat a solemn dinner in a large room, and to see always the same vapid faces, make up a dreary life, which the selectman of a New England village has no occasion to envy.

BOLOGNA — PICTURE GALLERY.

In Bologna alone, so far as my observation goes, can the genius of Guido be appreciated. That a man who could paint as he did should have painted as he did, can only be explained by his dissipated habits, and the needy condition in which they kept him. Entering the gallery with the expectation of meeting again the languid voluptuousness into which he so often declines, I was amazed at the power and grandeur which are here stamped upon his canvas.

The Victory of Samson is a noble work. The solitary figure in the foreground, it is true, is not so much a strong man as a seraph. There are no powerful muscles in the frame, and no evidence of exhaustion in the attitude. He has slain his foes by an effort of the will, and not by strength of arm. But the lightness, grace, and expression of the form, and the character of the distant landscape, touched with the rays of early morning, are most admirable.

The Crucifixion is a work of solemn and pathetic beauty. A dark landscape, a few figures struggling with love, adoration, and despair, are all the elements which art can use in dealing with such a subject, and Guido has here managed them with great power and great judgment. Of the numberless pictures of the Crucifixion, I should put this at the head, so far as my memory serves me, for dignity, pathos, and truth. No other artist gives to the scene such intense and overpowering reality.

The Massacre of the Innocents did not seem to me to quite deserve its great reputation. The kneeling mother in front is a beautiful and expressive figure, but the grasping of the hair by another is too violent an action, and the position of the lips — the mouth being open for a shriek — is revolting. The whole composition seems somewhat huddled and busy; but the subject is so painful, that it is not easy to judge of the picture dispassionately.

The Madonna della Pietà is a noble picture, of some twenty-five or thirty feet high, nearly filling the end of the hall. It is in two parts. Below, are the patron saints of Bologna, and the city in the background; above, the Saviour is lying on a bier, partially draped, the Madonna standing on the farther side, facing the spectator; her face raised to heaven, and filled with the deepest grief and the most trusting resignation.

In this gallery are three pictures by Domenichino, the Martyrdom of St. Agnes, the Madonna del Rosario, and the Martyrdom of St. Peter, the Dominican — all admirable; full of power and dignity; characterized by elevation of sentiment and purity of feeling, and flowing apparently from a serious, earnest, and spiritual nature. I was also much struck with a Deposition, by Tiarini, an artist of whom I had never heard before. There is also a beautiful work here by Perugino, the Madonna in Glory, with figures in the foreground; a little stiff in the attitudes and hard in the outlines, but full of sweetness, purity, and gentleness, with a wonderful light in the background. In the same pure and spiritual style are some very pleasing works by Francia and Innocenzio da Imola. The St. Cicilia of Raphael, the great treasure of the gallery, did not seem to me to deserve the extravagant praises that have been bestowed upon it. Nor did I find in the works of the Caracci, which are numerous here, any thing to tempt me away from those I have already named. From such examination as I gave them, they appeared to want vitality, to be faithful and conscientiously done, but rather manufactures than creations.

But the collection, as a whole, is one of the finest in Italy, or any where else. There are not only a great many good works, but, what is quite as important, there are very few that are not good. They are also in excellent condition, and have suffered little from the hand of time or of the restorer.

FOUNTAIN AND LEANING TOWERS.

The streets of Bologna are remarkable for their covered porticoes, or arcades, a convenient shelter from an Italian sun. The fountain in the public square, of which the figures are by John of Bologna, did not satisfy the expectations raised by the praises of the seldom-praising Forsyth. The chief figure — a Neptune — appeared to me to want dignity and expression, and the whole work, to be deficient in simplicity. The leaning towers of brick, one of which furnished to Dante a most picturesque and characteristic illustration, impressed me the more, as I had never happened to hear of them, and they quite startled me as I came upon them unawares. We read so much of the leaning tower of Pisa, that we feel something like a sense of injury at finding it does not incline more. These towers in Bologna are very ugly, and one half suspects them to have bent over on purpose to attract that attention, which, in their normal state, they could not command.

There are many interesting things at Bologna, but to see them would have required more days than I had hours at command. One of the first lessons of a traveller is renunciation — the stern resolve not to seize more than can be grasped. The mind, like a trunk, can hold only a certain quantity; and as an overcrowded trunk cannot be shut, so an overcrowded mind falls short of its natural capacity of retention. The things seen should be proportioned to the time at command. Choose what seems most interesting, and let the rest go. Hurry as we will, we cannot make one hour do the work of two.

THE UNIVERSITY.

No man, with any respect for learning and learned men, will leave Bologna without paying his respects to the shadows of departed greatness which still linger round the halls of her University, that once numbered ten thousand students, and diffused the light of cultivation all over Europe. Here the first dead body was dissected, and here the discovery of galvanism was made. This University has also had a peculiar honor in the number of its female professors. Here Novella d'Andrea, another Portia, lectured on the canon law, with a curtain before her face, lest the benefit of her teachings should be impaired by the intrusion of that 'doctrine,' which, as we read in Shakespeare, is derived from 'women's eyes.' Here at various times, Greek, mathematics, and, strangest of all, anatomy, have been taught by female professors. The University of Bologna, though much declined, is still honorably maintained; and the names of Tommassini and Mezzofanti are proofs that medicine and philology have not been neglected in our times.

This University, as is the case with similar institutions generally in Italy, is nobly lodged, and enjoys the luxuries of ample spaces and 'magnificent distances.' Long galleries, stately halls, immense staircases, and lofty ceilings are proofs of how much more an architect can accomplish who is not compelled, first of all, to guard against the cold. The necessity of furnishing artificial heat during two thirds of the year lays a heavy restraint upon our Palladios and Sansovinos. I had only time to walk through a number of rooms, including a noble library, an anatomical museum, and a chapel. The walls of the court are covered with monuments and armorial bearings of the distinguished men who have been professors. This seems a judicious and praiseworthy plan. The energies of the living professors would naturally be quickened by the hope of earning this posthumous honor. They could hardly see these memorials without the thought,

> 'Forsan et nostrum nomen miscebitur istis.'

The great difficulty would be to make the selection and draw the line of exclusion. It would be necessary, as the Romish Church does in canonizing its saints, to wait not less than fifty years after death, before the claims were passed upon.

PALACES.

In the Palazzo Bacciochi, the only palace I visited, there is one room full of interest and impressive teaching. It is a silent congregation of the Bonaparte family. There are full length statues of Napoleon and his mother, busts of his father, his two wives, his sisters, and their husbands. The bust of Pauline, by Canova, is an exquisite work of art. Several portraits, of no great merit, hang on the walls. From the evidence before us, the most bigoted legitimist must have confessed, that the Bonapartes were born to an inheritance of regal beauty.

The palace of Rossini is one of the most conspicuous buildings in Bologna. It is thickly covered with Latin inscriptions, in large gilt letters, not always in the best taste. They are said to have been put on by the architect in Rossini's absence, and that he has allowed them to remain, either from indolence, or from the satisfaction which the absurdity of the thing gives him.

SNOW-STORM ON THE APENNINES.

From Bologna to Florence I had the sharpest taste of winter that I have ever known, an experience for which we are hardly prepared in Italy. The distance is only about seventy miles, and yet I was three nights upon the road, detained by a snow-storm on the Apennines. From Pianoro, where I passed the second night, to Pietra Mala, the snow was in many places five feet deep upon a level. The carriage, drawn by four supplementary oxen, reeled and plunged like a ship upon a stormy sea. The country people were at work in opening the road and clearing away the snow, but they made a great deal of noise, and accomplished very little. It was in striking contrast with the silent energy of our people. The inns along the road were dreary and uncomfortable, and in former times had a very bad reputation. One of them was the scene of a frightful series of robberies and murders, of which Forsyth gives a detailed account, quite as fearful in its simple statement of facts, as the highly wrought horrors of the celebrated adventure in a forest, in Smollet's novel of Count Fathom. But the traveller will now meet nothing more formidable than damp sheets and indigestible suppers. There is as little danger upon this road as between Boston and New Bedford. The people are poor, but probably as honest as most men; and they certainly have sense enough to know that, in the long run, honesty is the best policy, and that, thronged as Italy now is with travellers, it is safer to fleece them all moderately in a lawful way, than to cut the throat of now and then a solitary victim, and thus kill the goose that lays the golden eggs.

The scenery of the Apennines is not very striking. There is none of the grandeur and sublimity of Swiss mountains. The outlines are not bold and marked, but drawn in gentle and unexpressive undulations. But in fine weather the valleys and deep gorges, thickly covered with trees, among which the oak predominates, must present many pleasing scenes. As I saw them, they wore a different expression — of wild and gloomy desolation — with snow, and brown, leafless woods, enclosed by dark-browed hills; above, a sullen canopy of leaden clouds, while near the horizon were strong gleams of brassy light, falling in vivid masses upon the glens and kindling the distant summits. The landscape was stern and wild; and the region seemed to be the appropriate nurse of those manly qualities of strength, endurance, and fortitude, of which Italy has so much need.

CHAPTER V.

Florence — Florentine Architecture — The Cascine — Piazza del Gran' Duca — The Tribune — Statues in the Tribune — Pictures in the Tribune — Autograph Portraits of Painters — Busts of the Roman Emperors — Group of Niobe — Churches in Florence — The Cathedral, Campanile, and Baptistery — Works of Michael Angelo in San Lorenzo — The Medicean Chapel — Santa Croce — Santa Maria Novella — The Annunziata.

FLORENCE.

THE beauty for which Florence is so celebrated is more in its situation and its environs than in itself. It occupies the central point of that longitudinal basin of the Arno which extends from Arezzo to Pisa. This valley of the Arno, which is only about one sixth of the whole extent of Tuscany, is a middle region between the mountains and the extensive plain of the Maremma which slopes in a south-westerly direction down to the sea; and it partakes of the character of both. Thus, Florence lies in the centre of an elevated plain or gently depressed valley, but the surface in the immediate neighborhood rises and swells in the most picturesque manner, and the Apennines, upon the north and west, interpose their brown and wooded crests. From any of the heights around, and especially from the hill of Fiesole, the view is enchanting. The eye encounters no unsightly blots in the landscape, nor is it wearied by any dreary monotony of forms. The earth itself here seems to be endued with something of the soft flexibility of water, so infinitely diversified are the outlines, and such various characters of grandeur, picturesqueness, and beauty are assumed by the mountain peaks, the gently rounded hills, the long ridges of verdure, and the sloping plains. Florence itself is but the central point of interest in this delightful panorama. The whole region smiles and glitters with villages and country-houses, which crown the summits and nestle in the valleys, marking all the prominent features of the landscape with lines and points of light, and breathing into its inanimate forms the charm of a living expression. Through this smiling region the Arno steals to the sea, a slender, thread-like stream, which has but little influence upon the landscape.

FLORENTINE ARCHITECTURE.

The streets of Florence are generally narrow, the fronts of the churches in many cases unfinished, and the prevalent architecture gloomy, massive, and frowning. The palaces carry back the mind to a period when a man's house was necessarily his castle, and was furnished with the means of resisting a sudden assault or a siege. The fronts of many of these edifices, however, are imposing from their simplicity, grandeur, and strength. A plain wall of dark stone, with hardly any embellishments or decorations, surmounted by a heavy but appropriate cornice, seems little calculated to awaken any suggestions or associations, other than those of shelter or defence; but yet, when under the shadow of these sombre structures, all the effect of the best architecture is produced upon the mind. We see that a certain form of beauty, even, is the result of careful adaptation of means to ends, and that as much of ornament has been bestowed as was consistent with the primary and essential idea of security. There are no graceful porticoes, no projecting oriels, no 'coignes of vantage,' no colonnades, nothing to interrupt the lights and distribute the shadows; but, on the other hand, there are no incongruous decorations. The façade is not broken by capricious or irregular inequalities. It is severely simple, but not monotonous; and a deep cornice, the size of which is always proportioned to the height of the building, gives to the whole front an expressive meaning, similar to that which a commanding brow imparts to the human face.

THE CASCINE.

In Florence, beauty is always at hand and within call. Fiesole is within an hour's walk, and the nearer heights of Bello Sguardo and San Miniato, which are indeed just outside of the walls, command fine views; as do the elevated portions of the Boboli Gardens, which are attached to the Pitti Palace. Towards the west, along the banks of the Arno, at a distance convenient to very stout gentlemen or very fine ladies, lie the Cascine, an extensive tract of land belonging to the Grand Duke, and open to the public, who have the good taste to profit largely by their privileges. Two carriage roads, a mile and a half long, run parallel to each other, one near the Arno, and the other at a considerable distance from it. These are bordered with hedges of laurel, myrtle, and laurestinus, and between them are plantations of wood, pastures for cattle, and game preserves, in which troops of quick-eyed pheasants are seen darting about with the security of barn-door fowls. A tract of level ground, extending along a stream which has no claim to be called beautiful, affords no great opportunity to the genius of landscape gardening, but it is laid out with good taste, and a person disposed to be pleased will find much to gratify that amiable trait, which is the best of travelling companions. If his taste be for woodland solitude, he can bury himself in the shadow of forest-trees, which, though planted by the hand of man, breathe the spirit of nature as fully as the oaks and chestnuts of the Apennines. He will hear no sound of human life, and, only from the smooth velvet turf and the many winding walks, which glide and turn and tempt the willing feet to explore recesses yet untrodden, and penetrate to browner shades, will he know that the hand of man has contrived this pure pleasure for him; and he will be grateful for the provident kindness, which has thus brought the voices of the forest to refresh the ear and the spirit that are wearied with the din of humanity.

If, on the other hand, his tastes are for companionship and society, he will find the Cascine, during a portion of the day, a most agreeable place of resort. Here, in the afternoon, assemble all the gay world of Florence, native and foreign, some in carriages, some on horseback, and some on foot. Here may be seen the equipages and the manners of all Europe. An Italian prince drives four showy horses, for his own amusement and their exercise, in a sort of drag, looking like an omnibus with the roof taken off. Russia and France are also represented; but, as is the case all over the continent, the largest portion comes from England, that country which is loved by its people with such pugnacious patriotism, while they are always running away from its taxes, its dull climate, its sea-coal fires, and the grim exclusiveness of its society. Perhaps three quarters of the carriages are unmistakably English. They are known to be such by their air of finish and good taste, the excellent condition and sleek coats of the horses, the completeness of the harness and appointments, the modest reserve of the colors, the well-fed respectability of the coachmen, and the overdressed women and haughty countenances inside. A wide circular space near the Arno is dedicated to the purposes of a sort of social exchange. Here the carriages draw up and the inmates descend or chat with their friends through the window. The flirtations of the previous evening are resumed, or new ones are begun. Smiles and greetings are interchanged, and even the solitary stranger cannot fail to catch something of that genial sunshine which is diffused over a company of well-dressed and well-mannered persons, speeding the lingering hours by hearing and saying pleasant things. This is the great resort of the flower-girls, so numerous in Florence, few of whom, however, commend their delicate wares by youth, good looks, or modest manners. Most of them are forward and intrusive, with features from which all expression, save that of hardy importunity, has been rubbed out by the grinding pressure of poverty. Woman is, herself, a flower, to whose bloom and sweetness the sheltered air of peace and security is essential. A losing struggle with life crushes the gentle and hardens the rebellious.

Among the crowd of heavy and substantial equipages which plodded along the Cascine while I was in Florence, was to be seen an airy fabric, whose slender body and gigantic wheels, giving it the likeness of an immense tarantula, proclaimed at once its transatlantic, or rather cisatlantic origin. It was one of those New York wagons, if that be the respectful name, built mostly of hickory, which are as slight, wiry, and elastic as if made of steel rods — the skeleton of a carriage disembodied of flesh and blood, looking as if it might be folded up after use and put into a great-coat pocket. The horses attached to it were in proportion. Instead of the heavy, burgomaster look, and up-and-down tramp of their substantial English cousins, their limbs were delicate, their heads and feet small, and their movements graceful. There was that about them which suggested at once the fire of youth and the wild freedom of the prairie. They darted to and fro among the other equipages as a swallow might frolic among a respectable flock of wild geese. The whole thing seemed emblematic of the country from which it had come; its flexibility, its youthful and unworn energies, and its go-ahead propensities.

The Cascine are themselves an unbroken plain, but on all sides the landscape is shut in by hills. The sunsets are seen here to peculiar advantage on that account. Towards the east towers a range of the lower spurs of the Apennines which, at the time of my visit, were often covered with snow. Upon these there lingered, long after the sun had set, those hues of purple and violet — a delicate veil of changing color — which, though not peculiar to Italy, are more often found there than in any country which travellers are in the habit of visiting. The sunsets of Italy are not, on the whole, finer than those of our own land; but every where west of the Apennines there are either ranges of hills, or a solitary peak, on the eastern horizon, on which 'parting day lingers and plays' in evanescent hues, upon which the artist gazes with admiration and despair.

PIAZZA DEL GRAN' DUCA.

One of the first places which a traveller visits in Florence is the Piazza del Gran' Duca, a place not imposing from its size, but interesting from its historical associations and the works of art which are here assembled. The prominent and central object is the Palazzo Vecchio, a massive and imposing structure, with enormous projecting battlements, and a lofty bell-tower stuck upon the walls in defiance of proportion, and partly overhanging them, and disturbing the passers-by with a constant sense of insecurity.

After the attention has been withdrawn from this dizzy fabric, and the eye returns to the earth, it rests upon a variety of works of art, and finds no mean museum in the open air. The most prominent is the equestrian statue of Cosmo I., by John of Bologna, and one of his finest works. Near the Palazzo is the imposing Fountain of Neptune, by Ammanato, representing a colossal figure in a car drawn by horses, while nymphs, satyrs, and tritons sport around the margin of the basin, pleading by the grace and spirit of their attitudes, and not in vain, in behalf of the cold pedantry of the design. On either side of the doorway of the Palazzo is a work which holds a distinct place in the history of art. One is a group, Hercules slaying Cacus, by Bandinelli, in which connoisseurs profess to see some signs of the ferocity and haughtiness which characterized that artist, whose uncomfortable temper seems to have been at least equal to his genius. The other is a colossal figure of David, by Michael Angelo, which, unfortunately, I could not see, as for some reason or other it was shut up under a covering of wood, during the whole of my visit.

On the right hand, facing the Palazzo Vecchio, are three arcades, or porticoes, entered by five or six broad steps, noble in size, harmonious in proportion, and tasteful in decoration. They were erected by Orgagna, in **1375**, for the transaction of public business, and served at once as a town-hall and an exchange. Here the magistrates were inducted into office, and here the democracy of Florence were harangued by their orators. Under the Medici, this spacious loggia was degraded into a lounging-place for the troop of mercenary Swiss and Germans which was raised by Cosmo I. to give splendor to his state and security to his power. These arcades now shelter a silent company of statues. Conspicuous among them is the Perseus of the fiery-hearted Cellini, not more known from its own merits, than from the graphic account of its casting which the artist gives in those memoirs of his, which are written with as much fire and fervor as if he had dipped his pen in the melted bronze. The figure is erect, holding aloft the head of Medusa, and trampling on the misshapen monster at his feet. Some critics object to the form as too robust, and to the attitude as wanting in simplicity, but no one ever denied its animated life. Corresponding to this is a group in marble, by John of Bologna, a young man holding a maiden in his arms, with an old man at his feet, which, for want of a better name, is called the Rape of the Sabines. It is a daring and successful effort to put such a conception into marble, and shows at once the artist's powers, and his confidence in them ; but there is something strained, violent, and unnatural in the whole composition, and the eye grows weary in gazing at such overtasked muscles. Judith slaying Holofernes, a group in bronze by Donatello, suffers by its proximity. It is of the natural size, while its neighbors are colossal ; and it has more the air of an actress playing the part of Judith than of Judith herself.

Attractive, however, as this square is, few persons linger long in it, during the first days of their residence in Florence, for through it they pass to reach the celebrated gallery of pictures and statuary, occupying the upper story of a building called the Uffizii. Here, for the first time, the traveller from the North is made to feel the full power of art, for though Paris, Dresden, Munich, Vienna, Venice, and Bologna are rich in pictures, yet in sculpture there is comparatively little till we come to Florence. In the galleries and corridors of the Uffizii, we understand, as never before, what is meant by the antique, and see the Greek and Roman mind as it expressed itself in bronze and marble.

THE TRIBUNE.

At first, every one hurries to the Tribune, and probably no one ever opened the door of that world-renowned apartment, for the first time, without a quickened movement of the heart. The room is in shape an octagon, about twenty-five feet in diameter. The floor is paved with rich marbles, now covered with a carpet, and the vaulted ceiling is inlaid with mother-of-pearl. It is lighted from above. Here are assembled some of the most remarkable works of art in the world. There are four statues, the Venus de Medici, the Knife-Grinder, the Dancing Fawn, the Apollino, and a group, the Wrestlers. On the walls are hung five pictures by Raphael, three by Titian, one by Michael Angelo, four by Correggio, and several others by artists of inferior name.

When the emotions of surprise, delight, and astonishment which seize upon the mind on first entering this room, and take captive the judging and reflecting faculties, have somewhat passed away, and reason resumes the throne from which she had been for a moment displaced, we are forced to admit that objects too numerous and incongruous are forced upon the attention at once. First of all, it is not well to have the eye, and the mind, wooed at the same time by statues and pictures of the highest merit. The passionless and lunar beauty of sculpture has something that is common with, but more that is alien from, the sunny glow of painting. In the natural day, moonlight and noonday are separated by a considerable interval of time, and by soft gradations of changing light. Could we pass from one to the other in a moment, the shock would be nearly as great as is felt on stepping from air into water. And in the second place, the pictures themselves are not congruous; at least, Titian's Venuses have no business to be in the same small room with Raphael's Madonnas. If we must have such works, let them not breathe the air of celestial purity which plays round those drooping brows and those serene lips.

STATUES IN THE TRIBUNE.

The Venus de Medici is the presiding genius of the place. She faces the door, and, from her central position, and the general inclination of her figure, seems extending a gracious welcome to all who enter. I hardly dare to set down the impressions which this celebrated statue made upon me. The courage with which Cobbett assails the supremacy of Shakespeare is a quality of doubtful value, and not to admire the Venus de Medici seems a solecism in taste nearly as singular. Perhaps my expectations were raised too high for any form hewn from marble to reach; at any rate, with a feeling like that of a single dissenting juryman in an exciting case, I confess to a disappointment at first, which, though lessened by subsequent visits, never entirely disappeared. The statue is but four feet eleven inches in height, which gives a sort of doll-like character to the whole figure. The hands — a modern restoration — are unnecessarily bad: the head is small in proportion to the body; and there is a sort of vacant simper upon the face. There is certainly wonderful beauty in the undulating outline of the whole form. The lines flow into each other as softly and delicately, as if the winds of summer had moulded the frame. But this seems hardly enough to call forth the raptures into which so many intellectual men have fallen over her. Admirable as is the workmanship, the expression has in it more of earth than of heaven. She is not a goddess, unconscious alike of her beauty and her nakedness — into whose bosom no ray of human passion or human weakness has ever darted — but a lovely woman, who knows her power and enjoys her triumphs.

If I was disappointed in the Venus de Medici, I found in the figure of the Knife-Grinder quite a new revelation of the power of art. As is well known, this statue is an enigma, to which no satisfactory solution has ever been offered. Indeed, whether he is whetting his knife, seems somewhat doubtful. But as to its power there can be no doubt. The figure is unideal, and the face and head coarse, but every line glows with the fire of truth. It is a striking proof that a great artist may imitate commonplace nature without falling into vulgarity. The attitude is full of ease, and the face looks up with so penetrating a gleam of expression, that nothing can come between it and speech. This is perhaps not high art, but it is the living truth, and is well worth a wilderness of unexpressive wood-nymphs and round-cheeked Bacchuses. No artist could have achieved such a work, without long habits of observation, the most patient attention to details, and the greatest skill with the chisel. It seemed to me that a single look at this figure had given me a new insight into Roman life and manners; as if one of Terence's characters had been turned into marble for my benefit. The Wrestlers is a group of the same class, and of kindred excellence.

After the vivid truth and speaking nature of these two remarkable works, we are hardly prepared to do full justice to the soft, ideal beauty of the Apollino. It is like taking up the Phèdre of Racine, after laying down the first part of King Henry IV. The Dancing Fawn, a work full of spirit, and admirably restored by Michael Angelo, is a sort of connecting link between the two.

PICTURES IN THE TRIBUNE.

The pictures by Raphael, on the walls of the Tribune, are not ranked in the very first class of his works. Three of them are portraits; one is of an unknown Florentine lady, evidently an early work, not painted with a very confident touch, but full of delicacy and sweetness. Another is the head of Pope Julius II., that warlike and vigorous old man, whose active brain and fiery temper, untouched by the snows of seventy winters, are so familiar to those who are acquainted with the history of art during his time. It is an admirable picture, evidently painted with a pencil which took pleasure in its work, rich and deep-toned in color, and with so much expression and character, that we feel a perfect assurance of its being a faithful likeness. There is also a female portrait, which bears the name of La Fornarina, but is supposed by Passavant to be that of Beatrice Pio, an improvisatrice of that period. It is not an ideal head, but one of rich, glowing, and luxuriant beauty, suggesting perfect health, an impassioned temperament, and a pleasurable organization — a face not made for solitude and contemplation, but for feasts, courts, and spectacles. The tone in coloring is Venetian, and had I been asked to guess the painter's name, I should have said Giorgione.

Of ideal pictures there are two, — a Holy Family, called the Madonna of the Goldfinch, from a bird held in the hand of the infant Saviour, a picture of great sweetness, purity, and elevation; and a St. John preaching in the Desert.

These two pictures are not penetrated with that maturity and vigor which Raphael's genius subsequently attained, but they are full of those winning and engaging qualities which belonged to it in every stage of its development. Raphael is perhaps overpraised by those admirers of art who are not artists, and who judge of paintings not by their technical merits, but by the effect which they produce; in other words, subjectively and not objectively. All the fine arts, poetry, painting, sculpture, and music, have something in common; something which all persons of sensibility feel, though such airy resemblances are not very patient of the chains of language. In the expression of this common element, Raphael has no rival. Maternal love, purity of feeling, sweetness, refinement, and a certain soft ideal happiness breathe from his canvas like odor from a flower. No painter addresses so wide a circle of sympathies as he: no one speaks a language so intelligible to the common apprehension. There is something in his pictures at Florence which recalls the early poetry of Milton. Like that, they flow from a mind into which none but forms of ideal beauty had ever intruded; like that, they are full of morning freshness, of the sense of unworn energies, of the most exquisite sensibility; and, like that, they glow with a light as pure as that which sparkled in the eyes of Beatrice in Paradise. Towards the painter, the dark cloud which overshadowed the closing hours of the poet was never turned. His life was a summer's day cut off before the noon. He is the Achilles of art, and his image is fixed in our minds as that of a youth, of immortal energies, ever aspiring, ever struggling, and ever conquering. Beautiful as are the works of Raphael, none surpass the perfect picture of his life. All contemporary testimony dwells with enthusiasm upon the gentle grace of his manners, the sweetness of his temper, his freedom from envy, and the readiness with which he communicated his knowledge to others. He breathed the atmosphere of love and admiration. In his behalf the common laws of man's imperfect moral nature were reversed. Before his transcendent genius, and the meekness with which its honors were borne, malice was silent and envy disarmed.

In Raphael's hands, art performs its highest, and indeed its only legitimate function, because it helps to make us better men. There are many pictures extant — some by eminent artists to their disgrace be it spoken — which degrade and sensualize the mind, filling it with impure suggestions, and giving strength to down-dragging impulses, already too strong in most natures. There are others that are, morally speaking, neither good nor bad, that please for the time, and then leave us as they found us. They entertain us like a brilliant spectacle or clever pantomime, but they do not haunt the mind with images of remembered beauty. They do not float before us in our twilight walks, or paint themselves upon the wall, in visionary colors before our eyes, as we look up from our work. But the pictures of Raphael, and of every artist who combines genius with purity of feeling, are positively elevating and purifying influences. Nor is it necessary for the securing of these influences that the artist should have a distinct moral purpose in view; or should appeal directly to the sentiment of religion, as the early Italian painters do so exclusively. It is enough that the tone of his mind should be pure and elevated. Take, for instance, the Beatrice of Allston — that admirable artist in whose soul the highest graces of painting, so long wandering and homeless, found a congenial abode. Here is merely the head of a beautiful young woman, but how full it is of the most persuasive moral power. The purity of soul expressed in those gently drooping lids and softly closed lips derives fresh attractions from so perfect a representation of its moulding influence upon the clay in which it is enshrined. The mere sight of such a face is an argument in favor of a spotless life. Such influences are indeed momentary, but of good influences how few there are that are not momentary, or at least evanescent? Temptation comes upon us suddenly and powerfully, like a tempest, but the virtue which resists it successfully has been slowly built up from a thousand nameless elements. Nothing is so small as to be despised ; nothing so trivial as to be rejected. The influence of works of this class is like the influence of nature. There is no necessary and inevitable relation between the beautiful scenes of the visible world, and moral well-being or well-doing, but it is certainly true that just so far as a man cultivates a taste for nature, he cultivates a susceptibility to moral impressions. A lover of nature is not likely to be a bad man, because such a love preoccupies the mind so as to arm it against evil approaches. A vacant mind invites dangerous inmates, as a deserted mansion tempts wandering outcasts to enter and take up their abode in its desolate apartments.

There are three pictures in the Tribune which confirm, by contrast, what has been said both of the engaging qualities of Raphael's genius and of his purity of sentiment. These are the Holy Family, by Michael Angelo, and the Two Venuses, by Titian. The Holy Family is, obviously, a work of remarkable power, which an artist would examine with attention and improvement, but it is quite wanting in those graces which make the works of Raphael so attractive to those who are not artists. It is hard, cold, and rigid, and probably few persons ever look at it a second time. If we do more than justice to Raphael, we do less than justice to this picture of Michael Angelo. The great merit of Titian's paintings as works of art, and especially the magic of their coloring, no one can deny. The carnation hues of youth and beauty, and the soft undulating outlines of the female form, are painted as none but Titian could paint them, and the effect is so dazzling and striking, that we can hardly persuade ourselves that it has not been produced by some process now lost to the pencil, or by the use of colors that modern chemistry cannot replace. But, as we look at them, we cannot help asking ourselves whether it would not have been better, on the whole, that they had never been painted. Is their excellence so transcendent, as to absorb the dangerous element involved in their subject? Is the unobjectionable range of art so limited, that in order to secure all its legitimate triumphs it must wander into such slippery regions? These are questions which every one must decide as he feels: they belong less to the reason than to the primitive intuition. It is impossible to argue upon them, as they must be settled by the instinctive sense of fitness and propriety. It is not enough to say, that to the 'pure all things are pure.' The rule itself has its limitations, and, unhappily, all men are not pure; and for this, bad books and bad pictures are much to blame. An artist should never light his torch at the fires of sense. No subject should ever be painted, which a man would hesitate to look at in the presence of his children, or of the woman that he loves, — and who will say this of a naked Venus?

Between these two pictures of Titian there hangs, in by no means a becoming proximity, a Holy Family, by Andrea del Sarto, a painter not of the very first class, but of great merit, and who would have been a better painter, had he been a better man, and not had a bad wife. The chief defects of his paintings arise from a want of elevated devotional feeling. The picture which hangs in the Tribune is esteemed the best of his oil paintings, and is full of sweetness, grace and tenderness — in short, of all the purely human qualities which belong to the subject.

I have no intention of writing a catalogue, and therefore pass over a number of pictures both in the Tribune, and the neighboring rooms, which are worthy of careful study, either from their own merits or their relation to the history of art. The Medusa's Head, by Leonardo da Vinci, is a very curious work — elaborately painted, as all his pictures were, and attracting the gaze by a strange species of fascination. The hair is changed into serpents, and the contrast between the pale beauty of the lifeless countenance, and the hissing and undulating activity of the reptiles, render it one of the most extraordinary pictures ever painted. What could have induced a man of such various and wonderful powers, with an organization so sensitive to beauty and all pleasurable sensations, to give so much time to a picture which we are afraid to look at steadily, lest it should start into life in our next troubled dream ?

AUTOGRAPH PORTRAITS OF PAINTERS.

One of the most interesting parts of this collection is to be found in the rooms devoted to the portraits of painters, executed by their own hands. Here is that well known portrait of Raphael, which has been so often copied and engraved, that in the minds of most persons the idea of Raphael always embodies itself in that form. There is an expression of melancholy in the countenance, which is more in unison with his early death, than with the splendid success of his career. It is a face of feminine beauty, showing great delicacy of organization and refinement of feeling; but not, it seems to me, doing justice to the power, energy, and endurance, which, in this great artist, were so remarkably combined with the finest attributes of genius. Dying before he had completed his thirty-seventh year, he is said to have left behind him two hundred and eighty-seven pictures and five hundred and seventy-six drawings and studies. To have done all this must have required not only unflagging industry, but a temperament of great activity and uncommon patience of labor, qualities which do not shine through this sentimental and dreamy countenance. Not less interesting is the noble head and face of Leonardo da Vinci, calm and serene, showing a tranquil consciousness of superior power, and looking like a man who could do great things without an effort. Nor will the English or American visitor pass by, without an honoring pause of contemplation, the scholarly and gentlemanly countenance of Sir Joshua Reynolds, who has the good fortune to be remembered alike by his pencil and his pen, and whose discourses still remain the most sensible and judicious work on the principles of painting, in our language. The head of Vandyke, which looks at the visitor over the shoulder, has that air of refinement which we should naturally expect in one who was eminently the painter of high life. These, and a few others, will attract and reward attention, but the great mass of the collection is composed of names of very little note, — the illustrious obscure, who have died and made no sign;

and if the beholder be of a moralizing mood, he will think of the vanity of human wishes and the uncertainty of human hopes. Of the many who start in the race, how few reach the goal! On what a broad tableland of mediocrity do Raphael and Correggio stand! Nature is prodigal of her germs, so that the life of every species may be prolonged, in spite of all sorts of exterminating influences: and, in the same spirit, she creates a swarm of inferior artists, so that we may pick out of the crowd, here and there, one whose works are worthy to live.

BUSTS OF THE ROMAN EMPERORS.

The long corridors of the Uffizii are occupied with a great variety of works of art. Multitudes of paintings cover the walls, most of them of little intrinsic value, though of interest to any one who would study the progress of painting. There is an immense collection of portraits, rarely looked at except by some one in search of a particular countenance, and numerous works in sculpture. Of these last, the most interesting is a series of busts of the Roman emperors. Most of them are curiously illustrative of the characters of the originals, as history has transmitted them to us; and furnish strong arguments in favor of the general truths of phrenology. In many of them we mark the square head, the short massive neck, the low narrow forehead, and the flat crown, which are the types of the animal nature — the signs of gluttony, lust, intemperance, and cruelty. Such heads and faces throw light upon the pages of Suetonius. We observe also a progressive decline in the art of sculpture as the series goes on, the later busts being of inferior workmanship to the earlier. Mingled with these are many heads of the wives and daughters of the emperors, remarkable for the hideous style in which the hair is dressed. The taste which could have tolerated such deformities was so bad, that it could not have existed without the support of bad morals. A virtuous people would never have endured such disfigurements. Upon no part of the human frame has fashion laid such ruthless hands as the head, and we cannot be too thankful that we live in an age in which the hair is not defiled by powder and pomatum, nor built up into those turreted and battlemented structures which provoked the wrath of Juvenal and the delicate satire of Addison.

THE GROUP OF NIOBE.

The group of Niobe has, very properly, a room to itself, for a work of such great excellence and such depth of feeling should be left to address the heart, unmixed with inferior or even different matter. Much has been written about this group, and much learning and ingenuity have been expended in conjectures upon its original disposition,* but all this curious research is

* Mr. Cockerell, an English architect, published in 1816 an essay, accompanied with a drawing, in which he maintained that the statues must have originally been placed in the tympanum of a temple. His arguments are ingenious and plausible, and his conclusions are generally adopted in England. M. Fulchiron, an intelligent and accomplished French traveller,

not necessary to a comprehension of its essential excellence. The statues are of various merit, and perhaps by different hands, but they are of a kindred style in art, and are conceived in the same spirit. They make at first glance a strong impression of truth, earnestness, and sincerity. I should say that the man or men who wrought these statues really believed in the legend commemorated. In drapery, attitude, and form, several of the figures are open to criticism, and have been admirably discussed by Mr. Bell, but I was well content not to observe these defects of detail. I seemed to be in the presence of a touching domestic tragedy, told in marble. The artist appeared to be swallowed up in his work. Nothing was done for mere display, or for the purpose of showing the skill of a practised hand. The majesty of the subject seemed to brood over the chisel, and guide its edge. Judging ignorantly, and by the natural light alone, I should say that they were the work of a period in which art was culminating, but had not reached its highest point of excellence. The grief of Niobe is feminine; deep, overwhelming, and hopeless, but not fierce or struggling. The dying youth is one of the most admirable figures in the world, full of expression, without distortion or extravagance; a serene image of death, at once mournful and soothing. This exquisite group is not very happily placed. The figures are arranged in the form of an oval, the Niobe making the central point of interest, a disposition which

however, dissents from this view, and reasons with much force in favor of the conjecture that they were arranged against a wall, at the height of the eye.

seems formal and unnatural; besides that it forces the attention upon the separate figures, and breaks up the unity of the whole, which is directly contrary to the artist's design.

CHURCHES IN FLORENCE.

I was somewhat surprised to find so many of the churches of Florence unfinished. In nearly all, the façade is wanting, and instead of a rich covering of marble, wrought into graceful outline and dappled with light and shade, the eye is disheartened by a dead wall of brick or stucco, without form or color. Too much has been attempted, and the zeal of the builders has cooled, or their resources have fallen short, before the vision of beauty or grandeur has been completed. This disproportion between the aspiration and the performance may be a republican defect. To bring a vast design to its ripe completion requires perhaps the steady uniformity of monarchical institutions, and a political atmosphere undisturbed by the warring breath of popular faction.

THE CATHEDRAL, CAMPANILE, AND BAPTISTERY.

The Cathedral, a work which occupied a hundred and sixty years in building, owed its origin to the devotional spirit of the people of Florence, while their liberties were yet in their own keeping. The decree of the Council, committing the enterprise to the charge of Arnolpho di Lapo, is framed in a strain of noble simplicity worthy of the best days of Rome.* Its crowning glory is the dome, the bold conception of Brunelleschi, the whole merit of which none but an architect can appreciate, though none but a common apprehension is needed to feel its overpowering effect. Rising from the smaller cupolas which cluster round its base, it appears to the eye the 'bright consummate flower' of architecture, encircled by its unexpanded buds. As

* The following is the decree, as quoted by Valery:

'Atteso che la somma prudenza di un popolo grande, sia di procedere negli affari suoi di modo che dalle operazioni esteriori si riconosca non meno il savio, che magnanimo suo operare; si ordina ad Arnolpho capo maestro nel nostro commune, che faccia ill modello o disegno della rinnovazione di Santa Reparata, con quella più alta e sontuosa magnificenza, che inventar non si possa, nè maggiore, nè plu bella dall' industria e poter degli uomini; secondochè da più savi di questa città è stato detto e consigliato in pubblica e privata adunanza, non doversi intraprendere le cose del comune, se il concetto non é, di farle correspondenti ad un cuore, che vien fatto grandissimo, perché composto dell' animo di più cittadini uniti insieme in un sol volere.'

'Whereas, the high wisdom of a people of noble origin demands that in the conduct of their affairs, they should proceed in such manner that their magnanimity, as well as their prudence, should be shown in all external works, it is ordered that Arnolpho, the chief artist of our borough, make a model or design for the restoration of Santa Reparata, in such fashion of exalted and sumptuous magnificence, that nothing greater or more beautiful can be contrived by the industry and power of man. And this is done in conformity with the resolution, publicly and privately expressed, of the wisest inhabitants of this city, that no works of common interest should be undertaken, unless there be a fixed purpose to do them in a manner corresponding to that great and general heart, which flows from the united minds of all the citizens, who, in this, have but one will.'

some great men are properly judged only at a distance from their own times, so this dome is most imposing when seen from some one of the many heights in the neighborhood of Florence. There, the grandeur of its bulk and the symmetry of its proportion disengage themselves from the objects around, and are felt in their full force. It seems a presiding presence over the whole city, and all inferior edifices pay homage to it, and recognise its higher claims.

The interior of the cathedral, imposing from its dim light and great extent, is full of that interest, so common to churches in Italy, derived from its being a mausoleum of greatness and a museum of art. Here reposes the dust of Giotto and Brunelleschi, in spots marked by commemorative busts; and the same honor is paid to the remains of Ficino, the great restorer of the Platonic philosophy. Upon the north wall is a portrait of Dante, of doubtful authenticity, representing him in a standing posture, in a robe of red, his head crowned with laurel, and holding an open book in his hand. The countenance is intellectual and melancholy, showing marks of pride, sensitiveness, and suffering; and whether an ideal head or a likeness, it is that which has been made familiar by Morghen's engraving and the outlines of Flaxman, and which rises up spontaneously before the mind's eye, whenever the name of Dante is mentioned.

The choir, an architectural structure of marble, is adorned with bas-reliefs by Bandinelli and his pupil, Giovanni della Opera, and behind the choir is an unfinished Pieta by Michael Angelo, whose fervid and impatient genius designed so much more than it could execute, in spite of industry, temperance, enthusiastic devotion to art, and a life of ninety years.

In the square where the cathedral stands, are the Baptistery and the Campanile, or Bell-Tower, structures which, so often in Italian towns, serve as architectural satellites to the principal church. The Campanile, the celebrated work of Giotto, rises to the height of nearly three hundred feet. It is Grecian, or rather it resembles the architecture of Greece by its regular outline, its uniform size, and its imposing cornice; but the lofty windows are Gothic in their ornaments. It is built of light-colored marble, adorned with statues and mosaics, and the whole execution is in the highest degree exquisite; but yet it seems to fail in the proper effect of architecture, and to be more admirable for the beauty of the details than for the imposingness of the whole. Its narrowness and regular outline give it an air of primness and monotony. Nor is uniformity of size in harmony with such loftiness of elevation. The Gothic Cross, which narrows as it soars, and ends in a point, is more satisfying to the eye. According to the original design of Giotto, a lofty spire was to have sprung from the top of the present structure; but the great expense of a work of such costly materials probably prevented its being executed.

The Baptistery is best known by its three bronze doors, one by Andrea Pisano, and two by Ghiberti. Of the latter Michael Angelo said, that they were worthy to be the gates of Paradise. From this I had supposed them to be of large size, and my first impression was one of disappointment at finding them so small. The execution is certainly marvellous. Skill, patience, and genius are indubitably stamped upon the work; but, after all, they seem but an inadequate result of forty years of labor; for that is the period Ghiberti was occupied upon them, according to Vasari. The figures are too small, the divisions are too numerous, and the bas-reliefs themselves have too large a share of the proper characteristics of painting. A gem, a mosaic, or a cameo may be examined with minuteness, but the patience becomes exhausted when this microscopic process is to be applied to so many compartments forming one surface. In such labors, the only compensation must be derived from the love of art itself, for the harvest of applause can bear no proportion to the laborer's toil.

WORKS OF MICHAEL ANGELO IN SAN LORENZO.

The church of San Lorenzo is interesting from its associations with the Medici family, and from the light shed upon it by the genius of Michael Angelo. In the sacristy, the traveller from the north first feels the peculiar power of this great artist. The room was designed by him, but it did not strike me as having much architectural merit. It has a formal, rectangular look, and too little shadow for a monumental chapel. Few persons, however, waste their attention upon the casket in which such treasures of art are enclosed. Here are two monuments in marble, by Michael Angelo; one to Lorenzo de Medici,* the grandson of Lorenzo the

* Madame de Staël confounds him with his grandfather, a mistake more natural and excusable than her unlucky blunder

Magnificent, and the father of Catharine de Medici, and the other to Giuliano de Medici, the third son of Lorenzo the Magnificent. They are essentially similar in character and design: each consisting of a sarcophagus surmounted by a statue, and supported by two colossal reclining figures, one male and one female. Those on the monument of Giuliano are called Day and Night, and those on that of Lorenzo, Morning and Evening; though there seems to be no reason why these appellations might not be interchanged.

These remarkable productions take deep hold of the mind, and supply materials for much reflection and some criticism. In the first place, we are inclined to ask, why did an artist of such prodigious inventive power place two works, so similar in conception and design, so near each other? This fact can only be explained by the indolence, the impatience, the carelessness, or the preoccupation of mind, which pass sometimes like spots over the disk of the brightest genius. A similar solution must be applied to the use by Shakespeare, in 'Much Ado About Nothing,' of the same trick to melt the coldness of both Benedick and Beatrice. Again, what is the meaning and significance of the colossal figures? What have Day and Night, or Dawn and Evening, to do with sepulchral monuments in general, or with the lives and fortunes of Lorenzo and Giuliano de Medici? Did Michael

in supposing Leonardo Aretino, a most respectable scholar and writer, to have been Pietro Aretino, a licentious poet and worthless man; which is like confounding Sir Thomas Browne, the author of the 'Religio Medici,' with Tom Brown, of facetious memory.

Angelo mean to allegorize time and eternity, death and the resurrection, or the active and contemplative elements in the human soul, in these gigantic forms? He himself has left no interpretation of them, and his critics and biographers can only surmise and conjecture. And, lastly, the attitudes of these figures are harsh and constrained, for they seem to be kept in their places only by some violent muscular effort. A contagious weariness passes into the beholder's limbs from long looking at them. The forms, too, are exaggerated and redundant in muscle.

So much for criticism. But much more remains for admiration. If these monuments show the characteristic defects of Michael Angelo, they are stamped with all the grandeur and power of his original and unequalled genius. Here is nothing borrowed or derivative: no cold imitation of the antique and none of the pipe-stem meagreness of mediæval art. A great artist has great ideas to express, and he uses marble for his medium; and the material becomes in his hands what the Italian language became in the hands of Dante.

The four colossal figures are of essentially the same character. Day is much unfinished, and probably none of them ever received the last touches of the chisel. But so strong is the expression of thought and intellectual power, that neither the colossal size, nor the want of perfect finish, lessens the authoritative grasp upon the mind of the observer.

But of a still higher order of art is the statue of Lorenzo. He is seated, and in armor, the face resting upon the hand. The figure is so full of character and expression, that all the details are unobserved. It has the dignity and repose of sculpture, and the individuality of a portrait. The mind is too much moved to stoop to the contemplation of a fold of drapery, or the position of a limb. The air of the figure is thoughtful and contemplative. It is that of a man meditating and absorbed by some great design, and not without a dash of the formidable. There is something dangerous in that deep, solemn stillness and intense self-involution. Deadly will be the spring that follows the uncoiling of those folds. I recall no work in marble which leaves the same impression as this remarkable statue. Its power is like that of a magician's spell. Without losing the peculiarity of sculpture, it secures to itself some of the triumphs of painting. It is an entirely original work, and a distinct enlargement of the limits of the art: such a work as would have been pronounced impossible to be executed in marble, had it not been done.

In the same room is another work, also unfinished, by Michael Angelo, a Virgin and Child, a powerful work, and conceived in a reverential spirit, but not pleasing to the taste.

The first sight of these great works is a distinct epoch in the progress of one's training in art. Innumerable as are the antique statues which have come down to us, they have something in common, not easily described, but distinctly felt; just as the scholar perceives a kindred element in the history of Thucydides, the speeches of Demosthenes, and the tragedies of Sophocles. But these statues of Michael Angelo take us into a new world of genius. He is the Columbus of sculpture. He is

'the first that ever broke
Into those silent seas.'

In his hands, form is subordinate to spirit, and is made to represent and express an idea. He awakens not serene or melancholy images of grace and beauty, but thoughts of life, death, and immortality. It is the Christian element speaking to us in marble, and claiming affinity with the Divina Commedia of Dante in poetry, and the Cologne Cathedral in architecture.

These great works are not happily placed. They are too near the eye, and thrown forward into too strong relief by the light colored wall against which they are placed. Put them in a Gothic chapel, shroud them in becoming and monumental gloom, and remove them to the proper distance, and their whole power will be felt.

As I have before remarked, Michael Angelo, in spite of his long life and immense capacity of labor, left many unfinished works. In him, genius was tempered with sternness, impatience, irritability, and self-dissatisfaction. His conceptions seized upon him with a sort of demoniac possession. They became a presence not to be put by. He labored to escape from their overmastering tyranny. He flung himself upon the marble with that fervor and passion with which love embraces, and hatred grapples. But when the thirst of the soul began to be slaked, and the vision to be realized — when he had torn from the block the form which was concealed in its mass — the divine ardor relaxed, and the frost of indifference fell upon the mind and the hand. The short-coming of his labor — the chasm, which there always will be, in imaginative natures, between the forms of things unknown, and the shapes into which they are converted — chilled and repelled him. He turned away in coldness from the block which had lost the morning beauty of hope and promise, to chase new visions, again to be disappointed.

THE MEDICEAN CHAPEL.

Appendant to this same church of San Lorenzo is the Medicean Chapel, a memorable monument of extravagance and bad, or, at least, questionable taste. It is an octagonal room, crowned by a beautiful cupola, painted in fresco by Benvenuti, a modern Italian artist, of whom Valery remarks, with delicate consideration, that it is to be regretted that his talents were not adequate to the opportunity afforded him by so noble a dome. The walls of the chapel are encrusted with the richest marble and precious stones, such as jasper, agate, and lapis lazuli, and ornamented with the armorial bearings of the various cities in Tuscany, executed in Florentine mosaic. The cenotaphs of the Medicean family, which are ranged around the walls, sparkle with gems. Rubies, turquoises, and topazes are lavished upon them with a profusion which recalls our youthful visions of Aladdin's palace. No less than seventeen millions of dollars are said to have been expended upon this costly toy, which is still unfinished, and likely ever to remain so; and yet, after all, the general effect is poor and unsatisfactory. This chapel confirms most impressively the lesson taught with inferior force, it is true, by the doors of the Baptistery and the Campanile of Giotto, as to the necessary limitations and restrictions of art. This principle may be expressed in an epigramatic form by saying, that in art two and two do not always make four. The goldsmith and the jeweller accomplish their results by elaborate details and patient efforts, concentrated upon a small space. The effect which they leave upon the mind is the result of continued impressions. Not so with the architect: with him the first impression is every thing. His art cannot endure a commentator. It must be its own interpreter, or else it cannot be understood. The natural use of gems is to embellish the female form ; to become a part of that beautiful whole, and to glow with the life which warms and colors the neck or the arm. For this reason, we cut them into angles, so that the rays of light may be broken, and a new element of mobility and vivacity given to them. The price of diamonds, as is well known, increases in a geometrical ratio with the increase of size; but this is because the largest diamond is not bigger than an English walnut. Were they to be found as large as paving-stones, there would be no corresponding advance in price. A wall of diamond would be hardly more valued than a wall of glass; and a slab of pearl, not more than a slab of porcelain. The designer of the Medicean Chapel reasoned, that if a Florentine mosaic of a few inches square, be, as it unquestionably is, a beautiful thing, one of many square feet will be just as much more beautiful as it is bigger, and therefore he made the whole side of the room a mosaic. But therein he forgot the essential distinction between the jeweller and the architect. He lost the legitimate triumphs of the former, without gaining those of the latter.

SANTA CROCE.

I went to the church of Santa Croce in the expectation of seeing something externally imposing and beautiful. The Westminster Abbey of Florence I supposed would have something noble and majestic in its aspect, not unworthy of the illustrious dead who have been committed to its charge ; but what was my disappointment when I saw a mere mountain of brick, with as little pretension to beauty or proportion as the gable of a barn — an ugly, unfinished façade, more suggestive of a cotton factory than a church. The interior is venerable and imposing, dimly lighted by long and narrow Gothic windows of stained glass, and shrouded in the gloom which seems appropriate to a church, of which the chief interest is in its tombs and its monuments. Here repose the remains of Michael Angelo, Machiavelli, Galileo, Leonardo Bruno, and Alfieri, and though partially eclipsed by these greater names, the visitor should not overlook those of Lanzi, the historian of painting, and Filicaja, the lyric poet: names not to be forgotten, so long as modest learning and poetical genius are honored among men.

'Ungrateful Florence! Dante sleeps afar!'

The people of Ravenna very properly refused to surrender to the tardy justice of the Florentines, the remains of the illustrious foreigner whose last sigh they had received ; and Florence could only show her sensibility to the genius of her greatest writer, by the empty honors of a cenotaph.

Of the monuments in the church of Santa Croce, no

one is in the highest style of art, and it is a little disconcerting to the stranger to find that the most magnificent of all is erected to the memory of a man of whom he probably never heard, the Chancellor Marsupini. Over all of them, the genius of allegory has breathed from her lips of ice. Painting, sculpture, and architecture appear as mourners around the urn of Michael Angelo. Italy weeps over the dust of Alfieri. A figure, which may serve either for Political Science or History, crowns the monument of Machiavelli; and Poetry deplores the death of Dante. For a monument in a church, a mural tablet with an appropriate inscription, surmounted by a bust or a statue, is all that gratitude, sensibility, or good taste can require, and is always safe. The attempt to do more than this often leads to something tasteless and reprehensible, and when this danger is avoided, the value of a monument, as a memorial, is apt to be impaired by its positive excellence as a work of art.

SANTA MARIA NOVELLA.

The church of Santa Maria Novella is completed, a rare thing in Florence. The façade, an incongruous assemblage of Greek and Gothic forms, did not please me, but the interior, from its extent, its simplicity, and the happy disposition of its lights and shades, is very fine. Here is a famous picture by Cimabue, a Virgin and Child, larger than life, painted upon a gold ground. It is pleasant to read of the prodigious enthusiasm which this work excited when first exhibited, nearly six hundred years ago, for the gratification of Charles of

Anjou, as he passed through Florence on his way to take possession of his kingdom of Naples; of the admiring throngs who rent the air with shouts of delight, and of the stately procession which bore it from the studio of the artist to its present place in the church. Much of this enthusiasm is to be ascribed to the fact, that the works of Cimabue were so much superior to those of his immediate predecessors, that painting in his hands seemed like the revival of a lost art. It was not merely that the sentiment of devotion and the sense of beauty were appealed to with a power unknown before, but the national pride of the people was gratified, and stirring hopes for the future awakened. As works of art multiply, they form the standard by which they themselves are tried. We judge, compare, and discriminate. Our admiration is more regulated and less ardent. It was just so with the first specimens of sun-painting. We had nothing to give but amazement and delight. But, now, we coolly measure the works of one man or one country with those of another, as we compare Titian with Raphael, or Morghen with Longhi. As for the work of Cimabue itself, looking at it with the natural eye of this period, it seems stiff and grim: more curious than beautiful; and yet with an expression upon the countenance in which sweetness and dignity are blended.

But the most obvious and interesting associations with this church are secular, not to say profane. It is here that the opening scene of the Decameron is laid. Here Boccaccio represents himself as meeting that knot of graceful Florentine ladies, who, wearied with the universal dislocation of society, occasioned by the ravages of the plague, resolved to retire awhile into a neighboring villa, and amuse themselves with innocent recreations. We read that these fair worshippers were shocked with the demoralizing effects of the pestilence which was raging around them, and yet we find them, as every reader of the Decameron knows, listening to stories, which, in our times, it would be impossible for one gentleman to read aloud to another. In this respect we have made progress. It is mere paradox to say that vice has fled from the lips to the heart. Out of the fulness of the heart the mouth speaks. The purification of literature is a sign of a higher moral standard, and is mainly due to the better position and greater influence of woman.

THE ANNUNZIATA.

The church and conventual buildings of the Annunziata contain many interesting objects. The frescoes in the vestibule or atrium, many of which are by Andrea del Sarto, are of high merit. The subjects of several of them are drawn from the life of an eminent saint, Filippo Benizzi. One of them is a curious instance of the power of religious bigotry to destroy the simplest elements of Christian morality. The saint is walking in the country. Some gay young men, playing at cards under a tree, laugh at his uncouth appearance ; whereupon, he prays to Heaven, and the young men are struck with lightning. It is strange that the ecclesiastics who invent such stories, and cause them to be painted, do not reflect that nine men out of ten who read such legends, and look upon such representations, will keep one half the lesson and throw away the other — will take the vengeance and reject the saintly life. Jesus of Nazareth, with lips convulsed with the agony of the cross, prayed that his murderers might be forgiven, but his disciples limit their forgiveness to sins which they themselves have committed.

In one of the cloisters of this church is the 'Madonna del Sacco' of Andrea del Sarto, a fresco painting of great merit, not only in drawing and coloring, but from the simple originality of the design. It brings out more fully the human element than is usual in the treatment of this subject. It is a family — father, mother, and child — disposed in a natural group, not as if sitting for their portraits, but as if the artist had looked in upon them where they were unawares.

CHAPTER VI.

Giotto's Portrait of Dante — Raphael's Fresco of the Last Supper — The Casa Buonarotti — The Pitti Palace — The Boboli Gardens — The Museum of Natural History — The Laurentian Library — The Academia delle belle Arti — Environs of Florence — Church aud Convent of San Miniato — Galileo — Poggio Imperiale — Bello Sguardo — Fiesole.

GIOTTO'S PORTRAIT OF DANTE.

WITHIN the last ten years two interesting discoveries have been made in Florence. One is the portrait of Dante in the Chapel of the Palazzo del Podestá, by Giotto. This Palazzo is a singular structure, built in a rambling and uncouth style; and now used as a prison. Upon the walls of the cortile are seen the armorial bearings of a long line of magistrates of Florence. The room in which the portrait was discovered had lost the aspect of a chapel, and had been used as a storehouse for the prison, or some similar office. Perhaps it is hardly correct to say, that the portrait was discovered, as there must always have been some persons who knew that this work and many others were there, and might be found if any one would take the trouble to remove the whitewash which had been daubed over them. Fond as the Italians are of whitewash — a fact which the traveller soon finds out, to his cost — it is quite inexplicable that the Florentines, with their reverence for Dante, should not have spared his portrait, or that any magistrate, or man in authority, should not have been deterred by a wholesome fear of public opinion, from committing or allowing such an act of sacrilege. But for many years — even generations — the portrait slept in its shroud of white, and there would have slept till the last syllable of recorded time, had its resurrection depended upon indigenous reverence, energy, and enterprise. A few English and American gentlemen — among whom, our distinguished countryman, the late Mr. R. H. Wilde, was conspicuous — resolved to make the attempt to uncover it, and after repeated applications, and all sorts of aiding influence, the supineness or distrust of the government was so far overcome as to give these gentlemen a reluctant permission to remove the whitewash at their own expense.

The result answered to their hopes. After a coat of whitewash, in some places an inch thick, had been taken off, the portrait was found. It represents the great poet in the prime of life, before sorrow and struggle had sharpened and deepened the lines of his face, and made it that record of outraged pride and wounded sensibility which it became in his declining years. The brow is ample, the nose straight, and the features regular: a countenance at once intellectual and handsome. The dress is a long, flowing robe, and the head is covered with a sort of hood, or cap. Whatever merits as a work of art it may have had have been sadly impaired by what it has been through; but no one will deny that it is a precious waif snatched from the wreck of time.

RAPHAEL'S FRESCO OF THE LAST SUPPER.

This fresco, by Raphael, is in what was once the refectory of the convent of St. Onofrio, used at the time of the discovery as a coach-maker's shop. It represents the Last Supper, and is an early work, painted before the great master had entirely thrown off the stiffness and hardness of the school in which he had been trained. Judas sits apart from the other apostles, as if already an outcast, or, at least, an object of suspicion. This is an obvious sacrifice of dramatic propriety to the imperative claims of the church. It will be remembered with what skill Leonardo da Vinci has met the two requisitions, and designated the traitor, as yet unknown, by his darkly-lowering countenance and the overturned salt. The fresco has the easily recognised quality of Raphael's genius — its purity, elevation, and tenderness. The faces are full of character and expression. In the background is a landscape representing the agony in the garden. The room in which the fresco is painted has been cleaned, furnished with seats, and, with the liberality so general in Italy, thrown open to the public without charge.

THE CASA BUONAROTTI.

One of the most interesting objects in Florence is the Casa Buonarotti, the residence of Michael Angelo, and still occupied by descendants of his family, who study to keep the house of their illustrious kinsman as nearly in the state in which he left it as possible. One of the rooms — the first into which the visitor is shown — is filled with paintings upon the walls and ceiling, illustrative of various events in the great artist's life. In the same room is a bas-relief, by Michael Angelo himself, representing a combat with Centaurs, and also an oil painting by him. In his study are several memorials of him : his sword and walking-stick, some arm-chairs, which, as we were told, belonged to his great-grandfather, and looking uncomfortable enough to justify any antiquity. The walls are hung with drawings from his hand. In another room is a bronze bust of him, by John of Bologna, hard and expressive, and a portrait taken a short time before his death. The arched ceiling of one of the rooms was designed by him, and has a very noble effect, showing that great space is not essential to produce the impression of grandeur. The rooms open into each other. Some of the original furniture is still sacredly preserved. It was rather odd to be conducted over the house of Michael Angelo, as I was, by an English maid-servant, who seemed to have rarely the privilege of using her own language, to judge by the extent to which she availed herself of the opportunity of my ears. The sensibility with which the Italians cherish the memory of their great men is a most honorable trait in the national character. The house in which Machiavelli lived is designated by a tablet, and nearly opposite to it is that of the historian, Guicciardini.

THE PITTI PALACE.

The Pitti Palace, a splendid structure, was commenced for himself, by Lucca Pitti, a vain, weak man, elevated to great power by a sudden turn of political fortune. It finally passed by purchase, and while yet unfinished, into the possession of the rival family of the Medici, and furnishes an instructive commentary upon the saying, that fools build houses and wise men buy them. Johnson might have found in the varying fortunes of the founder of this palace, a vivid illustration of the vanity of human wishes. Machiavelli paints, in energetic language, his short-lived splendor and his sudden fall, not omitting one characteristic touch of selfishness and ingratitude, which strongly marks the powerless obscurity into which he had declined, that many articles of value which had been pressed upon him as presents, in the brief day of his elevation, were reclaimed by the donors as loans, when the tide of fortune had turned.

Of all the royal residences which I have seen, the Pitti Palace is the most desirable to live in, particularly when the attractions of the gallery are taken into account. The architecture of the façade is heavy, massive, and sombre ; but that of the cortile is rich and magnificent. The rooms are spacious and imposing, and the whole air of the palace truly regal. There is nothing that speaks of decay or neglect : no faded splendor and no mouldering magnificence. It is a house to live in, as well as a palace to look at. But in visiting it, it is difficult to think of any thing but its treasures of art, as in recalling it to the mind, little else returns. Here are nearly five hundred pictures, many of them of the highest merit, and very few that are not good. No other collection of paintings, which I have seen, approaches it in excellence, with the single exception of the Dresden Gallery; and between these two it would not be easy to award the palm of superiority. If a person could see but one, I should advise him, on the whole, to choose the Dresden Gallery, because it comprises a greater variety of artists and schools, and because of the unique Correggios and the incomparable Madonna di San Sisto, which are there; but if, after having seen them both, the privilege were offered of seeing one, and only one, a second time, the decision would be embarrassing, and probably quite as many would take the Pitti Palace as the Dresden Gallery. So far as arrangement and position are concerned, the advantage is decidedly with the Florentine collection. The pictures are well-disposed and hung in favorable lights: the walls are not crowded: there are no gloomy vaults of shade and cold, to chill the heart and strain the eye, but the sun streams in through spacious windows in rich and enlivening masses. The noble apartments are furnished with comfortable couches and chairs for the repose of weary limbs; and a traveller soon learns that there is no employment so exhausting as walking through a gallery and looking at its pictures. This splendid collection, with a liberality worthy of the highest praise, is thrown open to the public every day, without fee, and the humblest stranger who visits it is treated as if he were conferring, rather than receiving a favor.

Here, as elsewhere, the generality of visitors first seek out the Raphaels. The most celebrated of his pictures in this collection is the Madonna della Seggiola, so widely known by engravings. It is a work of great sweetness, purity, and tenderness, but not representing all the power of the artist's genius. Its chief charm, and the secret of its world-wide popularity, is its happy blending of the divine and the human elements. Some painters treat this subject in such a way, that the spectator sees only a mortal mother caressing her child; while, by others, the only ideas awakened are those of the Virgin and the Redeemer. But heaven and earth meet upon Raphael's canvas: the purity of heaven and the tenderness of earth. The round, infantile forms, the fond, clasping arms, the sweetness, and the grace belong to the world that is around us, but the faces — especially that of the infant Saviour, in whose eyes there is a mysterious depth of expression, which no engraving has ever fully caught — are touched with light from heaven, and suggest something to worship as well as to love.

In the same apartment, upon the opposite wall, is another work by the same inspired hand — the Madonna dell' Impannata, (so called from a window closed by cloth instead of glass,) which, though impaired by time and restoration, impressed me as superior in power and originality to the Madonna della Seggiola.

In another apartment is the Madonna del Baldachino (of the Canopy.) The Virgin is seated upon a throne, raised upon three high steps, at the extremity of the temple. A canopy, suspended from the roof, hangs over the throne, and two angels draw aside the curtain, in order to show the Virgin. Four fathers of the church stand beside the throne, and two angels are reading a scroll at the bottom of the steps. This is one of Raphael's earlier works, and from its resemblance to the style of Fra Bartolomeo, was doubtless painted under his first impressions of the power of that great artist.

There are also four portraits by Raphael. The finest is that of Pope Leo X. with two cardinals. The pope is seated before a table covered with a cloth. A richly sculptured bell is within reach, and he holds a reading glass in his hand. The features are strong, but not fine: the expression is that of a man who had always had his own way, and always meant to have it. It is evidently not a flattered likeness. The attendant cardinals are most speaking and characteristic faces. This is a grand picture, and the figures, being portraits, have all the interest of history.

This gallery is also rich in the productions of Andrea del Sarto, a very pleasing artist, who came very near being a great one. But he is a decided mannerist, which no man truly great in art ever was. His pictures have the strongest family likeness, and even the dresses of his Virgins seem all to have been cut from the same piece of cloth. His Holy Families, as compared with those of Raphael, are like Lalla Rookh to Comus. Still, he is a delightful artist, and probably paints as well as a man can who never breaks loose from the passions and weaknesses of earth.

Among the other striking pictures of the collection, is a sublime St. Mark, by Fra Bartolomeo: the Three Fates, by Michael Angelo, hard, powerful, and impressive: the portrait of an unknown lady, very carefully painted, by Leonardo da Vinci — the hands, especially, most elaborately and beautifully finished: the Conspiracy of Cataline, by Salvator Rosa, a picture of considerable power, but wanting in dignity and elevation: a beautiful St. Francis in Meditation, by Cigoli, a Florentine artist of much merit, whose name I had never before heard. There are three works by Rubens here, all excellent in their kind. One is a group of portraits of himself, his brother, and the two philosophers, Lipsius and Grotius. The attitudes are easy and graceful, the coloring admirable, and the faces full of life and expression. The other two are landscapes — not transcripts of a beautiful or picturesque country, but carefully painted, and with an attention to details quite remarkable in an artist of such fervid power and inexhaustible invention. The coloring is not showy, but honest and natural. These two pictures grew upon me at every visit, not certainly as works of the first class, and never to be named in comparison with some of the splendid productions around them, but rather as instructive illustrations of Rubens's views of art. Certainly, no man ever wielded a bolder and freer pencil, but here he sits down to paint a homely landscape, and does it in as patient and conscientious a way, as if he were drawing from a camera lucida. Here are no pulpy rocks, no hills of canvas, and no velvety grass. The details are not slobbered over, nor is every thing sacrificed to the general effect. They are as true as a scene from the windows of a Flemish farm-house.

In the same apartment with the Madonna della Seggiola are two portraits, one of Cardinal Bentivoglio, by Vandyke, and one of an old man, sometimes called Cornaro, by Titian. Portrait painting can hardly go higher than it has done in these noble works. At first, the attention is more attracted to the portrait of Bentivoglio, the costume is so splendid, and the head is so full of intellect and refinement. The gentleman and the scholar are stamped upon every line of the countenance. The face of Titian's old man is not so elevated and intellectual, but with every look it draws the gaze more and more. Such truth, such power, such color! It is the perfection of portraiture. Between two such works, comparisons are particularly odious. It is an ungracious and ungrateful office to seek to exalt one at the expense of the other. They hang together like a young moon and the evening star in a summer sky. Neither loses, but each gains, by the other's presence.

A Magdalen, by Titian, has stamped itself upon my memory as deeply as any picture in the whole collection, and is quite characteristic of the manner in which that magnificent painter treated a subject. The Magdalen is a woman who has led a life of sin, and is now repentant. Hence, the idea of a Magdalen involves two elements, the previous sin and the present repentance. In the early painters the dominant feeling was of repentance. The forms are meagre, the cheeks wasted, and the bloom and grace, through which she fell, are gone. But Titian was a man of such exuberant temperament, and so full of strong life, that the beauty and the passion were the predominant ideas in his mind when he formed a conception of the Magdalen, and they guided his pencil when he developed it upon the canvas. The picture beams with betraying and bewitching beauty. The luxuriant fulness of the figure, the rich, ripe cheek, the eyes whose passionate fire is not quenched by the tears which fill them, and the wealth of golden hair — such hair as none but Titian could paint — have more of earth than of heaven, and breathe an atmosphere of moral enchantment, which fascinates and fixes the wandering gaze.

In the Hall of the Education of Jupiter, (so called from the painting on the ceiling,) is an anonymous female portrait, ascribed to Raphael. At any rate, it is a most excellent picture. The face is not one of rare beauty, nor is it in the earliest bloom of youth, but it is a winning and cordial face; breathing gentleness, warmth of heart, and resolute firmness of purpose, were it needed. It is, too, a domestic countenance, suggesting a happy wife and mother, and a home brightened by an active spirit and a loving nature. There is so much character and such marked individuality in the countenance, that we cannot pass it by as a mere 'Portrait of a lady.' We are constrained to pause and speculate, and to say to ourselves, 'Who were you that look out of the canvas with that loving, sensible, animated face?' But we ask in vain. It is a fragment of the past, telling no story and linked to no associations. Who she was — where and when she lived — with whom her fortunes and her affections were entwined — are left to conjecture. It is a face without a history.* Near it is a St. Andrew kneeling before the Cross, by Carlo Dolce, a feeble and affected picture, as most of the works of this artist are. Carlo Dolce is a

* The portrait is generally said to represent a mistress of Raphael, and it may be so; but the expression of the countenance does not confirm the conjecture, for it is pure and noble. It is a common trick of biographers and catalogue makers to give this appellation to every portrait of a young female which they cannot identify, and often with great injustice. Painters are not better than any other men, but certainly not worse.

painter against whom one gets in time to feel a sort of personal spite. His red-bordered eyes, his affected attitudes, and his sickly sweetness soon disgust and weary. A gallery of his works would be as cloying as a dinner of sugar candy.

Canova's statue of Venus finds a home in the Pitti Palace. She stands upon a pivot, and can be turned so as to be seen in various points of view. If I was a heretic before the Venus de Medici, I was a downright infidel before Canova's. It seemed to me that the artist had tried to produce something that should be more beautiful than beauty; as if a painter should try to paint a picture, which should be bluer than blue, or redder than red. The true line of grace is thus overstepped, and prettiness and affectation are the result. There is a want of simplicity and repose in the whole figure. She is huddling her drapery about her, and, at the same time, an expression in her face seems to says, 'Am I not doing it becomingly?' reminding one of a veteran belle who covers her face with her fan to hide the blush that should be there, and at the same time looks through the sticks to observe the effect. Canova's skill with the chisel was unrivalled, and the mechanical execution of this statue is exquisite; but this is small praise. If a statue does not speak to the mind and the heart, it is but a stone after all.

In one of the rooms is a picture of Judith and Holofernes, of no very high merit, and by an artist whose name I have forgotten, in which, however, contrary to the common practice of painters, the right moment is taken. This is a subject frequently painted, especially by Allori, one of whose repetitions is also in the gallery of the Pitti Palace; and another belongs to the Boston Athenæum. But how does he represent it? We see a woman of magnificent beauty, richly dressed, with a ghastly head in her hand, and attended by a servant; a picture powerfully colored, but with as little of sentiment or emotion in the figure, as if she were a butcher's wife, carrying home a calf's head to a customer. The artist has chosen the wrong moment. The deed has been done. The glow and excitement have passed away, and the languor of exhaustion has succeeded. Every action or incident has its point of most intense interest — its flowering moment, so to speak — and this the artist should select. In the case of Judith, that point is the instant when, her womanly weakness overcome by patriotism and devotion, she raises the sword to strike her sleeping victim. All before is preparation: all after is retrospect. This is the time chosen by the painter of the picture first mentioned.

The attractions of the Pitti Palace are not exhausted by the paintings that hang upon the walls. The ceilings are elaborately painted in fresco — in several of the rooms by Pietro da Cortona — the subjects being all sorts of fantastical and unintelligible allegories; and if one is willing to forget the allegory, and wrench his neck off his shoulders in examining them, he will find much to admire in the grouping and coloring. There are also some twenty or thirty tables of Florentine mosaic, in themselves works of art, representing fruits, flowers, animals, landscapes; and I remember one imitating a breakfast service in the natural disorder of a half-finished meal. These tables are so beautiful that it seems hardly fair to put them in the same room with pictures of such paramount attraction. They deserve to be examined without the intrusive proximity of superior claims. The grapes glow with the bloom and dew of life, and the flowers are as fresh as if they had just been brought in from the garden and laid upon the table. No mechanical manufacture produces such beautiful results as the Florentine mosaic. Of course, such tables are too fine for use, and can only be looked at; and when we are told that some of them have cost a sum of no less than eighty thousand dollars, it seems paying far too dearly for this pleasure of the eye, and the enjoyment of beauty is rebuked by the sense of disproportion.

THE BOBOLI GARDENS.

Behind the Pitti Palace are the Bob̀oli gardens, which are laid out in that artificial style which in our country we know only from description. All is formal and regular. Trees are planted in rectangular rows, and their branches so trained and interlaced as to form long cathedral aisles of foliage, as if a lateral shaft had been cut in a solid mass of fresh green. In these very gardens, Milton may have had suggested to him his image of the Indian herdsman,

> 'that tends his pasturing herds
> At loop-holes cut through thickest shade.'

The whole fashion of the place speaks of the luxury of shade, and of defences against a tyrannous and intrusive sun. For this end are reared those high, verdurous walls to refresh the eye, dazzled with the fervors of a summer's noon; for this, grottoes are hollowed out of the rock, and sun-proof roofs of foliage are woven where the freshness and coolness of the morning long lingers and slowly retires. At every turn, the stranger encounters statues, standing singly or in groups — some colossal, some quaint, and some imposing — some carved by hands no less illustrious than those of Michael Angelo, and others, by John of Bologna. The ground is very irregular in its surface; and this inequality makes the formality of the style less offensive. From the heights in the rear of the palace, a fine view of Florence is obtained.

To me there was a great charm in these gardens. They are open to the public twice a week, and I never failed to visit them on those days. At noon, in that genial climate, the sun was warm enough to reconcile one to their peculiar character, and to aid the imagination in forming a picture of their summer fascinations. The rose still lingered about the walks in fearless beauty. At the end of the gardens is a fountain, or more properly, a small circular basin of water, in which are three colossal statues, which claim to represent rivers. This sheet of water is enclosed by a thick belt of trees and evergreen shrubbery; but a broad, smooth margin of marble and turf is left between the two, which was the favorite sporting-place of the English children in Florence, whose mammas and nurses made this spot a sort of infant exchange. Here they were found of all ages and sizes, from the baby of two summers, that could do little more than crow and clap its hands, to the little damsel of ten or twelve, already beginning to draw herself up and look dignified. Their animated movements and happy voices gave life and music to a scene worthy of the pencil of Correggio or Albano. There are no children so beautiful as English children. The good constitutions they are born with, the great care with which they are reared, their simple food, their abundant supply of fresh air, and their living and sleeping in cool rooms, not poisoned by the breath of furnaces, give them a vigor, bloom, and energy of movement, easily distinguishing them from their continental contemporaries. I did not 'sigh for their sakes that they should e'er grow older;' for the notion that mature life brings with it more of suffering than of satisfaction is a disparagement of the wisdom and goodness of God, who has made a world which men and women are to carry on, and which, as Paley says, 'is a happy world, after all.' And yet there was a sigh called forth by the sight of these fairy creatures. It did not flow from recollections of blessings given and withdrawn, once bitter, but long since mellowed into softness and tenderness, but rather from that mysterious law in our nature which mingles a shade of sadness, or, at least, of pensiveness in our finest emotions.

'As frighted Porserpine let fall
Her flowers at the sight of Dis,
Even so the dark and bright will kiss:
The sunniest things throw brightest shade,
And there is even a happiness
That makes the heart afraid.'

THE MUSEUM OF NATURAL HISTORY.

This noble institution, which is daily open to the public, occupies a building immediately adjoining the Pitti Palace. The collections in mineralogy, geology, and ornithology, are said to be good, and to be constantly increasing by the liberality of the Grand Duke. But to the casual visitor, at least, the most striking part of the collection are the models in wax, which are distributed through fifteen apartments. They comprise preparations of every possible variety, colored with the utmost fidelity, and elaborated with the most patient minuteness of detail. The arrangement, to my unscientific eye, seemed excellent; presenting the muscular system, the blood-vessels, the organs of sense, and, in short, all the details of the fearful and wonderful mechanism of the frame of man, in separate portions and in their natural succession. There are also several whole length figures. The preparations are arranged in glass cases distributed around the walls, and over the cases are drawings corresponding to the models. One of the most interesting of the rooms contains a collection illustrative of comparative anatomy. Here are dissections of the leach and the lobster: a representation of the progress of incubation, from the egg to the chicken, and of the successive stages in the life of the silkworm.

The art of imitating the living form by wax was first used by Zumbo, or Zummo, a Sicilian, who came to Florence at the invitation of Cosimo the Third, one of the Medici family. His genius, like that of Rabelais and Swift, had a diseased fondness for revelling in those disgusting images, from the contemplation of which most men instinctively recoil. The representations which he has left of the plagues of Florence are doubtless hideously and repulsively real; certainly, it is difficult to look at them a second time, and that perhaps is the best tribute to their fidelity. Indeed, were they of the size of life, they could not be looked at at all.

The value of such anatomical preparations is hardly commensurate with the great labor and expense requisite in their preparation. The surgeon can never learn his art by mere ocular inspection. He must dissect, and read with the knife in his hand. The unprofessional world, with other pursuits and alien tastes, will hardly expend many precious hours of a short life in a painful and minute study of details, which only become attractive in the light of a knowledge comprehensive enough to grasp and combine them into an harmonious whole. The laws of health cannot be too generally known and too carefully taught; but these are neither numerous nor complicated. The dyspeptic need not go to a dissecting room, or to an anatomical museum, to learn that mince-pie is injurious to him; and a conviction of the benefit of exercise may be imparted, without showing the manner in which the heart is stimulated, and the circulation quickened, by muscular effort. Besides, there is another class of considerations to be taken into account, when we propose to admit the universal public, young and old, behind the veil of nature. We know that we are fearfully and wonderfully made. We know that there is not a fibre or a process in the frame of man, which should not awaken reverent and solemn reflection; but we also know that such is not the result in all natures. Such revelations are to the giddy and thoughtless but trifling toys, while the coarse and vulgar extract from them only debasing and degrading associations. Things are now not quite so bad as they were in the days of Forsyth, when all the sacred mysteries of reproduction were laid open to the general gaze, without distinction of sex; but, perhaps, even now the privilege of access is too indiscriminately accorded.

THE LAURENTIAN LIBRARY.

The Laurentian Library is nobly lodged in a building designed by Michael Angelo, so rich and stately, that it seems hardly respectful to entrust any thing smaller than a folio to its keeping. Here are some of the most interesting manuscripts in Europe. As a lawyer, I gazed with reverence upon that world-renowned copy of the Pandects, which is said to have been discovered at Amalfi in the twelfth century. The notion, long entertained, that, in consequence of this discovery, the study of the civil law was revived, and its influence extended throughout Europe, is now generally abandoned; but it is certain that the volumes were long regarded with a religious veneration, accorded to no other relic of profane antiquity. They were transferred from Pisa to Florence by the fortune of war in 1406, and never shown but by the special permission of the magistrates, and by torch-light. Here is also a manuscript of Virgil, of the fifth century, in excellent preservation.

In Italian literature, the most interesting specimens are a copy of the Divina Commedia of Dante, transcribed by Filippo Villani, within twenty years after the poet's death; and a copy of the Decameron, made from the original autograph, by Francesco Mannelli, the godson of Boccaccio. The autograph of Petrarch appears in a copy of Horace, and a volume of Cicero's Epistles is said to have been written by his hand. This has been doubted. The handwriting is remarkably neat and regular. There are also some splendid missals.

THE ACADEMIA DELLE BELLE ARTI.

This institution is contained in a spacious building which was once a hospital. The gallery of paintings is particularly rich in specimens of early Tuscan art, and the progress of painting may be seen from the rigid stiffness of the Byzantine school to the grace and freedom of the sixteenth century. Here the celestial genius of Fra Angelico fills the air with the spirit of devotion. There are also some very pleasing specimens of Pietro Perugino, and two admirable pictures of St. Francis, by Cigoli, in which the weakness of the worn-out man and the ecstatic fervor of the saint are most powerfully represented. When I visited this gallery, I had not read the works of Lord Lyndsay or Mr. Ruskin, nor Mrs. Jameson's Legends of the Monastic Orders (indeed, the last had not been written), and hardly knew the worth and value of what was before me. I should see it with more profit now.

'’Tis the taught already that profit by teaching.'

Here, too, the manufacture of Florentine mosaic is carried on at the public expense. The materials used in this beautiful art are gems and the half precious stones ; and great taste and skill are shown in imitating the colors of fruits and flowers in the natural hues of the mineral kingdom. The process is very tedious, and said not to be favorable to the health. One man whom I saw was at work upon a fragment of a table which was to occupy him for five years. Some of the specimens of the art which are shown to visitors are extremely beautiful. In a lower room was a porphyry sarcophagus, very elaborately carved, which was destined for a monument to the late Grand Duchess.

ENVIRONS OF FLORENCE.

The environs of Florence are all beautiful. Go where we will, we cannot go amiss. Out of whichever gate we pass, we come upon something attractive or interesting, either in nature or art. Every where the surface is broken into expressive irregularities, and the eye is never out of sight of a picturesque landscape. Churches, convents, neat villas, some of which are almost palaces in extent and architectural beauty, crown the heights and nestle in the hollows. The pine, the olive, and the vine blend their forms and foliage in soothing and animating eye-harmonies. The city is so compact, also, that a short walk will always bring one face to face with the tranquillizing aspect of nature, before a touch of fatigue has dimmed the sense of enjoyment. I believe that the Italians are not very sensitive to natural beauty. If this sensibility be wanting to the people of Florence, they lose a large amount of cheap and pure satisfactions.

CHURCH AND CONVENT OF SAN MINIATO.

A brisk walk of a few minutes out of the Porta San Miniato, brings the traveller to the church and convent of that name, a mass of buildings conspicuous from their position and castellated appearance. The church, parts of which belong to the eleventh century, is an imposing structure, and is, to a considerable extent, built of the fragments of ancient Roman edifices, which, when we compare their original destination with their present position, remind us of a palimpsest manuscript from which a hymn to Apollo has been expunged, and a holy legend written in its place. It is well to have Christian churches rather than ruined temples, if the latter must be sacrificed to the former; but, in a country so abounding with accessible building materials as Italy, there is no excuse for the indolence or parsimony which destroys the monuments of antiquity, in order to use their fragments for incongruous modern structures. Here are many curious and interesting works of art, especially by Luca della Robbia, who expended fine powers of invention and design upon the strange material of glazed blue and white terra cotta. The medallions by him in the Chapel of St. James are esteemed among the best of his works, but the material is so suggestive of soup tureens and tea drinking, that the legitimate effect of art is in a great measure lost. The remains of the fortifications raised around the convent by Michael Angelo, during the last unsuccessful struggles of the citizens of Florence to throw off the rule of the Medici family, may still be traced.*

GALILEO.

At a short distance from the convent is a tower, which was used by Galileo as an observatory, and near the tower is a villa in which the illustrious philosopher resided, and where Milton is said to have visited him. Milton's expression in relating this Incident, is, that he 'visited the famous Galileo, grown old, a prisoner to the Inquisition, for thinking in astronomy otherwise than the Franciscan and Dominican licensers thought.' He was never actually incarcerated in Florence, and Milton's words, probably, mean no more than that he had been directed to confine his movements to his own house and grounds, or that he preferred a voluntary seclusion on account of the annoying supervision with which his steps were followed. Could the inexorable past be made to yield up its spoils, with what delight should we read a record of the interview † between the aged philosopher and the youthful poet — so unlike in

* Was it from one of his expedients that Butler took the hint of his well-known couplet,

> 'feather-bed twixt castle-wall,
> And heavy brunt of cannon-ball'?

He hung heavy woollen cloths around the Campanile, by which the force of the cannon-shot was lessened, and the building saved.

† Landor has made this interview the subject of one of his 'Imaginary Conversations;' but it is not one of the most successful efforts of his uncertain genius.

mental organization, but so like in purity of life and manliness of soul — the former, as we may imagine, grave, wise, didactic, and cautious, shadowed with sadness and touched with infirmity; the latter in the bloom and flower of his manly beauty, radiant with his splendid genius, overflowing with life and hope and power, as yet untouched by sorrow, disappointment, poverty, or blindness. That the poet listened with reverence to the words of the philosopher, we may feel assured; nor can we doubt that the wise, old man was touched by the graceful deference of his accomplished guest, and moved by the power and eloquence of his discourse, so rich in learning, so vital with genius. His heart may have throbbed with that feeling, with which Schiller represents Wallenstein as stirred, when he saw before him the morning purity of Max Piccolomini.

'He stood beside me like my youth,
Transformed for me the real to a dream,
Clothing the palpable and the familiar
With golden exhalations of the dawn.'

An Italian biographer of Milton, with that sensitive regard to the honor of his country for which the literary men of Italy have always been distinguished, has supposed that he may have derived from his conversation with Galileo some astronomical hints, which were reproduced in the Paradise Lost; but of this there is no proof, nor is it even probable.

POGGIO IMPERIALE.

A short distance outside of the Porta Romana is the Poggio Imperiale, a country palace of the Grand Duke.

The approach to it is by a noble avenue of cypresses, oak, and larch, some half a mile in length. That man is fortunate who can call such an avenue his own. It matters little what is at the end of it, whether a palace, a villa, or a cottage. It includes in itself all the elements of a landscape. The restless play of light and shade, the majestic canopy of foliage, the wind-music that storms or whispers through it, the trunks regular but not monotonous and ever revealing fine accidents of perspective, are full of fresh suggestions and unworn exhilaration to a mind at all sensitive to natural beauty. The palace itself is an imposing building, containing a multitude of apartments, which are well furnished and neatly kept. From the windows of the upper story a noble landscape may be seen. In the cortile is a marble statue — the wounded Adonis — generally ascribed to Michael Angelo, and quite worthy of his chisel, for it is full of life, power, and originality. In the dining-room is a small statue of Apollo, by a Greek artist, and of great beauty ; one of the finest relics of ancient art, and well worthy of a more conspicuous and accessible position.

A field near the Poggio Imperiale is the scene of Redi's wild dithyrambic of 'Bacchus in Tuscany,' a poem which foams and sparkles like newly poured champagne. Redi was a learned physician, and is said to have rarely indulged in the wines which he celebrates with such lyric fervor.

BELLO SGUARDO.

About half a mile from the Poggio Imperiale is the hill of Bello Sguardo, crowned by a villa in which the historian Guicciardini once resided. From this villa there is a very fine view of Florence. I was there at sunset on the fourth day of December, but there was no breath of winter in the air, which was soft and balmy like that of an early October day in New England. In the garden, roses and camellias were blooming as boldly as if there were no such thing on earth as frost. The towers and domes of Florence burned in the rich light of the setting sun, and the Arno flowed like a river of gold; and I could hardly comprehend that a villa commanding so enchanting a prospect should be, as it was, unoccupied.

LA PETRAJA AND CASTELLO.

The Grand Duke of Tuscany is rich in dwelling-places, each so attractive that his difficulty must be to decide not which he will use, but which he can stay away from. Within a short distance from Florence, driving out of the Porta al Prato, are two pleasant villas belonging to him, La Petraja and Castello, both well worth visiting. Attached to each are elaborate gardens, with terraces, fountains, and statues, formal walks of shrubbery and walls of verdure. The cypress, oak, and laurel blend with the more delicate forms of the orange, lemon, and myrtle. In the grounds of La Petraja is a beautiful fountain, in which the principal figure is a bronze Venus, by John of Bologna, who is represented as wringing the water from her hair. These villas, and the grounds appurtenant to them, like every thing belonging to the Grand Duke, were in good order, and showed the results of a generous expenditure and a careful supervision.

FIESOLE.

Fiesole, the cradle of Florence, occupies the summit of a steep hill, which it takes an hour's brisk walking to reach. The latter part of the way is much like mounting a flight of steps, and is very trying to those that are 'fat and scant of breath.' Every foot of the road is interesting, either from the beauty which it reveals, or from the associations which it awakens. It passes near the Villa Palmieri, which was the scene of the Decameron of Boccaccio. Fiesole is a place of remote antiquity, as is attested by a piece of massive Etruscan wall, composed of immense stones, of irregular shape and various sizes. Old as this is, it bears its years well, and seems as likely to endure as any structure of man's hands now upon the earth.

In Fiesole, as in most Italian towns, there are churches and a convent, in which are doubtless many things worthy of being seen; but the traveller, unless he can spend much more time than I had at my disposal, will hardly linger under any roof, while so enchanting a prospect tempts him without. Language breaks down in the effort to fix upon paper the impressions awakened by a landscape of such beauty, such variety, and such extent. A genius like that of Byron, from which words flash with the sudden and illumining power of lightning, or of Shelley, who paints with a pen dipt in the rainbow, can alone fasten the scene and arrest the emotions to which it gives birth.

CHAPTER VII.

La Certosa — The Brethren of the Misericordia — Society in Florence — Robert and Elizabeth Browning — Powers and Greenough — Departure from Florence — Pisa — The Leaning Tower, Cathedral, Campo Santo, and Baptistery — Beggars — Leghorn — Steamer to Civita Vecchia — Civita Vecchia — Arrival at Rome.

LA CERTOSA.

ONE of the pleasantest days of my residence in Florence was that devoted to a visit to the monastery of La Certosa, about four miles distant. It is beautifully situated, crowning a gentle elevation covered with olives and vines. The buildings are quite extensive, and there are gardens, courts, cloisters, and chapels; in short, quite a little village. Here are several paintings in oil and fresco, some of them of considerable merit; and a small cloister glazed with beautiful stained glass from the designs of Giovano da Udine, illustrating events in the life of St. Bruno, showing great purity of feeling and delicacy of touch. In the refectory is an elaborately carved stone pulpit. But the most interesting part of the whole is a subterranean chapel, in which is the tomb of the founder Niccolo Acciajuolo, by Orgagna, a work of the fourteenth century. It is a canopy, resting on four twisted columns, and under it, the figure of the deceased, in full armor. On the pavement are tablets to his father, sister, and brother, all with recumbent figures. These works are particularly interesting from the details of the costume, which are very faithfully rendered. In the same chapel is another monument, to a bishop, of the same family, by Donatello, an elaborate piece of sculpture in bas-relief with a rich border of fruit and flowers. In the principal chapel there are some good pictures, and a beautiful floor of porphyry, jasper, and verd antique. The cells of the monks are small detached houses, spacious and comfortable, with trim gardens attached to them.

This extensive establishment is now occupied by only eighteen monks, and though every thing is kept in good order, there was an obvious air of declining fortunes around the whole. A deep silence, like that of the grave, brooded over the scene. The only sound that was heard was the play of a fountain in the open space around which the cloisters ran, and there was a touch of melancholy, even in its murmur and movement. It was like the last child in a nursery, playing by itself. The monk who attended me was dressed in a flowing robe of white woollen. He was in the prime of life, but his face wore the expression of one to whom there was no future; and his speech and manner were those of one so long and so much accustomed to the gloom of solitude, that the light of society dazzled and confused him. The discipline is very strict. The only other monk, whom I saw, was kneeling at his devotions in the chapel; silent and motionless as the marble around him.

This visit to La Certosa made a strong impression

upon me, and the muffled voice and subdued manner of my guide long dwelt in my thoughts. He was evidently one of those commonplace persons in whom the wrongs of the monastic system are most distinctly seen. Minds that can draw deeply, either from the fountains of genius, or the cisterns of learning, can endure solitude without sinking into torpor. A spirit sublimed into ecstasy by religious enthusiasm can bear it, for all absorbing passions sustain the mind which they consume. In either case, interest and companionship are supplied from unfailing sources. But a man of an average understanding and a commonplace temperament, shut up in a monastic establishment, turns in time into a human vegetable. Light is not more essential to the eye than is the discipline of life to such men. They need occupation, the alternation of hope and fear, the glow of success, the sharpness of defeat, the attrition of chance and change; and, above all, the family affections, to train them up to their just stature. The wing of an eagle does not more presuppose the medium of the atmosphere to play in, than does the nature of man demand the relations of son, brother, friend, husband, and father. My poor monk seemed to me a wingless bird. Monastic institutions have had their day. They have done their work, and it was a good work in its season. It is now unseasonable, and therefore not good.

THE BRETHREN OF THE MISERICORDIA.

The stranger in Florence will soon encounter, in the course of his walks about the city, an uncouth figure enveloped in a black robe — the face and head covered with a hood, in which are glass spaces for the eyes. He goes about, soliciting alms, never speaking, but inciting attention by rattling the box which he carries. The disguise is so perfect, that a man would not detect his father under it. This person, who may be the wealthiest nobleman in Florence, perhaps the Grand Duke himself, is a member of the Brotherhood of Mercy, engaged in collecting charity; voluntarily, or imposed as a penance by his father confessor. This institution, which had its origin in the thirteenth century, and was then substantially what it is now, is one of the forms in which the spirit of religion mitigated the rigor of feudal distinctions, and enforced the perfect equality of all men before God. It is an association composed, mainly, of the wealthy and prosperous classes, whose duty it is to nurse the sick, to aid those who have been injured by accident, and to secure decent burial to the poor and the friendless. They are summoned by the sound of a bell, and when its warning voice is heard, the gay guest glides from the ball-room or dinner-party, slips on his black robe, and aids, perhaps, in carrying to the hospital some poor laborer who has broken his leg by a fall from a scaffold, and waits to assist the surgeon and nurses in their care of the patient. Such institutions, worthy of praise and imitation at all times, were invaluable at the period when they were founded; and they are always to be remembered to the credit of the Romish church, which so carefully guarded the principle of humanity against the encroachments of caste, during the middle ages, and thus helped to prevent the sparks of freedom from being trampled out by the iron heel of nobility.

SOCIETY IN FLORENCE.

There is quite an agreeable English society in Florence, and the little I saw of it made me regret that I could see no more. I went to a ball, one evening, given by an English lady of rank and fortune, where nearly all the guests were either English or American. All balls are much alike, but still they have their points of difference. With our small houses, we never think of a ball without thinking of a crowd, but Lady S——, who lived in a palazzo, could give to her guests the first of luxuries, that of space. In an endless suite of capacious and lofty apartments, there was no squeezing, no crushing either of dresses or satin-slippered feet, no loud tumult of voices; and the dancers could dance as freely as peasant girls at a vintage. And then the pleasure of breathing pure fresh air to the last, and of not seeing cheeks, which were damask roses at nine, become peonies at eleven! And let me also mention, with due encomium, another element of this ball, and that was the simplicity of the entertainment. I will not vindicate my Yankee birth by calculating how many, or rather how few dollars the supper must have cost, but simply say, that it was tasteful, abundant, sufficient, and not expensive. It answered the legitimate purposes of such an entertainment. It served to refresh those who had become weary with the exercise of dancing, or exhausted by the excitement of society; but there was nothing to tempt an epicure, or to attract any one to the ball for the sake of the supper. And this I hold to be becoming and worthy of imitation. When shall we learn that our luxurious and costly entertainments are not only opposed to the true ends of society, but are vulgar in their spirit? I use the word advisedly, for they are not only ostentatious displays of wealth, but they make the mind secondary to the body. It is Cicero, I believe, who adduces an argument in favor of the higher intellectual character of the Romans, as compared with the Greeks, from the fact that the Latin word, *convivium*, means a 'living together,' while the corresponding Greek term, *symposium*, means 'a drinking together.' Society is a living together, and not an eating or drinking together; and if we do eat and drink together, it is only to make us live together more cordially.

At this ball there were many blooming English girls, with countenances giving assurance of good qualities that will last long and wear well. As a class, they are less lovely and delicate than their American cousins, but they have a more helpful look. They seem to have more of reserved power; more of that which will enable them hereafter to walk cheerful and erect under the burdens of life, if any should be laid upon them. For the honor of my country, I am glad to add, that the most beautiful woman at the ball was an American; a lady past the bloom of early youth, but with a face and form which time had as yet not only not despoiled, but enriched.

ROBERT AND ELIZABETH BROWNING.

It is well for the traveller to be chary of names. It is an ungrateful return for hospitable attentions, to print the conversation of your host, or describe his person, or give an inventory of his furniture, or proclaim how his wife and daughters were dressed. But I trust I may be pardoned if I state, that one of my most delightful associations with Florence arises from the fact, that here I made the acquaintance of Robert and Elizabeth Browning. These are even more familiar names in America than in England, and their poetry is probably more read, and better understood with us, than among their own countrymen. A happier home and a more perfect union than theirs it is not easy to imagine; and this completeness arises not only from the rare qualities which each possesses, but from their adaptation to each other. Browning's conversation is like the poetry of Chaucer, or like his own simplified and made transparent. His countenance is so full of vigor, freshness, and refined power, that it seems impossible to think that he can ever grow old. His poetry is subtle, passionate, and profound; but he himself is simple, natural, and playful. He has the repose of a man who has lived much in the open air; with no nervous uneasiness and no unhealthy self-consciousness. Mrs. Browning is in many respects the correlative of her husband. As he is full of manly power, so she is a type of the most sensitive and delicate womanhood. She has been a great sufferer from ill health, and the marks of pain are stamped upon her person and manner. Her figure is slight, her countenance expressive of genius and sensibility, shaded by a veil of long brown locks; and her tremulous voice often flutters over her words, like the flame of a dying candle over the wick. I have never seen a human frame which seemed so nearly a transparent veil for a celestial and immortal spirit. She is a soul of fire enclosed in a shell of pearl. Her rare and fine genius needs no setting forth at my hands. She is also, what is not so generally known, a woman of uncommon, nay, profound learning, even measured by a masculine standard. Nor is she more remarkable for genius and learning, than for sweetness of temper, tenderness of heart, depth of feeling, and purity of spirit. It is a privilege to know such beings singly and separately, but to see their powers quickened, and their happiness rounded, by the sacred tie of marriage, is a cause for peculiar and lasting gratitude. A union so complete as theirs — in which the mind has nothing to crave nor the heart to sigh for — is cordial to behold and soothing to remember.

POWERS AND GREENOUGH.

No American went through Florence without visiting the studios of these distinguished sculptors, and no one could see their works without a glow of national pride. Powers is still in Florence, reaping that harvest of success which his talents and industry have so fairly earned. Greenough, as I need hardly say, is no longer upon earth; having been called away, suddenly and mysteriously, just as a new career of distinction and usefulness was opening before him in his own country.

Powers enjoys a high reputation, and he deserves it, but I have seen nothing from him which gives proof of imagination or high invention. From one who has seen the swarms of naked nymphs and goddesses in the galleries of Rome, his Greek Slave will not receive the enthusiastic praise which has been lavished upon it in England and America. His Fisher Boy is beautiful, but not original; and I should pass the same judgment upon his Eve, from merely having seen the model in plaster. His great power resides in his imitative faculty, and the patient skill with which he manipulates the surface of the marble. No modern artist has succeeded so perfectly in giving to his statues the peculiar and indescribable look of flesh, equally removed from the roughness of stone and the glossy polish of porcelain. His elastic muscle seems as if it would yield to the touch. His busts cannot be too highly praised: none better have been made since the days of antiquity. He is, himself, attractive from the frankness and simplicity of his nature, which he has preserved unchanged through all his foreign life. His conversation on art is instructive, because he speaks from his own experience and observation, and never affects a faculty or knowledge which he does not possess. He is a shrewd observer of men and manners, with a keen perception of the ludicrous; and relates, with admirable humor, the odd traits of character and manner, which are exposed to the glance of an artist, through whose studio all the travelling stream of England and America passes.

As between Greenough and Powers, the former seemed superior to his works, but not so, the latter. In Powers, the whole man appeared to have been passed out through the hand and the chisel. Humor excepted, there was nothing in him which was not in his marble. Greenough was a man of large powers and various accomplishments, in whom the practice of his art was but one mode of intellectual expression. His conversation was very instructive and entertaining. He had read and thought much upon art, and those laws of beauty which art interprets. His general cultivation was ripe and full, and his manners courteous and dignified. No one could meet him casually, without feeling that he was a superior man. The principal work in his studio, at the time of my visit, was the colossal group of the Western Settler struggling with an Indian, destined for the capitol at Washington; in which, so far as could be judged from its unfinished state, the difficulties of the subject were most triumphantly met. There was also a bas-relief, of touching beauty and expression, representing a sculptor, in an attitude of dejection and discouragement, before his work, while a hand from above pours oil into his dying lamp; an allegory illustrative of the struggles of genius and the relief which timely patronage may extend to it.*

The death of Greenough was a great shock to those who valued him; for his vigorous frame and unworn energies seemed to promise many years of successful

* This bas-relief is now in the possession of Mr. George Ticknor, of Boston.

action. It was also, humanly speaking, a public calamity; for with his genius, his reputation, his manliness of mind, his love of his profession, and his independent position, he could not have failed to exert a strong and favorable influence upon the growth of art in America. He did not die, like Masaccio and Giorgione, before his prime; but, like Vandyke and Raphael, in the full maturity of his powers: though, from a comparison of his mind with his works, it is probable that, had he lived, he would have attained to a higher elevation in art than he had previously reached.

DEPARTURE FROM FLORENCE.

I entered Florence on the twenty-second of November, and left it on the thirteenth of December, with many regrets and a countenance often reverted. Three weeks are far too short a time for a city so crowded with objects of the highest interest, and I left much unseen and undone; but let me be only grateful for what I did see and did do. I confess that what I was obliged to omit in Florence itself, cost me fewer regrets than what I was constrained to leave unexplored out of it. While at the height of Fiesole, I turned with deep longing to the distant Apennines. There were Vallombrosa — that word of music — and Camaldoli, and La Verna. There were wild mountains crowned with the pine and the oak, savage solitudes, pastoral glens, and sheltered valleys populous with vines and olives. There were many spots which the genius of Dante had touched with idealizing light; and who would not gladly see even a rock or a fountain which had been embalmed in his immortal poem? There were the Val di Chiana,* in Dante's time a pestilential swamp, but since made healthy by drainage; the mountain Falterona,† the well-head of that river Arno, whose name the poet suggests, but does not mention; the valley of Casentina, ‡ for a draught of whose sparkling rills Adamo of Brescia so longed, in his torment of hopeless thirst. I wished to penetrate into the heart of Tuscany — to trace the many-winding Arno to its parent source — to converse with that rural population, which is unpolluted by the stream of foreign travel — to learn something of their way of life, and how shadow and sunshine were distributed among them. But for such an enterprise, time and another season of the year were necessary, and thus that sylvan region remained and still remains unexplored, save in dreams and visions.

Firenze la bella — Florence the beautiful — thus it is called by its inhabitants, and thus it dwells in my memory. I recall no place which I would sooner select for a residence, were I required to choose among European cities. Its clean quiet streets, its lovely environs, its incomparable Cascine, its treasures of art, so near at hand and so accessible, its ample libraries, its agreeable society, and — pardon the bathos — its cheapness, present an aggregate of attractions hardly to be met with elsewhere.

The climate of Florence, I believe, is capricious. It

* Inferno, xxix. 47. † Purgat, xiv. 17.
‡ Inferno, xxx. 64.

was my good fortune to bask in its smiles. The weather, with the exception of two days of rain, was absolutely perfect; cool enough in the morning and evening to make a fire pleasant, and invite to a long brisk walk; but, at noon, warm enough to sit under a tree, or by an open window, and dream of summer and the songs of vintagers. Under the rich sunshine which rained from the clear blue sky, the world without was so inviting, that it required all the attractions of Raphael and Titian to keep me within doors. The sun made pictures every where, for every where there were picturesque forms, waiting to be waked into life by the touch of his 'fiery rod.' I have never seen any where in such perfection, as in my walks from Fiesole, that 'peculiar tint of yellow green' upon the western sky at the hour of sunset, of which the fine-eyed Coleridge speaks.

PISA — THE LEANING TOWER — CATHEDRAL — CAMPO SANTO — BAPTISTERY.

I left Florence at noon in the diligence for Empoli, and arrived there at about three, having passed through a country apparently well cultivated, and which must be very pretty in spring, summer, or early autumn. At Empoli, the familiar presence of a railway station greeted me, and taking a seat in the cars, I arrived at Pisa at half-past five. At the table d'hote dinner of the hotel where I lodged, there were ten persons seated; and of these, five were Americans and five were English. Such is the state of Pisa, once so powerful and prosperous; and, indeed, of a large part of the whole country to which it belongs. In Italy, strangers seem to be at home, and the natives to be exiles. The former amuse themselves with the imposing monuments of past greatness, as with the curiosities of a museum, but the Italians must look upon these, much as the representative of a decayed and impoverished family looks upon the portraits of his ancestors, who were powerful and rich. Indifferent eyes may value them as works of art, but to him they have another meaning, and address other feelings. They are not pictures, but symbols; not forms, but memorials.

At Pisa, all that the traveller need see is comprised within a few acres, and is embraced with one glance of the eye. Here are those four buildings, 'so fortunate,' as Forsyth has well remarked, 'in their solitude and their society' — the Cathedral, the Campo Santo, the Baptistery, and the Leaning Tower.

The Leaning Tower, as it rose before me on a bright sunny morning, seemed at once a new vision and a familiar fact. This piece of architectural eccentricity was, and I suppose is, one of the commonplaces of geography, and is put into the same educational state-room with the Wall of China, the Great Tun of Heidelberg, and the Natural Bridge of Virginia. I cannot recall the time when its name was not known to me; and now, here it was, bodily before me; no dream, no illusion; but a very decided fact, with a most undeniable inclination on one side; so much so, that a nervous person would not sleep soundly in the house that stands under its lee, on a windy night.

This singular structure is simply a campanile or bell-tower, appurtenant to the cathedral, as is the general custom in Italy. It is not merely quaint, but beautiful; that is, take away the quaintness and the beauty will remain. It is built of white marble, wonderfully fresh and pure, when we remember that nearly seven centuries have swept over it. I will not describe it, nor give its dimensions, for these may be found in every guide-book, and nearly every book of travels; nor will I condense the arguments which have been called forth by the question, whether the inclination be accidental or designed. To one who has been on the spot, and observed the spongy nature of the soil, as evidenced by the slight subsidence of portions of the cathedral, there is really no room for argument or doubt.*

The ascent is very easy and gradual. The summit is secured by double rails, and the inclination is less perceptible when on the top than when it is observed from the ground. There is no peculiar sense of danger to interfere with the full enjoyment of the beauty of the view, which embraces mountain and plain, land and sea; a combination at once varied, extensive, and picturesque. This was my first sight of the Mediterranean, whose blue waters blended in the distant horizon with the blue of the sky. To the eye, it was but common water reflecting the universal sky, but a man must be very insensible, not to recognise peculiar elements in his first view of that many-nationed sea,

* M. Fulchiron, however, the intelligent French traveller whom I have before cited, maintains that the inclination was the result of design and not of accident.

upon whose shores so much of the poetry and history of the world has grown.

The cathedral is one of those buildings, so common in Italy, rich with the spoils of centuries, which would justify, and indeed requires, in order to be comprehended, a study of many days. The façade of five stories is rich and imposing, and the stately bronze doors are of admirable workmanship. The general effect of the interior is noble and impressive, from its great extent, the grace and originality of the architecture, and the dim light diffused through painted windows. The columns of the nave, transept, and aisles, are seventy-four in number. They are not uniform in style, and are evidently the spoils and fragments of other edifices. The ceiling of the nave and choir, of carved and gilded wood, seems to be rebuked by the rich magnificence of the pavement, which is of marble, white and yellow. The works of art here are numerous and interesting. If the visitor be limited for time, I advise him to devote himself to the bronze statues by John of Bologna, to the pulpit, the masterpiece of John of Pisa, to the pictures of Andrea del Sarto, and the wood-work of the stalls.

The Campo Santo is a cemetery, enclosed by cloisters opening into the contained space by Gothic arches, with a roof supported by open-work of timber. It is a parallelogram in form, being about four hundred and fifteen feet in length, and one hundred and thirty-seven in breadth. The earth with which the interior is filled was brought from the Holy Land, in the days of the great Saladin, and was long supposed to have some peculiar power of rapidly decomposing the bodies which were deposited within it. Burials rarely take place here now, and only by the special permission of the Grand Duke.

The cloisters form an interesting museum of art, Greek, Roman, mediæval, and modern. The collection of sepulchral monuments is curious and extensive; among them, sarcophagi of Greek workmanship, some very fine. Among the works of modern artists, is a female figure by Bartolini, called L'Inconsolabile, but looking more sulky than inconsolable. There is also a bas-relief, by Thorwaldsen, to the memory of the distinguished physician, Vacca. Algarotti and Pignotti are buried here, and both have monuments; that of the former having been erected by Frederick the Great of Prussia, as the inscription shows. It has been said, that the thrifty monarch omitted the ceremony of paying for the work which he had ordered. A lawyer of some note in his time, Filippo Decio, reposes here. He caused his own monument to be erected before his death. Perhaps his professional experience had given him distrust, and taught him how soon the dead are forgotten by their heirs, and lawyers by their clients.

The frescoes on the walls of the Campo Santo are of much importance in the history of art, and are now much studied and deservedly valued. They are so well described in Kugler and Murray, that any account of them here would be superfluous; to say nothing of the presumption of undertaking to give any details upon so extensive a series of works from a single hurried visit. I was most struck with the 'Triumph of Death,' by Andrea Orgagna, a set of allegories, strange and uncouth, but full of dramatic power and a certain intense reality. A group of youth and maidens amusing themselves in a garden, with the angel of death hovering over them with a scythe, is overflowing with the expression of light-hearted mirth and joyous unconcern; and, with equal power, the artist has represented a company of the maimed, blind and diseased, vainly entreating the grim presence to end their sufferings. The whole composition reminds one of the mysteries or miracle-plays of the middle ages.

The Baptistery is a circular building of white marble, about a hundred feet in diameter. The exterior presents a singular combination of Grecian and Gothic elements. There are two orders of Corinthian columns, the lower being twenty in number and engaged in the wall, and the upper, sixty; all supporting semicircular arches. But above the arches of the upper order, the Grecian character of the structure, thus far resembling that of the campanile, ceases, and we have a row of pinnacles and pediments, with figures inscribed in the latter, in the Gothic style. Above the pediments, surmounting the second order of columns, the circular figure ends, 'and the building becomes a polygon of twenty sides, each of which terminates with a pediment between two clusters of pinnacles, which conceal the base of the dome.'

From this discrepancy in the style, it has been conjectured that the building was the work of different architects, and erected at different periods. However opposed such a combination may be to the unities of architecture, its general effect is animated and pleasing to an uninstructed eye.

The interior, with its double row of inexpressive arches, is by no means equal in effect to the exterior. Here is one of the earliest examples of a double dome, afterwards introduced by Sir Christopher Wren in St. Paul's Church. Both domes are of brick; the interior shaped like an ugly funnel. In the centre, is a font formerly used for baptism by immersion, fourteen feet in diameter. Its form is octangular; it is composed of a variety of marbles, and embellished with sculpture and mosaics. The great ornament of the interior is the pulpit, by Nicola da Pisa. It is hexagonal in form, supported by seven columns, one at each angle, and one in the centre. The central column rests upon the back of a man in a crouching posture, with an eagle in his right hand. The columns at the angles are supported by animals — lions, tigers, or griffins. The capitals of these columns are highly carved, with a very sharp and delicate chisel. Over the columns is a cornice which runs round the pulpit, and at each angle above are three small columns, between which are panels, decorated with bas-reliefs admirably executed. One, especially, representing the Last Judgment, is a miracle of patience and skill.

Forsyth, whose strictures upon this group of buildings in Pisa are too harsh, and show the bias of a mind too deeply tinged with Greek ideas to be just to mediæval art, says of this building, 'Who could ever suppose that such a structure and such dimensions were intended for a christening? The purpose of an edifice should appear in the very architecture.' Without pausing to inquire how a building could be so contrived, as to reveal by its architecture that it was intended for the baptism of children, a moment's reflection will show that a circular building, with a font in the centre, is the best adapted for such a ceremony as a christening; because it affords the greatest possible space to the spectators who might be desirous of witnessing it.

It was my fortune to see this ceremony performed upon a very young pilgrim on the path of life. It lasted some ten or fifteen minutes, and was done in a very awkward manner; and once or twice I thought the child would have slipped from the priest's clumsy grasp and fallen into the water. He was evidently not accustomed to the care of children. The infant behaved extremely well, and uttered no cry of remonstrance.*

BEGGARS.

These buildings at Pisa were haunted by a swarm of most importunate and intrusive beggars. They were of all ages and both sexes; some suffering from infirmities, and all with those hard, gaunt faces, which speak of a desperate and losing battle with life. They darted out from every hiding-place which the structures furnished, and seemed to rise up from the very earth itself. These beggars are the dark shadows

* There is a story in one of the French Ana, of a priest who was called upon to perform the ceremony of baptism when in rather too genial a condition, and finding himself much embarrassed in his task, exclaimed, 'Bless me, this is a very hard child to baptize!' The little Pisan, if it had been endowed with the gifts of observation and speech, might well have remarked, 'This is a very hard priest to be baptized by.'

which haunt all the bright points in Italy, and are not only a teasing annoyance at the moment, but (with those who have means) awakening perplexing conflicts of duty as to denying or giving. This is a question not quite settled by the iron edicts of political economy or social ethics, which bid the axe fall though the naked heart be under it. The effect of the 'everlasting No,' upon one's own nature is not to be overlooked. To see suffering which we are determined not to relieve, or which presents itself in such formidable masses as to render all thought of relief hopeless, petrifies the feeling. The heart that is not moved by the aspect of wretchedness has lost its finest grace; and, unhappily, in this as in all things, familiarity blunts the sense, and the poor blind beggar is in time passed by as if he were no more than an unsightly weed by the roadside. Happy is the man who, with with a willingness to succor, approaches suffering in manageable forms — not so huge as to paralyze benevolent effort and turn the stimulus into a narcotic — but with 'hope's perpetual breath,' to fan the flame of charity. He has within his reach the best influences for the growth of the character, and the most soothing anodyne for the pain of a wounded spirit.

LEGHORN.

I passed three days at Leghorn, in a very comfortable hotel, kept by one of the ubiquitous family of Smith, a man whose gentlemanly and amiable deportment would commend an inferior house. The cause of this detention was the failure of the steamer from

Genoa. I was comforted by the assurance, that such an interval of delay never had happened before, and never would happen again. But the days did not pass heavily by. The weather was delicious, and a man must be unreasonable not to find contentment under such a sky and such a sun, and although Leghorn is uninteresting as compared with other Italian cities, it is by no means barren. The most attractive object is the English chapel and the adjacent burying-ground. The latter is crowded with marble tombs and monuments. The hope and flower of many an English family lies buried here, borne to Italy in search of health, but finding only a grave. Valery remarks with justice upon the good taste, the simplicity, and the religious tone of the inscriptions. Smollett is buried here, and a plain monument is erected to his memory, with an inscription in Latin (not of the first quality), which should have been English. Here, too, reposes a calmer and purer spirit — Francis Horner — one of the most admirable public characters of his time, whose serene career of duty contrasts with the wayward course of the irritable and undisciplined Smollett, as the light of the stars with that of the meteor which shoots across their field. His monument is a marble tablet, with a bas-relief likeness by Chantry, of the size of life; a head, at once, amiable, dignified, and intellectual.

There is one striking work of art in Leghorn, a colossal statue of Ferdinand I., in an open space by the harbor. At the four corners of the pedestal are four Turkish slaves in bronze, modelled from captives taken in the battle of Lepanto. Their hands are chained behind them, and their countenances are stamped with the most touching expression of melancholy and despair. The merit of this noble group is enhanced by comparison with two or three modern statues in marble in other parts of the city, which are very indifferent.

Leghorn is a mosaic of races and creeds. Its growth and prosperity spring, mainly, from the wise and liberal policy of Cosmo I. and Ferdinand I., Grand Dukes of the Medici family; and are arguments in favor of religious toleration and unfettered commerce. Leghorn, in the sixteenth and seventeenth centuries, was a general city of refuge to the persecuted and oppressed of of all climes. Here fled the Jews in great numbers, chased from every part of the Spanish empire by the pitiless bigotry of its councils. At this day, nowhere on the continent of Europe, do the Jews hold up their heads so high as at Leghorn. They form about a fourth of its population, and comprise more than a fourth part of its intelligence and activity. Here, too, came many families from France, driven out by religious persecutions or civil wars. Many inhabitants of Corsica, impatient of the Genoese yoke, took refuge in Leghorn. Cosmo II. attempted to establish here the last remnants of the Moorish conquerors of Spain, who were driven out of that country by Philip III.; but the African blood proved too fiery and unmanageable for the success of the experiment, and they were transported to the land from which their ancestors had originally come.

Leghorn has a general air of business and progress. The shops are full of goods from every part of the world, and the manufactures of England and France may be bought there as cheaply as in those countries themselves. Coral and alabaster are wrought with much taste. Houses were building in many places; a thing to be seen in no other part of Italy. I had the curiosity to go into one of them which was nearly completed. It was of moderate dimensions, but combined taste with convenience; a modification of English with Italian notions. It would rent, as I was told, for about half of what would be paid for similar accommodations in Boston.

Commerce, which formerly enriched Florence and Pisa, has long since deserted those cities and transferred its fickle smiles to Leghorn. From my own observation, I should say that the ancient and honorable character of Tuscan commerce was well sustained in its present home. At the house of a Leghorn merchant, I found generous hospitality commended by cultivation and refinement, and the pursuits of commerce dignified by various knowledge and literary taste.

In Leghorn, also, I renewed my acquaintance with an English gentleman, who had been a fellow-passenger in the steamer from Boston. He occupied a pretty villa in the outskirts of the city, to which was attached a spacious garden, under good cultivation. His wife was the daughter of an English gentleman long settled in Leghorn. She and her sisters spoke Italian and English with equal facility, and from my experience of their discourse in Italian, I should say that the sweetest of all tongues was 'la lingua Toscana in bocca Inglese.' Good conversa tional voices are rare in Italy, and the music of its language is never so well apprehended as when conveyed in the low and gentle tones of refined English women.

In my walks about Leghorn, I noticed large piles of massive oak timber; a product which I had not associated with the soil of Italy. I was told that it was exported in considerable quantities, mainly for the use of the British navy, and that large contracts were in force for the supply of a material which the progress of industrial civilization is rendering more and more scarce. The trees are felled in the Apennines. Would that there was more of the oak and less of the myrtle in the character of the Italians themselves!

In Leghorn a most painful spectacle is presented by the gangs of convicts which are every where encountered in the streets. They are employed in various ways upon the public works, making excavations, and sweeping the streets. Their dress varies according to the crimes for which they have been condemned. There were some hideous faces among them. The wolf and the tiger glared from them, but nothing of the man. Compared with these, the convicts in the State prison at Charlestown look like reputable members of society. It is singular that this way of disposing of criminals should be retained in a country so (comparatively) well governed as Tuscany. The aspect of such a mass of crime, living and moving before the eye, cannot but have a demoralizing influence, especially upon the young. What parent among us would not think, with the liveliest alarm, of having so foul a spectacle daily before the pure eyes of his children?

An incident occurred while I was at Leghorn, which brought home to me a lively sense of the blessings we enjoy in living in a land at once of liberty and law. One night, at about twelve o'clock, I was awakened by the entrance of a number of men into my room. It proved to be my host, attended by three armed officers. The latter approached the bed, examined my features attentively by the light of a lamp, and, remarking that I was not the person they were in search of, left me with a cool apology for the disturbance; which, however, was no substitute for either sleep or patience. It seems that they went through the whole house in the same way, and entered every apartment 'without distinction of sex.' They exhibited no warrant, except that which they wore by their sides; and gave no intimation of the name or condition of the person for whom they were in search.

STEAMER TO CIVITA VECCHIA.

The steamer at last arrived, and on the evening of December 18th I went on board. From the long delay, there was an unusually large number of passengers: many more than the small boat could accommodate. Among them were about a dozen Americans. The weather had been threatening during the day, and dull gray clouds were mustering their forces in the air. As soon as we got out of the harbor it began to blow heavily and knock up an angry sea; and the overladen boat plunged and pitched in the most distressing way. Nearly every body yielded to the despotic power of the roused waters; and though myself in a very solemn frame of spirit, I had some compassion to spare for my neighbors. Nobody can measure all the horrors of sea-sickness, who has not seen Italians under its power. They do not believe in 'silent griefs,' but are accustomed to give vent and breath to every emotion. Some wept, some groaned, and some almost shrieked aloud. But over a night of much suffering and some danger, a veil of oblivion may well be drawn.

By morning, the wind had lulled under the influence of a heavy rain. A more pallid and woe-begone set of faces were never seen, than those that greeted the welcome light. We reached Civita Vecchia at about eleven, but were not allowed to land till an hour after.

CIVITA VECCHIA.

Nowhere is the temper of mortal and imperfect man put to severer proof than at Civita Vecchia; and nowhere is there more scolding and swearing done. It is merely a gate of entrance to Rome; and the inhabitants depend mostly on what they can fleece from the traveller during the brief space of his sojourn. The various devices under which money is obtained furnish a striking illustration of the inventive powers of the human mind. The force of extortion can no farther go. He pays the porter who carries his luggage to the custom-house: he pays for two examinations, one by the custom-house officers, and one by the police: he pays another porter for putting his trunks upon the diligence: he pays for a visa to his passport: he pays an unreasonable bill at the inn; and, finally, when he draws a long breath of relief and thinks that this generation of horse-leeches has at last sucked their fill, he is stopped at the gates and obliged to pay for liberty to quit the town: a liberty worth gaining at almost any price. Imagine a testy and impatient Englishman, with little French and no Italian, going through this ordeal, and the words with which he will piece out his imperfect vocabulary are easily supplied. The author of Murray's Hand-book, after recounting the above extortions, adds in a very mild way: 'It will hardly, therefore, be a matter of surprise, that in many instances the recollections of Civita Vecchia are not of the most agreeable kind.' I am afraid that if the town were sacked and destroyed, and the inhabitants carried into captivity, the news would be received by every traveller who has landed there with a certain savage satisfaction.

The great lion of Civita Vecchia is the bandit Gasperoni, who is confined in prison here. This wretch, who owns to thirty murders, receives visits and even presents in money from travellers: a diseased curiosity quite inexplicable in men of any moral thoughtfulness. And yet among his visitors was that enthusiastic philanthropist, Sir Thomas Fowell Buxton, who has recorded the incident in his diary, in a paragraph which I never can read without amazement.

ARRIVAL AT ROME.

The friends who were with me being equally impatient with myself to quit Civita Vecchia, we took a carriage and started for Rome, though it was late in the afternoon before we could get off. Nothing is lost, however, by travelling over this road by night, as a subsequent journey by day revealed. A more monotonous, dreary, and uninteresting country cannot be imagined. There are neither striking scenery nor inhabitants. The marshes between Boston and Lynn are not more unattractive.

We reached Rome at midnight, entering it by the Porta Cavalleggieri, in the immediate neighborhood of St. Peter's. The night was dark and stormy, and just before reaching the gate the clouds gathered for a storm of thunder and lightning, which lasted for a considerable time. As we drove by St. Peter's, the dome and colonnade were revealed by gleams of lightning and then shrouded in gloom, and the dash of its fountains was heard mingled with the pattering of the heavy rain-drops. Amid this war of the elements we passed by the Castle of St. Angelo, over the bridge, and through the narrow streets that lead to the Piazza di Spagna; and I felt that it was under no inappropriate conditions, that I was first brought face to face with the grandeur and mystery of the Eternal City.

CHAPTER VIII.

First Impressions of Rome — St. Peter's — The Piazza, Obelisk, and Fountains — Façade and Vestibule — Interior — Monuments — Ascent to the Dome — General Character of the Building — Christmas in St. Peter's.

FIRST IMPRESSIONS OF ROME.

To the traveller who enters Rome with any sort of preparation, — who has any thing like a due perception of its multitudinous claims upon the attention, — the first few days of his residence there will usually be passed in a sort of bewildering indecision, endeavoring to fix upon some plan by which he may comprehend the mighty maze of interests that lies before him. Will he follow the stream of chronology, and beginning with the morning twilight of history, come down through the kingly period, the republic, the empire, the night of the dark ages, the new dawn of power and influence in more recent times, and trace this last to its present lengthening shadows of decline — studying each period in its monuments, binding the present to the past, and observing how each age is the parent of its successor? Or will he divide Rome into subjects, and take up painting, sculpture, architecture, separately, and resolutely exclude every thing but the matter in hand?

Will he cut it up territorially, and exhaust one section before he approaches another? Will he make the circuit of the walls, and get the general contour and leading features stamped upon the mind, before he descends to particulars? While thus deliberating, accident or indolence or caprice will probably determine for him, and, in the impatience of doubt, all plans will be abandoned, and the impulse of the moment be his guide.

It may be stated, as a general rule, that, in proportion to the stranger's susceptibility to all that is characteristic and peculiar in Rome, will be his disappointment at first. Most persons enter Rome by the Porta del Popolo, which opens upon the spacious Piazza del Popolo, an irregular area, in which there is no very striking object, except the obelisk in the centre. In front, two twin churches, of moderate size, and no great architectural merit, divide the three streets which diverge from the piazza, like three outstretched fingers from the palm of the hand. The traveller will probably be driven only a few steps further, to one of the hotels in the Piazza di Spagna. He will find himself surrounded with shops, coffee-houses, and lodging-houses. In fine weather, he will see stout gentlemen in drab gaiters, and fair-complexioned ladies with parasols, and superfluous flounces on their gowns. He will hear English spoken all around him. He will say to himself, 'All this is well, but it is not Rome; it is London or Paris or any other metropolis. The majestic shadow of the past is not here. It is modern, comfortable, and business-like. This is what I left at home, not what I came here to see.'

Nor will these unexpected impressions be dissipated by the first exploring expeditions which he will make in search of the ideal. The greater part of inhabited Rome is, comparatively, a modern city, occupying the once open spaces of the Campus Martius; and the most thickly-peopled part of the ancient city is now inhabited only by ruins and memories. The streets of modern Rome are narrow, dark, and gloomy: without sidewalks: frequently crooked; and rarely presenting fine continuous façades of architecture. They are not kept clean; and, in wet weather, it requires no common resolution to walk in them. An indescribable air of mouldiness and decay haunts a large proportion of them. They seem withered and wrinkled by time. The passenger, too, must keep all his wits about him, to avoid being run over; for the Roman Jehu thinks that he has done his duty, if he gives notice of his approach by a sort of warning yell, and that, afterwards, the responsibility is yours and not his.

Nor does the first aspect of most of the ruins in Rome satisfy the longings of the heart. In all probability, the visitor will have formed some notion of these, or, at least, the most prominent of them, from engravings; and these are rarely true. To lie like an engraving would be as good a proverbial expression as to lie like a bulletin. Not that the size, dimensions, and character of the object delineated are falsified, but liberties are taken with all that is in immediate proximity to it. Many of the Roman ruins are thrust into unsightly neighborhoods. They are shouldered and elbowed by commonplace structures, or start out, like excrescences, from mean and inexpresssive walls.

They are surrounded by decay which has no dignity, and by offensive objects which are like discordant notes in a strain of music. All these are swept away by the engravers; and the effect upon the particular object is idealizing and untrue. Every thing is smoothed, rounded, and polished. Holes are filled up, inequalities are removed, backgrounds and foregrounds are created, the crooked made straight, and all deformity erased. Hence, though there is truth enough to suggest the resemblance, there is untruth enough to excite vexatious disappointment. The image of the beautiful seems ever to be flitting before the traveller's weary steps. The light fades as he draws near, and the 'shining trails,' which he has followed, go out in darkness.

But let him bide his time. The Rome of the mind is not built in a day. His hour will surely come. Not suddenly, not by stormy and vehement movements, but by gentle gradations and soft approaches, the spirit of the place will descend upon him. The unsightly and commonplace appendages will disappear, and only the beautiful and the tragic will remain. And when his mind and heart are in unison with the scene around him, a thousand happy accidents and cordial surprises lie in wait for him. Upon the Pincian Hill, on the summit of the Baths of Caracalla, under the arches of the Claudian Aqueduct, beneath the whispering pines of the Villa Pamphili-Doria, influences will drop into his soul, not merely soothing and reposing, but elevating and tranquillizing—pictures will be stamped upon the memory, which will ever shed around them the serene light of undecaying beauty, never dimmed by the disappointments, the burdens, the torpid commonplaces, and the dreary drudgeries of future years.

But this supposes a fitting frame of mind in the traveller himself. As Rome cannot be comprehended without previous preparation, so it cannot be felt without a certain congeniality of temperament. Something of the imaginative principle — the power of going out of one's self, and forgetting the actual in the ideal, and the present in the past — the capacity to sympathize with the dreamer, if not to dream — a willingness to be acted upon, and not to act — these must be wrought into the being of him, who would catch all the inspiration of the place. The traveller must leave all his notions of progress and reform at the gates, or else he will be kept in a constant state of protest and rebellion; as unfit to receive the impressions which are around him as a lake ruffled by the storm, to reflect the heavens. He must try to forget such things as a representative government, town-meetings, public schools, railways, and steam-engines. He must learn to took upon pope, cardinal, and monk, not with a puritan scowl, but as parts of an imposing pageant, which he may contemplate without self-reproach, though without approving; as the man of peace may be innocently amused with the splendid evolutions of a review. He, whose spirit is so restless and evanescent as to forbid repose, whose zeal for progress admits neither compromise nor delay — he, who sees, not the landscape, but the monastery which blots it, not the church, but the beggar on its steps — he, who, in the kneeling peasant, finds all idolatry and no devotion — may have many good and great qualities, but he is out of his place in Rome.

He is an exotic, and will only languish and pine in its uncongenial soil.

ST. PETER'S.

When Rome is viewed from a distance, the dome of St. Peter's is the central point of observation, and seems to be gathering the rest of the city under its enormous wings. It is so with thoughts and associations. St. Peter's is the first object of interest, around which all others group themselves. Here the traveller hurries as soon as the dust of the journey is shaken from his feet; and here he comes, at the last moment, as the spot from which he is most reluctant to part.

A work so vast and various must be approached in the spirit of knowledge and docility. Most buildings have an unity of plan; and their different parts, and the successive changes in structure and detail, are like variations upon one musical theme. Not so with St. Peter's. It awakens no ideas of unity or simplicity. It is a great representative structure, which gathers within itself the convergent rays of innumerable lights. It is a temple, a museum, a gallery of art, and a mausoleum. If a fanciful comparison may be pardoned, other churches are gardens, but St. Peter's is a landscape. Its growth and history embrace nearly three hundred and fifty years, from the time of Nicholas V. who began it in 1450, to that of Pius VI., who built the sacristy in 1780; and it expresses, not only the will of different popes, the tastes of successive architects, but the changes and revolutions of time itself. Its foundation was nearly coeval with the invention of printing: before the sacristy was completed, the splendid researches of Watt had been crowned with success; and, in the interval, had occurred the discovery of America and the Reformation. Religion, politics, literature, art, and manners had gone through whole cycles of mutation, and the web of society had been unravelled and rewoven. All these considerations should be borne in mind by him who would form a true judgment of this unique building. It should be examined in that historical spirit in which we study the Roman law or the English constitution.

As early as the fourth century, a church had been erected by Constantine the Great, upon the site of the Circus of Nero, to commemorate the spot which had been hallowed to the Christian world, as the burial-place of St. Peter, and the scene of many of the early martyrdoms. This church having fallen into decay in the course of eleven centuries, Nicholas V. resolved to erect another in its place, which should rival the glories of Solomon's temple. The plan adopted by him, which was that of the Roman basilica, was changed by Bramante, in the early part of of the sixteenth century, who first conceived the sublime idea of a cupola, in conjunction with a Latin cross. Between his death, in 1514, and the appointment of Michael Angelo, as architect, in 1542, the plan of a Latin cross had been abandoned, and returned to by successive architects. Michael Angelo adopted the Greek cross, and designed the dome, the tribune, and the transepts, substantially as they now are; and, down to the beginning of the seventeenth century, the spirit of this great man presided over the work, and ruled it from his tomb. Afterwards, Carlo Maderno returned to Bramante's idea of the Latin cross, and by him the façade was also built. The colonnades were added by Bernini, who is responsible for many of the details of the interior.

The distance from the Piazza di Spagna to St. Peter's is about a mile. There are two ways of reaching it on foot. One is through a succession of narrow and unsightly streets, and over the bridge by the Castle of St. Angelo, ending in front of it. The other is by crossing the Tiber, in the ferry-boat, from the Via Ripetta and proceeding across the fields, and entering the Porta Angelica, by which the building is approached on the side. The latter, in fine weather, is the more agreeable walk; but the effect of the building is much more imposing, when seen from the front, and this should always be the visitor's first view.

THE PIAZZA, OBELISK, AND FOUNTAINS.

The site of the building is not in all respects happy. It is near the base of a gently sloping elevation, and, thus, has the disadvantage of a rising background. When first seen, however, the attention is drawn to, and almost absorbed by its accessories, rather than itself; by the piazza, the obelisk, the fountains, and the colonnades. It is impossible by any statement of numbers, extent, or dimensions, to convey any notion of the sublime effect of this combination of objects. Let the reader imagine himself in the centre of a spacious ellipse, of which the longer diameter is about eight hundred feet. On either hand, semicircular colonnades, supported by four rows of columns, enclose space enough between the two inner rows, for the passage of two carriages abreast. One extremity of each semicircle is united to the ends of the façade of the church, by covered galleries, similar in construction to the porticoes themselves. The galleries and porticoes, together, are not unlike in form to sickles, of which the galleries make the handles. The galleries are not exactly parallel, but they converge as they recede from the façade. All these structures are of the most colossal size. The porticoes are sixty-four feet high, and the holy army of saints which crown the entablature, nearly two hundred in number, are eleven feet. But so harmonious are the proportions, that, when seen from the centre of the piazza, the whole effect is light, airy, and graceful. Nothing could have been devised more calculated to add dignity and expression to the front of the church, or to screen from the view of the spectator the buildings on either side which would have been an incongruous element in the scene. The galleries and porticoes seem like all-embracing arms of invitation extended by the church to the whole Christian world, summoning it to come and worship under the roof of the most majestic temple ever made with hands. The combination of the straight line of the galleries with the circle of the colonnades — of the entablature with the statues above and the columns below — meets all that the mind requires, both of unity and variety. The eye slides delightedly along the majestic curves and lines — nowhere wearied with monotony, nowhere disturbed with incongruity — till it rests upon the façade to which it is so gracefully drawn. I have seen this incomparable piazza under all conditions; in the blaze of an Italian noon; at the silence of midnight; swarming with carriages and foot-passengers; occupied by soldiers at their drill; and, under all, it retained the same aspect and character. It never seemed crowded; it never seemed desolate. Men and women, however numerous, never appeared but as fringes and embellishments. Its contents never were commensurate with itself. They stood in the same relation to it as vessels to the harbor in which they ride.*

After having contemplated the scene as a whole, the visitor may pause, for a moment, to examine those details which, at first, were hardly observed. He will not fail to commend the taste which marked the central point of the piazza by an obelisk. This form, heathen in its origin, has been appropriately adopted by Christianity; for it expresses that element of aspiration, which, natural to the heart of man, finds solution and repose only in the Christian faith. It is a solid mass of red granite, eighty-three feet high, without hieroglyphics, resting on a pedestal or base of about fifty feet. Its removal from its former position, † and its

* Many buildings were destroyed to make space for this colonnade; among them, the house which Raphael built for himself in the Borgo Nuovo, which belonged to the Priory of Malta at the time of its destruction. The expense of the colonnade and galleries was eight hundred and fifty thousand dollars; not including the pavement, which cost eighty-eight thousand dollars.

† This obelisk formerly stood on the Circus of Caligula, near the site of the present sacristy of St. Peter's. It remained standing during fifteen centuries, and is the only obelisk in Rome that was never thrown down. The exact position it occupied is marked by a square stone, in the passage leading

erection on its present site, was, as is well known, a miracle of engineering skill, triumphing over incredible mechanical difficulties; but it is not easy to imagine it, when on the spot. It springs from its base and pierces

from the church to the sacristy, with the inscription, 'Sito del obelisco fino all' anno MDLXXXVI.' The plan of removing it had occurred to several popes, but was only accomplished through the energy of Sixtus V. aided by the genius of Fontana. A commission appointed by the pope invited proposals and plans from all Europe, and upwards of five hundred were sent in. These comprised, of course, a great variety of opinions and suggestions. The great point of difference was, whether the obelisk should be removed in an upright position as it then stood, or whether it should first be lifted from the pedestal and laid upon the ground. Most of the plans were in favor of the former method; but Fontana zealously maintained the expediency of the latter. The pope required him to make an experiment of his scheme of transportation, upon a small obelisk formerly belonging to the Mausoleum of Augustus. This proved entirely successful; and the execution of the enterprise was entrusted to him by a papal edict, dated October 5, 1585.

The great difficulty in the removal arose from the enormous weight of the obelisk, which was nearly a million of pounds. On the 30th of April, 1586, this immense mass was slowly and successfully lifted two feet above its pedestal, by the strength of nine hundred men, aided by thirty-five windlasses. It remained thus suspended in the air till the 7th May, when, by the same agency, the still more difficult task of swinging it sideways out of its perpendicular position, and laying it upon rollers placed on the ground to receive it, was also happily executed. Between the 7th of May and the 10th of September, the obelisk had been transported on rollers to its present site, and the greatest feat of all — that of elevating it and placing it upon its pedestal — remained to be done. Eight hundred men, one hundred and fifty horses, and forty-six windlasses the blue air with its slender spire, as if from a spiritual and natural impulse, as lightly as a palm-tree rises from the soil. It points to the heavens with silent finger, lifting up the eye and the thoughts, as if to teach us that the beauty and grandeur around us are unworthily enjoyed, if they do not elevate our contemplations above the earth. On either side of the obelisk, between it and the semicircular portico, but nearer the latter than the former, are the fountains. Among the many fountains in Rome, these are remarkable for the simplicity of their construction. The jet of water, which rises sixty feet above the pavement, is received into a basin of oriental granite, and, flowing over its sides, falls in a silvery sheet into a larger

were employed. The work began at early dawn; and at an hour before sunset the obelisk was securely resting in its present position. The gratitude of the pope was in proportion to the greatness of the enterprise and its splendid success. He caused two medals to be struck in honor of the event, made Fontana a knight of the golden spur, gave him five thousand crowns in money, and settled upon him and his heirs a pension of two thousand crowns a year. He also gave him all the ropes, timber, and other materials which had been used, which produced the sum of twenty thousand crowns.

The story so commonly told — that the enterprise had nearly failed through the stretching of the ropes under the enormous weight, and that a voice from the crowd called out 'water,' and that the ropes were drenched from the fountains near at hand, and thus, from the shrinking produced by the wetting, enabled to perform their office — is not found in any contemporary author. It is, as Platner remarks, probably one of those inventions which spring from a wish to disparage the triumphs of genius, and to lower its claims in comparison with those of the common mind.

one below. The basins supply form, and the water, drapery; art thus performing its legitimate function, in multiplying the surfaces over which water may glide or break. Nothing can be more impressive than the contrast between the restless play of these fountains, and the monumental repose of the obelisk. The former expresses the undecided struggle between aspirations and passions — stern resolves bending under the weight of temptation — the central strength of virtue, and the yielding weakness of temperament; while the latter is like a noble life on which death has set the final seal of excellence, and which is forever rescued from the grasp of chance and change.

FAÇADE AND VESTIBULE.

When the visitor, after pausing to contemplate these imposing objects, passes on to the church itself, he will gather, from the time it takes him to reach the portico, an impression of the size of the piazza which the eye alone fails to communicate. As he draws nearer, he will notice the two prominent defects of the plan; the lengthening of the nave consequent upon the adoption of the form of a Latin cross, and the very inferior architecture of the façade.

By the lengthening of the nave, the base of the dome is cut off from the eye; and thus there is no point in the piazza, from which the whole of its sublime proportions can be seen. In this respect, the common prints of St. Peter's are deceptive; the point of sight being always above the plane of the eye, more of the dome is represented in them, than is really visible to any one of mortal stature. The façade is hopelessly and irredeemably bad; ill-adapted to its position, as being palatial rather than ecclesiastical in its style, and of no essential merit independent of its unfitness. By the multiplication and intersection of the pilasters, windows, bands, and cornices, an air of crowded uniformity has been given to the whole front, making it resemble an enormous chequer-board. There is no boldness in the projection of the portico and pediment; and nowhere a chance for the light to be broken into massive shadows. The whole is deficient in dignity, simplicity, and expression. The lengthened nave, and the façade, are both due to Carlo Maderno, 'a wretched plasterer from Como,' as Forsyth indignantly calls him; and for both he has been severely, perhaps too severely censured. For the former he may plead in justification the wishes of the Pope, Paul V., who determined to include within the new building the whole space occupied by the old basilica. For the defects of the façade he may urge in extenuation the necessity of a balcony, from which the papal benediction may be given; but, surely, that might have been gained, and not so much lost. The balcony might have been made the central object, around which all the rest should be disposed; or, it might have been blended with the other details of the front, without too much prominence, and without impairing the general effect.

The vestibule is a noble and spacious building, in itself. Standing in the middle, an architectural vista of more than two hundred feet, on either hand, is opened to the eye; terminated on the right by an equestrian statue of Constantine, and, on the left, by a similar one of Charlemagne ; neither worthy of the splendid position it enjoys. Nor will more than a rapid glance be vouchsafed to the celebrated mosaic of St. Peter walking on the sea, which is over the central entrance of the vestibule, — a work hallowed by the name of Giotto, though little of his handy-work is left in it.

INTERIOR.

We are now about to enter the church itself. He must be of a singularly insensible temperament, who can move aside the heavy leathern curtains of the entrance, without a quickened beating of the heart. When the visitor has passed into the interior, and so far recovered from the first rush of tumultuous sensations which crowd upon him, as to be able to look about him, he will be struck with, and, if not forewarned, disappointed at the apparent want of magnitude. This, deemed by some a defect, and by others a merit, is, strictly speaking, neither the one nor the other ; but the inevitable result of the style of architecture in which St. Peter's is built. This structure, like every work of art, should be judged with reference to its aim and purpose. It is not in the form of a basilica, and we violate an elementary canon of criticism, when we apply to it the rules by which the excellence of a basilica is tried. In this, we demand unity and simplicity ; but in the style of St. Peter's, harmony, variety, and proportion, are the graces aimed at. There is certainly something very effective in the severe purity of the basilica. How airy and graceful are the columns of the nave !

how, like a musical accompaniment, the side-aisles flow along! how naturally the walls rest on the arches of the colonnade! and how fitly the roof crowns and binds the whole! The first impression satisfies and elevates the mind. The elastic glance leaps, at a bound, from the pavement to the roof, and follows the unbroken line of the perspective without a pause of discontent. Some persons have regretted that a form of ecclesiastical architecture, so hallowed by the traditions of the church, was not adopted in this greatest of Christian temples. But, besides that the magnitude of the building, and the immense weight of the superincumbent mass, required the support of piers and arches, it would have been impossible to procure the requisite number of monolith columns for a basilica of the first class. The majestic porticoes and temples of antiquity had been plundered of their pillars of granite and marble, to decorate earlier churches; and there were no more left for either rapacity or devotion to seize upon. Nor could the crowning glory of the dome have been combined with such a plan. Thus, in entering St. Peter's, we must leave behind us the prepossessions derived, either from a Gothic cathedral, or a Roman basilica. In a Gothic cathedral, for instance, the statues are of the size of life, because, by the natural standard they furnish to the eye, the apparent height of the roof and the shafts is enhanced; but, in St. Peter's, the statues are all on a colossal scale. The cherubs which support a vase of holy water, near the door, are of seemingly infantile proportions, but they are really upwards of six feet high. Not only is harmony of proportion an essential attribute of a building like St. Peter's, but its immense size makes it unnecessary to enlarge its apparent dimensions.

It is true, that so far as the first impression is concerned, which is so important in architecture, a building like the Milan cathedral, or the church of Santa Maria Maggiore, has the advantage of St. Peter's. But in the former, successive visits do little more than renew and deepen the first image ; in St. Peter's, the visible objects seem to grow and expand as we gaze. It is a mighty volume, in which every day we read a new page. The eye becomes the pupil of the mind ; and the proportioned bulk and harmonious grandeur unfold themselves by gradual and successive steps. A cathedral breaks upon us with the sudden splendor of a meteor ; but St. Peter's gains upon the mind by gradations, like those which mark the approach of day in temperate latitudes.

An objection which has been made to the nave of St. Peter's — that it contains too great a multiplicity of details — cannot be so satisfactorily met. The roof shadowed with sunken coffers and shining with gilded ornaments ; the enormous piers, with their Corinthian pilasters, their niches, and their statues ; the lateral and longitudinal arches ; the recumbent figures in stucco ; the medallions ; the innumerable ornaments in marble — confuse the mind with their number and mass. Had there been less profusion, and a severer taste in embellishment, the general effect would have been increased.

As we leave the entrance, and walk towards the dome, the eye is caught by the row of lamps, one hundred and twelve in number, which are grouped, in branches of three, upon a circular balustrade of marble. At a distance, their faint, tremulous gleams, struggling through the eclipsing light of day, present an impressive picture, and recall Shelley's fanciful image of 'a swarm of golden bees;' but their effect lessens as we draw near, and the lamps are revealed. From the balustrade, a double flight of steps leads down to the most sacred spot in the church, the tomb of the apostle to whom it is dedicated. At the bottom of the steps, in a kneeling attitude before the tomb, is a marble statue of Pius VI. by Canova; the only statue which I recall as being in a situation to be looked down upon by the spectator. It is a work of great beauty and expression, and its position is a source both of wonder and regret; of wonder, because not even the truly amiable and respectable character of Pius VI. would seem to entitle him to occupy a spot of such peculiar sacredness; and of regret, because its merits, as a work of art, are very much lost.

On the right side of the nave is the bronze statue of St. Peter, the foot of which has been reverently kissed by so many generations of devout Catholics. It is a story, often repeated by Protestant writers, that this identical statue is a work of antiquity; a representation of Jupiter, baptized anew in those transition ages, 'when Pan to Moses lent his pagan horn.' But in this statement there is more of Protestant zeal than of knowledge in art; for not only it has not that character of the head, and arrangement of the hair, always found in statues of Jupiter; but its inferior workmanship, the stiffness of the attitude, and the hardness of the outline, prove it to be of a later date than the classical periods of art. It is probably the recast of an antique statue.

The huge, uncouth structure, reared over the high altar, awakens, both from its ugliness and inappropriateness, a double effusion of iconoclastic zeal. It is a baldachino, or canopy, of bronze, ninety-three feet high, and resting on four twisted columns of the same material; the whole elaborately ornamented and richly gilded. It is difficult to imagine on what ground, or for what purpose, this costly fabric was placed here. It has neither beauty nor grandeur; and resembles nothing so much as a colossal four-post bedstead without the curtains. Its size is so immense, that it cannot be avoided, either by the eye or the mind. It is a pursuing and intrusive presence. Stand where we may — look where we will — it thrusts itself upon the attention. We wish it any where but where it is — under the dome, rearing its tawdry commonplace into that majestic space, and scrawling upon the air its feeble and affected lines of spiral.

The bronze of which this baldachino is constructed is said to have been taken by Urban VIII. from the Pantheon — a fact which gives a fresh coating to the dislike, which the mere sight of it awakens.

The pilgrim is now beneath the dome. The spirit of criticism, which has hitherto attended him with whispers of doubt and suggestions of improvement, goes no further. Astonishment and admiration break upon the mind and carry it away. To say that the dome of St. Peter's is sublime is a cold commonplace. In sublimity, it is so much beyond all other architectural creations, that it demands epithets of its own. There is no work of man's hands that is similar or second to it. Vast as it is, it rests upon its supporting piers, in such serene tranquillity, that it seems to have been lifted and expanded by the elastic force of the air which it clasps. Under its majestic vault, the soul dilates. To act like the hero — to endure like the martyr — seems no more than the natural state of man.

Under the dome, with the tribune before us, and the transept on either hand, we are face to face with the sublime genius of Michael Angelo. These are his conceptions, carried out by his successors in a spirit of becoming reverence. His mind was never in its element, unless when grappling with majestic designs and moving in wide spaces. As men like Cromwell and Bonaparte are turbulent and impatient when in an inferior sphere, but tranquil when they have risen to the heights of power, so the crowded and restless energies of Michael Angelo, which chafed and fretted in the narrow precinct of a single statue, or an oil picture, found repose in such gigantic tasks as the dome of St. Peter's and the frescoes of the Sistine Chapel.

The arts of painting and sculpture can offer no parallel to the dome of St. Peter's. Their range, so far as the sublime is concerned, is necessarily limited; and beyond that limit they degenerate into the monstrous or the grotesque. Music is too sensuous, too stirring, too passionate — too much felt in the blood — to lift the mind into regions so lofty and so pure. Poetry, alone, can awaken such emotions, and call up such shapes of grandeur. Michael Angelo has been often compared to Dante, whose works he is known to have studied and admired; but Dante's is not the name which the dome of St. Peter's first suggests. He is sublime; but that is not his greatest power. His leading characteristics are picturesqueness and intensity. The genius of Milton presents the most obvious parallel to that which reared this majestic dome. The first book of the Paradise Lost is in poetry, what that is in architecture. Both are marked by the same imaginative sublimity and the same creative power. Both raise the mind to the same exalted heights, and both by the same means.

MONUMENTS.

St. Peter's is a world of art; but the specimens, with a few exceptions, are by no means of the first class. The period at which the building was so far completed as to admit of interior decorations, was the Alexandrian age of art. Bernini was to Michael Angelo what Lycophron was to Homer. The monuments to deceased popes erected here are all of them costly, and many magnificent. Some separate figures and portions of them are of great excellence, but few soar to the dignity, simplicity, and feeling of high monumental art. Most of them are framed upon a uniform model. They are pyramidal in their general outline: the statue of the deceased pope, kneeling, sitting, or standing, being the central and crowning figure. Below, is a sarcophagus, ornamented with bas-reliefs, flanked or supported by statues, in which all the resources of allegory are exhausted. Prudence, Justice, Charity, and Religion, lean, sprawl, or recline; and all endeavor, with more or less of ill-success, to do what marble never can do.

The finest of these monuments is that erected by Canova to Clement XIII. at the end of the right transept. The pope is represented in an attitude of prayer: a figure full of expression. He kneels upon a cushion, and his tiara is on the space before him. Below, on the left, is the figure of Religion, a female holding a cross taller than herself. This statue, though admirably executed, is not of the highest merit. The general character of the form is too sturdy and masculine, and the attitude too rigid. The golden rays which encircle the head are a most unfortunate embellishment. In passing suddenly from the flowing outlines of the figure to a circle of radiating spikes, the eye experiences a painful shock; nor does the material harmonize with the purity of the marble. On the left, is the genius of Death, sitting with his torch reversed: the countenance and attitude beautifully expressive of the gentleness of grief. This is an admirable work of art; not original in its design, but such a statue as would have been admired in Greece, in the best days of Grecian art. The delicate symmetry of the limbs, the grace of the position, and the air of soft melancholy thrown over the whole figure, are stamped with the impress of Canova's genius in its best days, before he had fallen into the prettiness and affectation observable in some of his later works.

The lower part of the monument represents the door of a chapel. This is guarded by two lions; that on the left is represented as waking, and that on the right as sleeping. The latter is an incomparable creature — as noble a combination of strength and repose as art has ever created — a work to be praised only by superlatives, and without qualification. We wonder in looking at it why Canova did not do more in the same style; why an artist so capable of representing the sublime should have dwelt so habitually within the limits of the beautiful. Is it because the animal sublime, if such an expression may be allowed, differs from the human sublime, in kind as well as degree: the former being the result of material form, the latter, of intellectual expression?

Admirable as these lions are, one is tempted to question their appropriateness as embellishments to the monument of a peaceful ecclesiastic. We ask, what is their meaning, and what ideas do they represent? Pistolesi, the author of the great work upon the Vatican and St. Peter's, tells us that they typify the firmness of mind ('la fortezza dell' anima') which distinguished the deceased pontiff. On the other hand, M. de Stendhal, a clever French writer, says that they express grief in its different aspects of rebellion and submission.

The great name of Thorwaldsen will naturally attract attention to the monument of Pius VII.; but it is hardly worthy the genius of this illustrious artist. The figures are good, but, as a whole, the design is formal and rectangular, and leaves an impression on the mind that the sculptor had not put his heart into his work.

In the monument to Urban VIII. which is in the tribune, the genius of Bernini is seen in its most favorable aspect. The figure of the pope is in bronze, and full of expression; and the statues of Prudence and Justice, which are in marble, are fine specimens of cleverness and skill. They are not beautiful, still less, sublime. They want repose and dignity, but they are full of animation and spirit. They are somewhat exaggerated and redundant in their forms, like the pictures of Rubens; but they have the same vital energy.

In the same tribune — as if to give us the extreme points to which the genius of Bernini could rise and fall — is the most glaring offence against good taste in all St. Peter's; a fabric of bronze, in which is enclosed the identical chair in which St. Peter and his immediate successors officiated; that is, we are told to believe so. Four fathers of the church hold up the bronze covering with their hands, but, in their attitude and position, they resemble dancing-masters rather than saints and theologians. Above, there is a pictorial representation of the Holy Ghost, a confused hubbub of clouds, gilding, rays, and cherubs; the whole design from top to bottom being nothing less than detestable.

To those who speak the English tongue, the most interesting of the monuments in St. Peter's is that erected by Canova to the last three of the Stuart family, James the Third, Charles the Third, and Henry the Ninth, as they are designated in the inscription. It is a marble structure, in form resembling a truncated obelisk. The lower part represents the door of a mausoleum, guarded on either side by winged figures identical in design. The whole monument seems feeble and commonplace, but its interest is independent of its merits as a work of art. Here repose the last of a memorable race — a family, remarkable not for great virtues or great capacity, but for great misfortunes.

Misfortunes have their dignity and their redeeming power.

'Sunt lacrymæ rerum et mentem mortalia tangunt.'

No family ever underwent a more righteous retribution, or more distinctly sowed the harvest of sorrow which they reaped. But here is the end of a great historical chapter: nothing now remains but compassion. Over the dust which here reposes, neither puritan nor republican would cherish the remembrance of crimes committed or wrongs endured.

ASCENT TO THE DOME.

The visitor to St. Peter's should not fail to ascend to the dome: a long journey, but involving no danger and not a great amount of fatigue. From the church to the roof the passage is by an inclined plane of pavement, with so gradual an ascent that loaded mules pass up without difficulty. In stepping out upon the roof, it is difficult to believe that we are more than one hundred and fifty feet from the ground, or that so extensive an architectural surface could have been reared in air by the patient labor of men's hands. It rather seems as if a little village had been lifted up by some geological convulsion. Here are wide spaces to walk about in, houses for human habitation, a fountain playing, and all the signs of life. The views are every where fine, and one can fancy that the air is purer and the sky more blue than to those left below. The dome soars high above the eye, and a new sense of its magnitude seizes upon the mind. The two cupolas which flank the façade are upwards of one hundred feet high, and the five smaller ones which crown the chapels are of great size; but here they seem like dwarfs clinging about a giant's knee.

The dome of St. Peter's, as is well known, is double, and between the outer and inner wall is a series of winding passages and staircases, by which the ascent is made to the top. The length of these passages and staircases, their number, and the time it takes to traverse them, are a new revelation of the size of this stupendous structure. We begin to comprehend the genius and courage which planned and executed a work so novel and so bold. From the galleries inside, the view of the interior below is most striking. It looks as the earth may look from a balloon. The men moving upon the pavement appear like that 'small infantry warred on by cranes,' and even the badalchino hardly swells beyond the dimensions of a candelabrum.

At the base of the ball, a railing, unseen from below, enables the visitor whose nerves are tolerably good to enjoy an extensive and beautiful prospect, embracing a region interesting not merely to the eye but to the mind: the cradle of that mighty Roman race which here began its ever-widening circle of conquest and annexation. It comprises the Campagna, the Tiber, the distant Mediterranean, the Apennines, the Alban and Sabine hills, and the isolated bulk of Soracte. From no point on earth can the eye rest upon so many spots on which the undying light of human interest lingers.

From this place the ascent is made to the interior

of the ball itself, into which most travellers climb, probably more for the sake of saying that they have been there, than any thing else. Though the ball looks like a mere point from below, it is nearly eight feet in diameter, and the interior will hold a dozen persons without inconvenience. Although I visited it on a winter's day, the atmosphere was extremely hot and uncomfortable, from the effect of the sun's rays upon the gilded bronze. By means of an exterior ladder, it is possible to climb to the foot of the cross; a feat which few landsmen would have the nerve to undertake.

Enormous as is the mass of the dome, and high as it is raised in the air, there have been for a long time no indications of insecurity; and it seems to be as firm as the hills themselves. But it is fearful to think of what an earthquake might do; and in the volcanic soil of Italy, earthquakes are not very rare or very unlikely occurrences.*

GENERAL CHARACTER OF THE BUILDING.

Every great architectural structure has its peculiar character and power, which is independent of the particular parts which compose it; resembling the expression of a countenance, or the air of a figure. Some buildings are gay, some are grave, some are impressive, some are simple, some are affected. St. Peter's

* There is a story told of two Spanish monks having been in the ball of St. Peter's in 1730, when a slight shock of earthquake was felt, and that one of them was so affected with terror, that he died upon the spot.

is so vast, and it contains so much, that it has no one prominent characteristic. It cannot be defined by a single epithet. It is among buildings what Shakespeare is among poets: both are characterized by universality. In consequence of the immense extent of the interior and the thickness of the walls, the temperature is nearly the same during the whole year. Thus, we always experience an agreeable change in entering it. In winter, we leave behind the dampness and the cold, and pass into a dry atmosphere of vernal softness, which refreshes the frame and soothes the spirit. In summer, we escape from the fiery heat and dazzling sunshine, and breathe with a sense of luxury the cool airs which are stored up in those capacious caverns. The windows of the church are never opened. It has its own atmosphere, and needs no supply from the world without. The most zealous professor of ventilation would admit that there was no work for him to do here. Our notions of a future life are never quite purged of material grossness. We imagine our senses as passing with us beyond the grave. When we dream of the climate of heaven, we make it warmth without heat, and coolness without cold, like that of St. Peter's.

SUNDAY EVENING VESPERS.

My most delightful recollections of St. Peter's are connected with the Sunday evening vespers, which I never failed to attend. They were performed in one of the side-chapels, and lasted about an hour. Most of the time was taken up by the singing of a choir of male voices to the accompaniment of an organ. The music was of a peculiar kind, such as can hardly be heard out of Rome; not sombre and monotonous like that which we usually hear in Protestant churches, nor yet resembling those 'brisk and giddy-paced airs,' sometimes introduced to quicken the inexpressive drone of psalmody; but music which was at once elaborate, expressive, and sacred; weaving solemn airs into a complicated tissue of harmony, such as tasked both the voice and the mind to unwind. The voices were not of the first class, but they were admirably trained; and the performers sang with the unconscious ease with which common men talk. Without pretending to understand and interpret all the language which music speaks to a trained ear, I felt that the highest charm of music was there, and that the strains were in unison with the scene and the day. Before the close of the services, in the shortest days of winter, the shades of evening began to settle upon the church. The distant arches were shrouded with the gray veil of twilight. A silence, deep, palpable, and overpowering, came down upon the scene the moment the voices had ceased. The power of such moments and such influences can be felt but not described. What we see is blended with what we hope or what we mourn. The gloom is peopled with airy shapes, and visionary voices are mingled with the sounds which die along the arches. As forms grow dim and shadowy, the shadows become substantial. The imagination pieces out what the eye cannot complete. The living and the lifeless change places. The kneeling monk becomes a statue, and some wandering ray of light, falling upon the fluttering drapery of a female saint, gives to the marble a momentary touch of life.

CHRISTMAS IN ST. PETER'S.

The services in St. Peter's on Christmas day, in 1847, were attended by an immense concourse of people. Rome was at that time thronged by strangers from all parts of the world, and the zeal and interest of the native population were awakened anew by the universal enthusiasm inspired by Pius IX., at that time at the height of his short-lived popularity. It was indeed rather idolatry than popularity; and the wild hopes which he made to blossom in the susceptible hearts of his people, were such as neither the highest capacity nor the most favorable opportunities could have ripened into fruit. At an early hour on that day I found the church already occupied by a great crowd. A double row of soldiers stretched from the entrance to the altar, around which the pope's guards, in their fantastic uniform, looking like the knaves in a pack of cards, were stationed, while a series of seats on either side were filled by ladies dressed in black and wearing veils. The foreign ambassadors were in a place appropriated to them in the tribune. Among the spectators were several in military uniforms. A handsome young Englishman, in a rich hussar dress of scarlet and gold, attracted much attention. In a recess, above one of the great piers of the dome, a choir of male singers was stationed, whose voices, without any instrumental accompaniment, blended in complete harmony, and gave the most perfect expression to that difficult and complicated music which the church of Rome has consecrated to the use of its high festivals. We waited some time for the advent of the pope, but, with such objects around us, were content to wait. The whole spectacle was one of animated interest and peculiar beauty. The very defects of the church — its gay, secular, and somewhat theatrical character — were, in this instance, embellishments which enhanced the splendor of the scene. The various uniforms, the rich dresses, the polished arms of the soldiery, were in unison with the marble, the stucco, the bronze, and the gilding. The impression left upon the mind was not that of sacredness; that is, not upon a mind that had been formed under protestant and puritan influences; but rather of a gorgeous ceremonial belonging to some 'gay religion, full of pomp and gold.' But we travel to little purpose if we carry with us the standard which is formed at home, and expect the religious sentiment to manifest itself at all times and in all places, in the same manner. The Scotch Covenanter upon the hillside, the New England Methodist at a camp-meeting, worship God in spirit and in truth; but shall we presume to say that the Italian is a formalist and a hypocrite, because his devotion requires the aid of music, painting, and sculpture, and, without visible symbols, goes out like a flame without air?

In due season the pope appeared, seated in the 'sedia gestatoria,' a sort of capacious arm-chair, borne upon men's shoulders, flanked on either side by the enormous fan of white peacock feathers. He was carried up the whole length of the nave, distributing his blessing with a peculiar motion of the hand, on either side, upon the kneeling congregation. It seemed by no means a comfortable mode of transportation, and the expression of his countenance was that of a man ill at ease, and sensible of the awkwardness and want of dignity of his position. His dress was of white satin, richly embroidered with gold; a costume too gaudy for daylight, and by no means so becoming as that of the cardinals, whose flowing robes of crimson and white produced the finest and richest effect. The chamberlains of the pope, who attended on this occasion in considerable numbers, wear the dress of England in the time of Charles I., so well known in the portraits of Vandyke. It looks better in pictures than in the life, and shows so much of the person that it requires an imposing figure to carry it off. A commonplace man, in such a costume, looks like a knavish valet who has stolen his master's clothes.

High mass was said by the pope in person, and the responses were sung by the choir. He performed the service with an air and manner expressive of true devotion, and though I felt that there was a chasm between me and the rite which I witnessed, I followed his movements in the spirit of respect, and not of criticism. But one impressive and overpowering moment will never be forgotten. When the tinkling of the bell announced the elevation of the Host, the whole of the vast assemblage knelt or bowed their faces. The pavement was suddenly strewn with prostrate forms. A silence like that of death fell upon the church — as if some celestial vision had passed before the living eyes, and hushed into stillness every pulse of human feeling. After a pause of a few seconds, during which every man could have heard the beating of his own heart, a band of wind instruments near the entrance, of whose presence I had not been aware, poured forth a few sweet and solemn strains, which floated up the nave and overflowed the whole interior. The effect of this invisible music was beyond any thing I have ever heard or ever expect to hear. The air seemed stirred with the trembling of angelic wings; or, as if the gates of heaven had been opened, and a 'wandering breath' from the songs of seraphs had been borne to the earth. How fearfully and wonderfully are we made! A few sounds, which, under ordinary circumstances, would have been merely a passing luxury to the ear, heard at this moment, and beneath this dome, were like a purifying wave, which, for an instant, swept over the soul, bearing away with it all the soil and stains of earth, and leaving it pure as infancy. There was, it is true, a refluent tide; and the world displaced by the solemn strain came back with the echo; but though we 'cannot keep the heights we are competent to gain,' we are the better for the too brief exaltation.

I noticed on this occasion another peculiarity of St. Peter's. There was an immense concourse of persons present, but there was no impression of a crowd. The church was not thronged — not even full: there still seemed room for a nation to come in. In ordinary buildings, when they are filled to their utmost capacity, the architecture disappears, and the mind and eye are occupied only with the men and women. But St. Peter's can never be thus put down. Fill it full of human life, it would still be something greater than them all. Men, however numerous they might be, would be but appendages to its mountainous bulk. As the sky is more than the stars, and the wooded valley more than the trees, so is St. Peter's more than any amount of humanity that can be gathered within its arms.*

* The whole cost of the building of St. Peter's, from the foundation by Nicholas V. in 1450, to the completion of the sacristy by Pius VI. in 1780, is estimated to have been about forty-seven millions of dollars; a sum, representing, however, two or three times that amount, in exchangeable value, at the present moment. This does not include any of the monuments or works of art. The annual expense of keeping the building in repair is about thirty thousand dollars.

CHAPTER IX.

The Vatican — The Cortile of the Belvedere — Nuovo Braccio — Museo Pio-Clementino — Extent and Character of the Collections in Sculpture — Gallery of Pictures — Frescoes of the Sistine Chapel — The Stanze of Raphael — The Tapestries — The Loggie — The Library of the Vatican.

THE VATICAN.

The palace of the Vatican bears the same relation to other palaces, that St. Peter's does to other churches. It is, indeed, not a palace, but a congress of palaces. One of the stories with which every traveller in Rome is amused, is, that the Vatican with its gardens, and St. Peter's, occupy as much space as the city of Turin; and as it has never been contradicted, it is probably true. The Vatican comprises a papal palace, a library, and a museum; and is said to contain between four and five thousand apartments.

As a museum of art, it is the first in the world. In sculpture, it not only surpasses any other collection, but all other collections put together. The whole of Europe could furnish nothing to rival the Vatican. It also comprises the highest triumphs of painting, in the frescoes of Raphael and Michael Angelo. He who has seen the Vatican has seen the utmost point reached by the human mind and hand in these two arts. The world is no more likely to witness any thing beyond what is here visible, than to have a nobler epic than the Iliad, or a greater dramatist than Shakespeare.

Such an assemblage of buildings is no proper subject of architectural criticism. Built at different periods, by various architects, and for many purposes, it has no unity of plan and no uniformity of character. But no edifice presents so many fine architectural pictures; for such they may indeed be called, so wide are the spaces, so lofty the heights, so boundless the perspectives. Walking through the Vatican is like walking about a city: we learn here how noble is the effect produced by mere space. There is a perfect relation between the Vatican and its contents. The statues it contains amount to several thousands, and in any smaller building they would be crowded; but here they have ample verge, and seem only appropriate furniture and decoration to the galleries and apartments in which they are placed.

The first few visits to the Vatican leave the mind of the traveller in a state of whirl and confusion, producing at last entire exhaustion. He is like the shepherd in the Rambler who asked to have the river Euphrates flow through his grounds, and was taken off his feet and borne away by the stream. He naturally wishes to make a general survey of the whole, before descending to study the several details. He walks with resolute purpose right onward, hardly glancing at the innumerable objects of attraction around him, which are all postponed to a more convenient season; but long before the great circuit is completed, his knees knock together with fatigue, and his worn brain refuses to receive any new impressions. But time and patience, which conquer all things, conquer the Vatican. At each visit something is gained, and larger accessions made to that great assemblage of objects which need not be seen a second time; until, at length, the field of observation is narrowed to those few noble specimens which have come down to us radiant with the accumulated admiration of successive generations — each sight of them revealing new beauties and awakening fresh enthusiasm.

THE CORTILE OF THE BELVEDERE.

This is an octagonal space, surrounded by an open portico, with a fountain playing in the centre, and four small cabinets opening from it. These cabinets contain the most celebrated, if not the finest statues in the whole collection. In one is the Apollo Belvedere; in another, the Laocoon; in a third, the Belvedere Antinous; and the fourth is appropriated to three statues by Canova.

The Apollo Belvedere provokes criticism, because it appears to defy it. It seems to me to bear the same relation to the works of the school of Phidias, that Euripides does to Sophocles. Beauty is beginning to be divorced from simplicity. There is — shall I speak the word? — a little of the fine gentleman about the Apollo; and in the expression there seems to be a gleam of satisfaction reflected from the admiration which his beauty awakens. There is not enough of the serene unconsciousness of the immortal Gods. The disdain and triumph of the countenance are those of a mortal who had doubted his aim, and was surprised at his success. The glory of the statue is its airy movement. The chest seems to dilate and the figure to grow tall, before the spectator's eyes. The admirable lightness and elasticity of the form are, in a great measure, lost in casts. There are, doubtless, finer statues in the world than the Apollo — works proceeding from a deeper vein of sentiment, and breathing a more simple grandeur — but there are none more fascinating. In this statue, more than in any other work in marble, we recognise the grace and animation of a living form; a sympathetic charm which every one can feel. The Apollo Belvedere as compared with the Theseus in the British Museum — perhaps the best work now left to us of the best period of Grecian art — is like Dryden's Alexander's Feast as compared with Milton's Ode on the Nativity. The latter is the production of the greater genius, but nine readers out of ten will prefer the former.

The group of Laocoon and his sons — so justly denominated by Michael Angelo, at the time of its discovery, the miracle of art, 'il portento dell' arte' — is one of those productions which would have been pronounced impossible had they never been executed. It stands upon the very line by which the art of sculpture is divided from poetry and painting. There is no other work of Greek art, of high rank at least, which resembles it. It has two elements peculiar to itself — violent action and the expression of physical suffering: neither of which, as a general rule, did the Greeks admit within the legitimate province of plastic art. The subject, viewed by itself, can never be pronounced proper for marble or canvas. Imagine the group to be a father and his sons who, in a tropical forest, during their noonday repose, are seized and destroyed by two enormous serpents, and what is there but shuddering horror and physical disgust? There is no poetry, and nothing that exalts the fear and suffering into tragic grandeur. Such a work would be but little higher in the scale of art than the well-known picture of the Anaconda destroying a horse and his rider: a hideous image of brutal force and animal pain, not much more worthy of being painted than a butcher slaying an ox. But the Greek saw in this group the record of an awful mythological event. The serpents were not to him mere earth-born reptiles, but creatures divinely commissioned to punish an impious mortal. The form of Laocoon himself is invested with a dignity borrowed from courageous daring and a terrible retribution. He was of consequence enough in the eyes of the offended god, to be made the victim of a signal and conspicuous doom. It is easy to see how entirely these ideas must have modified the impressions made by this extraordinary group, and how the mere physical horror must have been swallowed up in higher emotions.*

* These remarks may be also applied to many of the subjects which the Italian painters have selected — such as The

In execution — in the successful overcoming of mechanical and material difficulties — this group is beyond any thing that antiquity has transmitted to us. The history of its conception in the mind of the artist, and of its embodiment in marble, would be an extremely interesting chapter in the literature of art. We must remember that the sculptor could not have had the aid of any model in representing the convulsive agony and terror of his figures, but must have relied exclusively upon a profound knowledge of anatomical development and a powerful imagination. The proportions are not correct; for the sons, judged by their apparent age, are on a smaller scale than the father; but this violation of proportion was common among the ancient artists, deliberately adopted in order to give prominence to the central figure in a group, or to increase the dignity of the human form when brought into proximity with animals. The surface of the marble is not polished, but finished with the chisel merely; by which the peculiar expression required in the flesh and muscles is enhanced.

There is something about the Laocoon which reminds one of Bernini; or of Bernini, as he would have been, had he been born a Greek. Phidias would have pronounced such a subject unsuitable for art, and given but faint praise to the adventurous skill which

Massacre of the Innocents, and the various repulsive forms of martyrdom which they have represented. These delineations of physical pain are idealized in the eyes of the devout Catholic by the faith which they sealed. The horror is lost in the victory.

had wandered so far and brought back such spoils. It would be interesting to know what other works were produced by so daring a genius and so skilful a hand; whether he ever pushed the tragic element further than in the Laocoon, and never fell into extravagance and caricature.

The Belvedere Antinous is an exquisite image of blooming youth. For soft and delicate beauty — beauty which, like that of the vernal rose, the sunset cloud, and the breaking wave, is suggestive of brief continuance and early decay — this statue has no superior, hardly an equal. The busts and statues of Antinous all have a certain expression of melancholy. Their beauty seems 'too ripe for earth.' We feel that the next step in the progress of change will be to impair what is now so perfect. In this statue, the softness of the limbs just stops short of languid effeminacy. It is beauty not like that of the Apollo, in action, but in repose; filled to the brim with sweet sensations; neither restless from desire, nor cloyed with enjoyment.

In the fourth compartment are three statues by Canova; the Perseus and the Two Boxers. The modest genius of the artist is said to have been opposed to an arrangement which brought his works into such direct competition with the masterpieces of antiquity. During the absence of the Apollo in Paris, under the rule of Napoleon, the Perseus was placed on its pedestal: an honor of which it was hardly worthy, as it is rather a fine than a beautiful statue, and is deficient in sentiment and expression. The Two Boxers are carefully executed in anatomical details, but they are wanting in refinement. This word is not misplaced, even when applied to such subjects as these. Nothing more marks the superiority of Greek sculptors than their treatment of such themes. A Greek sculptor, in executing a statue of an athlete, would have made him first, a man, and secondly, an athlete. The human element would have been recognised, as well as the professional. But in Canova's boxers we see only an accurate transcript of brute, animal force. We applaud the exactness of the imitation, but regret that such powers should, in this age of the world, have been wasted upon such a subject, and feel that sculpture is degraded when it stoops to represent a brawny prize-fighter.

MUSEO CHIARAMONTI.

Here are some seven hundred pieces of sculpture — all worthy of examination, many of them curious, and some of them of great merit. The bust of the young Augustus is one of the most beautiful things in Rome. It represents him about sixteen or eighteen years old. The face is of delicate and dreamy beauty. The brow is intellectual and thoughtful, but the chief charm of the work is in the exquisite refinement of the mouth. The maiden in the fairy tale, who spoke pearls and diamonds, must have had such lips. It is the face of a poet, and not of a statesman. The expression is that of one dwelling in a soft, ideal world. It looks as Virgil might have looked when the genius of Latin poetry met him on the banks of the Mincius, and threw her inspiring mantle over him.

NUOVO BRACCIO.

This noble hall is upwards of two hundred feet in length, and admirably lighted from a roof supported by Corinthian columns. It is impossible for works of sculpture to be better disposed, and out of seventy-two busts and forty-three statues which are here, there is hardly one which is not excellent.

The Minerva Pudicitia is a statue of great merit. The attitude is not easy, and the position of the feet hardly consistent with the disposition of the figure; but the drapery is admirable, and a marked expression of purity and delicacy pervades the whole. There is also another statue of Minerva here, called Minerva Medica, famous for its drapery and the dignity of its look. The breadth of the shoulders and the narrowness of the hips give the form a masculine character.

A statue of Domitian exemplifies the ingenuity of the artist in modifying the personal defects of his imperial sitter. The emperor was short and fat, but the sculptor has contrived to give an air of lightness to the figure by the most elaborate and deeply-cut drapery; showing a very patient and a very skilful chisel.

Here is a statue of Demosthenes, one of the noblest works of antiquity. The attitude is easy and dignified, the air of the head noble and intellectual, and the drapery absolutely perfect. With every visit this statue gains upon us. We persuade ourselves that it is a likeness, and thus find it doubly attractive. At any rate, it satisfies our imaginings of the great orator and statesman, and there is nothing he did and spoke that is beyond the serene majesty of this marble image.

The colossal group of the Nile is one of the most striking objects of this part of the museum. The principal figure is in a reclining posture, and represents a man in the ripe autumn of life, with a flowing beard and a grave expression, while around him sixteen children are sporting in every possible variety of attitude: some climbing on his knees; some clasping his neck; some nestling in his lap; some bestriding his arms; and some playing with his feet. Most of these little creatures are restorations, but they are very cleverly executed. They seem to be really enjoying the fun; and the 'fine, old gentleman' with whom they are frolicking, appears like an indulgent grandpapa, surrendering himself to a game of romps with his grandchildren. The number sixteen is said to be in allusion to the sixteen cubits at which the rise of the river begins to irrigate the land.

MUSEO PIO-CLEMENTINO.

This is by far the most extensive collection in the Vatican. Besides the Cortile of the Belvidere, already mentioned, it comprises the Hall of Animals, the Gallery of the Muses, the Circular Hall, the Hall of the Greek Cross, the Hall of the Biga, and the Grand Staircase. In point of architecture, these are the most splendid portions of the whole Vatican; and the visitor knows not which most to admire, the innumerable works of art which solicit his attention, or the spacious courts and the noble apartments, around and in which they are distributed.

In a square vestibule at the entrance is the celebrated

torso of Hercules, known as well by the admiration of Michael Angelo as by its own merits. The great excellence of a work crowned by the commendation of so many great names must be taken on trust by those who do not see it for themselves; but as some poetry seems written exclusively for poets, so this colossal fragment addresses itself to the trained eye of the artist. To represent with perfect accuracy the swellings and hollows of a finely developed muscular frame; to give to marble the peculiar roundness of flesh, and to create an image of heroic strength without the alloy of brutality, and in so small a portion of the human body — is unquestionably an effort of genius as well as skill; and they who have learned how hard the task is will give a generous tribute to the result which they cannot imitate. The mere amateur, who has never had a chisel in his hand, cannot appreciate an excellence so purely technical, and will miss sentiment and expression. I confess that I should hardly have looked at this torso a second time, had I not with the mind's eye always seen the shadowy brow of Michael Angelo bending over it with studious and admiring glances.

In the same room with this torso is one of the most interesting objects in Rome — the sarcophagus of gray stone found in the tomb of the Scipios — the shape of which is so well known by the many copies which have been spread over the world. The works of the republic are not numerous in Rome, and this venerable monument attracts us as well by its antiquity, as by its association with the illustrious family whose name it bears. Impressive as it is, it seemed out of place in this modern and airy room, so richly lighted and commanding so living a landscape. It was an exotic torn from its native soil. Half of its significance and meaning is lost by its being thrust upon the eye in the broad glare of noon, and surrounded by such different and exciting objects. How much better would it have been, had it been left in the gloom and silence of the vaulted niche for which it was prepared! How much more impressive would the simple inscription have been, if we had been compelled to spell it out, in sepulchral darkness, by the flickering light of a torch! Then, all would have been in harmony: the sombre walls of the tomb; the ashen gray of the sarcophagus; the partial and struggling illumination; the heavy air, and the palpable silence.

The Hall of Animals is a fresh revelation of the resources of Greek sculpture. Here is a motionless menagerie in marble; horses, dogs, centaurs, crocodiles, wild boars, lions, bulls, and serpents. In some cases, the colors of life are attempted in marbles of various hues; and in others, the material is wholly porphyry or basalt. In many of these specimens — especially of the nobler animals — the proportions are not correct. They had not been studied with the accurate eye of modern science. But the observation of the ancients, as far as it went, was admirable; and thus the general character of each type is given with nice discrimination. Their animals are always alive.

In the Gallery of Statues, so called, is one of the finest works of antiquity, the recumbent statue of Ariadne. The attitude is easy, graceful, and refined; the limbs have the languid flow of sleep; the head rests on the back of the left hand, while the right arm is thrown over the head and falls down behind in an easy curve. Although the size is colossal, the delicacy and grace of the female figure are not impaired. But it is especially admirable for the drapery, which hangs in the most natural folds, revealing the fine outline of the limbs which it veils, but managed with great refinement. How much superior to her bold-browed namesake at Frankfort, who comes flaunting forth in the eye of day, like a Godiva shorn alike of her modesty and her tresses!

This statue, the Demosthenes, and the Minerva Medica, in the Nuovo Braccio, are worthy of peculiar attention to the modern artist, as showing what may be done by a skilful management of drapery. What call is there for this perpetual reproduction of the nude? Why persist in a path of art in which the ancients can never be approached? With them, undraped figures were significant and becoming: they were in unison with all their ideas of life, education, and religion. But we have changed all this. With the Greeks, the body was a fact; with us, it is a symbol. The problem presented to the modern sculptor is so to deal with drapery as to make it enhance the characteristic expression of a face or form. In the solution of this, the highest triumphs of his art will be achieved. It is easy, comparatively, to make a naked nymph or Grace of a certain degree of excellence. All that is wanted are good models and mechanical skill: but to deal with drapery so that it shall reveal and not overlay the figure; to make it expressive, and yet not so elaborate as to attract attention to itself; to make it heroic, dignified, or graceful, according to the character of the form which it shrouds, — this requires skill, invention, and delicate creative power — qualities, in short, which distinguish the artist from the mechanic.

In this gallery are also two noble statues, both seated, and having some general points of resemblance; one called by the name of Posidippus, and the other, by that of Menander. They are evidently portrait statues, and are at once real and ideal, natural and yet heroic. They are to works in sculpture, what the portraits of Titian are to works in painting; combining the dignity and permanent interest of history with the truth of portraiture.

Whoever would seek for the luxury of architecture in its highest perfection, will find it in the Hall of the Greek Cross. The finest materials are used to embellish the noblest proportions. The architect has not scrupled to call to his aid the sister art of painting, and all the best effects of color are produced by the variety of tints offered to the eye. A superb doorway is flanked on either side by two colossal statues, in the Egyptian style, of red granite: the pavement is composed of rich, parti-colored mosaics: the compartments of the roof are gilded or painted. Shafts of gray or red granite are crowned by cornices and capitals of white marble or bronze. Statues, busts, vases, sarcophagi, and candelabra of marble and porphyry, are distributed around the hall with unerring taste. Every thing is rich, airy, and exhilarating. The style is daring, but perfectly successful. It would not suit a northern latitude or a weeping climate, and seems to demand blue skies, vivid sunshine, and a year of flowers. On entering this hall upon a bright, warm day, the effect was that of a joyous strain of music or a vernal landscape.

The prominent objects among the contents of this hall are two enormous sarcophagi of porphyry, covered with bas-reliefs of excellent workmanship. Considering the hardness of the material, it must have been a work of immense labor to execute these reliefs. The material being of a rich red color and highly polished, the general effect, though they are monumental structures, is cheerful, not to say gay, rather than sombre or funereal. They are very happily placed, being in perfect unison with the character of the hall.

The Hall of the Biga is a circular chamber, in which is preserved a representation in white marble of an ancient biga, or chariot, with two wheels. Very little of the original work remains, but it has been restored with great taste and skill, and forms a curious and interesting object. Such a vehicle must always have been a more agreeable thing to look at than to ride in. Indeed, a farmer's cart of the rudest description is probably a more comfortable mode of conveyance than the stables of Augustus or Nero could furnish. The body of the ancient carriages, without the intervention of any thing like a spring, rested upon a heavy axle, and the jolting and clattering must have been enough to drive a man of sensitive nerves frantic in the course of a day's journey. It is not to be wondered that the litter, or sedan, was so generally resorted to as a mode of conveyance by the rich and luxurious. The modern carriage, gratifying as it does both the indolence and impatience of man's spirit, is one of the finest results of the union of invention, science, and experiment, applied to the arts of convenience and utility — a department in which the moderns are far more superior to the ancients, than the latter were to the former in those which ministered to the sense of beauty.

EXTENT AND CHARACTER OF THE COLLECTIONS IN SCULPTURE.

While travelling in Europe I chanced to fall in with one of my countrymen who had a trunk full of miscellaneous objects, accumulated as memorials of the various places he had visited. He had been in Constantinople when the Church of St. Sophia was undergoing repairs, in the course of which some of its mosaics were destroyed; and he had brought away a handful or two of the fragments. I mention this simply as an illustration. In looking over what I have written of the museum of the Vatican, it seems to me to convey about as just an impression of its treasures of art, as these bits of colored and gilded porcelain, of the venerable mosaics of St. Sophia. But in a collection in which the separate objects are numbered by thousands, there must be a principle of selection. Many things must be forgotten, in order that a few may be remembered. The taste and temperament of the visitor will lead him into certain paths of observation rather than others.

When we consider that this immense collection is but a waif saved from the wreck of Rome — fragments, only, snatched from the relentless powers of time and war, the consuming grasp of fire, and every form of pillage and rapacity — what an impression does it give us of the treasures of sculpture which were accumulated in Rome in the days of the empire! Rome was for many generations the capital of the world. It was to the rest of the earth what Paris now is to France. Talent of all kinds was attracted to this central heart; and every aspiring artist felt that his reputation was provincial until it had received the imperial stamp of Rome. Here, too, flowed the wealth of the world; and the immense revenues of the patricians were expended in the luxuries of architecture and horticulture, in sculpture and painting. The gold which had been wrung from the African, the Gaul, or the Briton, stimulated the chisel of the artist whose early taste had been formed by the frieze of the Parthenon.

By whatever hands the works in the Vatican may have been wrought, the spirit of the collection is Greek. Indeed, until the time of Michael Angelo all sculpture was essentially Greek: in art, the Romans had no Lucretius and no Juvenal. We see various degrees of merit, but the merit is all of one class. Other things being equal, he who is most familiar with Greek literature is best prepared to profit by a visit to the galleries of the Vatican. The books and the statues illustrate each other. Greek literature is sculpturesque. Their poetry and their sculpture were alike rooted in the national heart, and drew from the same soil the same element of vital power.

GALLERY OF PICTURES.

The oil pictures in the gallery of the Vatican are not more than fifty in number, and although we can hardly assent to the remark in Murray's Guide-book, that 'It has more real treasures of art than any other collection in the world,' it has unquestionably many works of the greatest merit and of peculiar interest.

Foremost among them, and placed by general consent at the head of all the oil-paintings in the world, is the Transfiguration, by Raphael. As is well known, it was the last work of the artist, and not entirely completed at the time of his death. No one will venture to approach such a picture in the spirit of criticism; and this not only from deference to the consenting judgments of more than three hundred years, but on account of the touching interest thrown over it from the fact that these were the last lines traced by that immortal hand. Vasari describes with simplicity and feeling the scene which took place at his funeral — when this picture, with the colors yet wet upon the canvas, was hung upon the wall over his lifeless remains — and how his friends broke into tears and lamentations when they contrasted those forms of breathing life with the silent lips and motionless hands beneath. Many will recall the graceful lines, in which Rogers has commemorated this incident in his 'Italy,' and the exquisite sketch by Turner which accompanies them. This sketch had been familiar to me, long before I saw the original, and I never looked upon the picture without filling out, in the mind's eye, the design which I bore in my memory, and seeing below it a shadowy bier, a lifeless and graceful form covered with a painter's cloak, and troops of kneeling and weeping friends.

The picture has been criticised for its twofold action, which, it is said, makes of it, in reality, two pictures instead of one. But the subject necessarily involves two elements, the divine and the human, in order to give it completeness. The spectacle of the transfiguration would have been no more than a splendid vision, but for the connection thus established between the Saviour's glorified state, and the sufferings of humanity which were in him to find healing and relief. The contrasts afforded by such a subject — calling forth the two principles of worship and sympathy — were peculiarly suited to Raphael's genius, which was reverential, tender, and sensitive; and it is evident that he never threw more of his own individuality into any of his works than into this, and that no one is on the whole more characteristic.

The lower part of the picture is full of animation and expression, without any taint of bustle or caricature. In point of drawing, grouping, and dramatic power, in clearness of purpose and distinctness of self-interpretation, it is of the highest excellence. The heads of the apostles have a general air of dignity, and yet are stamped with the traits of individual character. The kneeling female in attendance upon the demoniac boy is a figure full of grace and feeling; and the natural contrast between her self-possession and the violent action of the demoniac is one of those fine dramatic points which Raphael makes with so much taste and skill, and with such temperance of touch, always stopping short of extravagance and exaggeration. The difference in the expression of the two females also distinguishes, with admirable discrimination, the relations of mother and sister. The attitude and countenance of the latter are glowing with an earnest appeal to the apostles in behalf of her afflicted charge, mingled with indignant contempt at their inability to relieve him; but the former is wholly absorbed by maternal suffering and sympathy, which leave no room in her heart for anger or remonstrance. In the upper part of the picture, the figure and head of the Saviour, in point of coloring, drawing, and expression, are among the very highest achievements of the art of painting. The dignity and serenity with which the form reposes on the air are a distinct expression of Divine power; and the light with which it is penetrated is also celestial. A painter like Correggio, a great master of light and shade, would have been tempted to make this element too prominent, and thus have, impaired the sentiment of the picture by a sort of theatrical contrast, involving wonders of technical skill. But Raphael's unerring judgment is here detected in making the figure luminous, but not overpoweringly so; and, thus, the sentiment and expression are not made subordinate to a trick of coloring.

The kneeling figures at the extremity of the mountain, which are supposed to be portraits of the father and uncle of Cardinal de Medici, by whom the picture was commissioned, are a blot in this magnificent work; and can only be excused by the custom of the times, and the deference which an artist naturally pays to the wishes of a powerful patron.

In the same room hangs another work by Raphael, the Madonna di Foligno, which is also an illustration of his power of blending things celestial and things terrestrial in such a way as to disarm criticism by the reconciling power of genius. Below are St. Jerome, St. Francis, St. John, and with them, Sigismondo Conti, by whom the painting was commissioned. The latter is an admirable portrait; and the figures of the saints, especially the kneeling St. Francis, are most characteristic and expressive. The Mother and Child, throned on clouds in the upper part of the picture, towards whom the countenances of the saints are turned, and the lovely child-angel who stands in the centre of the foreground, with a tablet in his hand, are painted as Raphael only could paint. This picture combines three great excellences; beauty of composition, delicacy of sentiment, and powerful expression of character.

Opposite to the Transfiguration hangs the Communion of St. Jerome, by Domenichino; a picture which is sometimes ranked as next in merit to the Transfiguration, of all the pictures in the world. Any attempt to classify paintings in this way, ranking them as first, second, and third, is nothing less than absurd. No two persons will agree in such an estimate; and there is no common standard to appeal to for a decision between conflicting judgments. Such scales of excellence are usually first propounded by some presumptuous critic, and then echoed and repeated merely on the strength of his name, without reflection or hesitation. Disputes about the comparative merit of pictures are like disputes about the taste of wines, or the flavor of fruits: certain distinctions are universally recognised, but individual preferences, from simple variety of temperament, are capriciously entertained, and often rest upon no other reason than that they are felt.

This picture by Domenichino is a remarkable instance of what may be accomplished without great natural genius; for this excellent painter was not born to that inheritance. I have always regarded the harsh language in which the author of the 'Modern Painters' speaks of Domenichino, as very unjust, and as showing an eccentricity of taste (to say the least) beyond any thing else contained in that daring and suggestive book. Ruskin sets so high value upon imagination in art, that he is not fair to unimaginative artists; and of all eminent painters Domenichino is, perhaps, the least imaginative. Conscientious, laborious, self-distrustful, of simple and retired tastes and mild temper, he made himself a painter by study, observation, and experiment. The fire of genius never burns along his lines; but skill, taste, correctness, judgment, and decorum always wait upon his pencil. The Communion of St. Jerome is not an ideal work: it is remarkable more than any thing else, for its truth and powerful reality. The emaciated form of the dying saint is painted with a painful fidelity to nature. Every thing is accurately delineated; costume, attitude, expression, and drapery. The unity of the subject is carefully preserved, and all the accessories are made subordinate to the simplicity of the main action. The composition is careful and natural, and the coloring rich and true. It is not a picture which moves us deeply by its pathos, or charms us by visions of celestial beauty; but we pay it a tribute of admiration which is increased by successive visits. We feel it to be the work of a truly conscientious artist, who did nothing carelessly, and, by his thoroughness and fidelity, accomplished all that can be accomplished in art without genius and invention.

In the same room with these three pictures are two others ascribed to Raphael, and, perhaps, in part, executed by him; both representing the Coronation of the Virgin. They are remarkable for delicacy of sentiment and purity of feeling; but in point of execution their merit is not conspicuous enough to bear the rivalry of the great works which are near them.

There are three other rooms devoted to oil paintings, and among the artists are some great names — Titian, Correggio, Perugino, Fra Angelico — but the attractions of the Vatican in sculpture and fresco painting are so manifold and so absorbing, that I never found the time or the will to give to the contents of these three rooms any thing more than that cursory examination which stamps no lasting images on the memory. Indeed, it always seemed to me that this collection of oil paintings was not happily placed for the full appreciation of its claims. There is already too much in the Vatican; and before we can reach the gallery, — unless we are led blindfolded, like the bearers of a flag of truce through the lines of a hostile army, — the fine edge of attention is dulled by the variety of objects which have been presented to it. Such pictures are fairly entitled to be seen and examined without the rivalry and disturbing influence of such various and powerful attractions.

FRESCOES OF THE SISTINE CHAPEL.

The religious character of this chapel, in the view of Protestants at least, is quite lost in the admiration awakened for that immortal artist who has left here such wonderful monuments of his genius. It seems really dedicated to Michael Angelo, and he is the presiding divinity of the place. The popes who employed him here for so many years could hardly have anticipated such a result. That was not an age of hero-worship, and art yet continued to draw its life-blood from the spirit of religion.

The end of the chapel opposite the entrance, and over the altar, is occupied by the great fresco of the Last Judgment, filling a space sixty feet high and thirty broad. The colors have been much impaired by the lapse of time, by dampness, and by the smoke of candles and incense; but the drawing, design, and expression remain, and are likely to be preserved and transmitted by engravings and copies, whatever be the fate of the original. The first impression which this work makes upon the mind is more overpowering than any thing which painting has ever accomplished. In this respect it is like the dome of St. Peter's in architecture. 'I have seen Michael Angelo,' said a French sculptor, 'and he is terrible.' He is indeed terrible here, and the power which he has put forth is something superhuman. The predominance of this element of power suggests an obvious criticism upon the general character of the work. It is too hard, too stern, too severe, too pitiless. The attention is naturally first turned to the principal figure — that of the

Saviour — and in what character does he appear? Not in that of the Consoler, the Redeemer, the Reconciler, but in that of the Judge; and not merely so, but an iron-hearted, almost a vindictive judge, a Minos or a Rhadamanthus, rather than Jesus of Nazareth. His arm is lifted as if to strike a blow. The figure, too, is brawny and coarse; and the attitude, which is neither sitting nor standing upright, wants both dignity and grace. On the other hand, the Virgin, who stands next to him, is a figure highly expressive of tenderness, sympathy, and compassion, and is admirably drawn.

Another objection to this great work is the want of unity. The Saviour does not form the central point of interest around which all others are grouped. There is no convergence towards him. The greater part of the personages seem to be unconscious of his presence. The composition is broken up into detached masses, like the scattered squadrons of a defeated and disordered army.

As is well known, strong objections were urged against this fresco, even before it was completed, on account of the nudity of so many of the figures; and these objections must ever remain unanswered and unanswerable. Michael Angelo's reply to Paul IV. that if he would reform the morals of the world the picture would be reformed of itself, does not meet the difficulty; for no one ever dreamed that any line of his pencil could minister to an evil impulse; but the question is one of decorum and propriety, and not of right and wrong. The sight of so many undraped forms gives to the whole scene a certain coarse and animal expression, wholly at variance with our conceptions of its solemn and spiritual character. We are reminded of a school of gladiators in training, rather than of an assemblage of the just and unjust, summoned to receive sentence according to deeds done in the body.

The lower part of the composition, in which the sufferings of the condemned are delineated, is that in which we find the least to object to; for there the tremendous power which is stamped upon the whole work finds its appropriate sphere and legitimate expression. Forms and faces more trembling and convulsed with despair were never embodied or conceived. It makes the heart sink to look upon them. No touch of pity hung upon the artist's hand. The justice of God, and the sinfulness of sin, were the only thoughts that his mind would admit. In the upper part, where saints, patriarchs, and martyrs are ranged upon the right hand and left of the Saviour, we miss the 'light from heaven.' Depth and tenderness of feeling, the purity of celestial love, the serene triumph of faith, the soft calm of inward peace, do not shed their gentle influences upon the scene. We look in vain for the rapt brows of Angelico, the ideal heads and finely-flowing draperies of Raphael, the worn but ecstatic forms of Cigoli, and those cherub faces of Correggio which beam like embodied smiles.

In looking at this fresco of the Last Judgment, no one can fail to observe how strongly Michael Angelo's mind was imbued with the spirit of Dante, and especially with the descriptions in the 'Inferno.' We see in both the overlaying of the spiritual by the material. In the time of the poet as well as of the painter, Christianity was invested with the terrors of the old dispensation, and yet darkened with the shadows of Paganism. Charon's boat was not deemed an incongruous element, and the fancy was allowed to run riot in all sorts of physical horrors, in delineating the punishments of the guilty.

It is somewhat to be regretted that Michael Angelo should have devoted so many years of his life to a subject of this class, which must lose its expression and significance as religious ideas grow more and more spiritual. A pictorial representation of the Last Judgment degrades a mental conception into a visible scene. When we bring to the aid of art the analogies drawn from earthly courts of justice; when we express immortal power by mortal frowns and gestures; when we spread over the canvas a world of muscular and struggling limbs — with exulting fiends and angels blowing trumpets, with distended cheeks — we may have done something for painting, but, certainly, nothing for religion or spiritual elevation. Granting, for a moment, that the judgment to be passed upon all deeds done in the body may assume the character of a visible and contemporaneous transaction, it is only dwarfed and debased by the efforts of art to embody it. What canvas, what wall, can reproduce the ideas of boundless space, countless numbers, dazzling light, and inconceivable motion, which dart into the mind when we open it to such visions? Such paintings were conceived and executed in the spirit of reverence; and we feel that faith and fear trace the lines and lay on the colors; but it is an unenlightened reverence, which is caught in the letter which killeth and does not soar to the spirit which maketh alive.

We appreciate the greatness of this fresco when we forget its subject. It is a work painted for artists; and the greater artist a man is, the more will he appreciate the difficulties which have been overcome and the excellences which have been reached. As a study of the human figure, nothing in pictorial art approaches it; and all the capacities of drawing are absolutely exhausted in it. Every line is expressive, and not a movement of the pencil has been wasted. The young artist cannot copy from it a hand or a foot without gaining something in art.

If we look upon the fresco of the Last Judgment with doubt and misgiving, we are conscious of no such feelings when we turn away from it and raise our eyes to the ceiling. Here nothing is called forth but wonder, admiration, and delight. Here the genius of Michael Angelo, always grand, is seen in its most engaging aspect, its sternness softened, and its power tempered, by gentler influences.

The ceiling of the Sistine Chapel is flat in the centre and curved at the sides. The flat central portion is occupied by four large and five small subjects, from the events commemorated in the Old Testament between the creation and the deluge. The curved portion of the ceiling is divided into triangular compartments, in which are twelve sitting figures, seven being prophets, and five, sibyls, placed alternately. In the recesses between these figures, and in the arches over the windows, are groups of the ancestors of the Virgin. These are all connected together by a painted architectural framework, so that each figure is enclosed in a setting of its own, giving it support, distinctness, and relief, and at the same time linking it with the rest of the composition. To this architectural framework are appended a great variety of figures, mostly youthful or infantile, in every possible attitude, which embellish and give an air of life to it, as the flowers of a creeping vine, to the support around which it twines. In the angles of the ceiling are representations of four events in the history of the Jews, which have a typical relation to the mission of the Redeemer.

This combination of subjects is not fanciful or arbitrary, but is founded upon the religious impressions of the artist's age, sanctioned by the traditions and authority of the Church. The pictorial decorations of the Sistine Chapel were intended to present a visible history of the ways of God to man; beginning with the creation, and ending with the advent of the Redeemer and the revelation of Christianity. As the commencement of this series, it was the purpose of Michael Angelo to paint on the wall, opposite the Last Judgment, a representation of the fall of Lucifer — the latter forming the initial chapter in the history of humanity, from its connection with the fall of man, and the former, its final close — but this intention was never carried into effect. When he began his labors on the ceiling of the Chapel, the upper part of the walls between the windows was already occupied by a series of frescoes, twelve in number, six on either side, representing passages in the life of Moses and of Christ, the purpose of which was to bring the old law into relation and contrast with the new. The lower part of the walls, now painted with representations of hangings, was intended to be occupied with the tapestries executed from the cartoons of Raphael. The sibyls are interspersed with the prophets, from the fact that they were supposed to have predicted the birth of the Saviour; and, in this view, they were at an early period clothed by the church with a sort of sacred authority; and that this impression might be confirmed, interpolations are understood to have been made in the received collections of their writings. These explanations of the decorations of the Sistine Chapel — for which I am mainly indebted to Kugler's Hand-book of Italian painting and the notes of the English editor — are necessary to a full comprehension of their purpose and spirit. The paintings were symbolical as well as actual. They were founded upon recognised ideas; spoke an intelligible language; and communicated religious notions by powerful impressions made upon the senses. Art was secondary to religion; and this is the secret of its power and vitality. In an age when few could read, it was proposed to paint to the eye the great events recorded in the Scriptures, and print a Bible in forms and colors. The change of feeling which has taken place in the course of three centuries, by which religious reverence has been lowered into artistic admiration, and the homage has been diverted from that which inspired the genius of the artist to the genius itself, has been before adverted to. Will the line of progress ever turn round and move in an opposite direction? And will men once more come into the Sistine Chapel and look upon its frescoes in that mood in which they were viewed by those who first beheld them, and make their shapes of beauty and grandeur the steps of a ladder on which the soul may rise to a nearer and clearer contemplation of God?

Looking at these works merely in a critical point of view, it is not possible to give them too high praise. There is hardly any excellence of which the art of painting is capable, which may not be found here in the highest perfection: drawing, composition, expression, dignity of sentiment, depth of feeling, and grace of movement. The creation of Adam is a miracle of art — his recumbent figure waked into sudden life by the touch of the Almighty's hand, could never have been painted by any one but Michael Angelo. For power of drawing, it is probably the highest achievement of the pencil. The figure of Eve, in the compartment representing her creation, is full of a beauty which is persuasive but not voluptuous; dignified but not austere; such as befits the mother of mankind. The prophets and sibyls are all admirable. The inspiration common to them all is expressed with unbounded fertility of invention; and the forms, attitudes, and draperies are in the highest degree noble and characteristic. Some of the sibyls are youthful and some are aged; but they all burn with the fire of prophecy, which in some takes the form of an impassioned flame, and in others, that of a fervid glow. Of the prophets a similar remark may be made. They are all noble figures, with intellectual heads stamped with the grandeur of supernatural knowledge; but no one is copied from or suggested by another. The element common to all is found in combination with passion, with contemplation, with melancholy, and with dignity.

So far we see Michael Angelo's genius moving in its natural and legitimate path of power and sublimity, without extravagance or exaggeration, guided by taste and controlled by judgment. But when we turn to the domestic groups between the prophets and the sibyls, and in the arches over the windows, and especially to the various infantile figures which support and adorn the architectural portions of the design, we see that softer and gentler aspect which it so rarely assumed, that but for these very compositions we should hardly have supposed him capable of putting it on. Here he is tender, airy, and sportive. The Graces wait upon his pencil, and he condescends to lay his invincible locks upon the lap of beauty.

The ceiling of the Sistine Chapel was finished in the year 1512, Michael Angelo being then thirty-eight years old. The fresco of the Last Judgment was completed in 1541, when he was sixty-seven. The difference between the two works — the unrelieved sternness in the latter; the severity unmitigated by any gleams of tenderness or compassion; the unsmiling terror which frowns upon us from every part of the composition — may have been in some measure the result of that change in temper and character which age so frequently brings with it. The life of Michael Angelo was shaped by the spirit of sculpture: it was cold, stern, self-withdrawn, self-dependent, and lofty. He was too proud to conciliate and yet too irritable to be silent. His relations with the various popes who filled the chair of St. Peter's during his time gave him ample opportunities of observing the weaknesses and infirmities of humanity. They brought him into contact with the brood of venal aspirants that crawl about the anti-chambers of greatness, full of ravenous wants and devoid of honor and truth. It is not unlikely, that in the interval between the two works a sense of the baser elements of humanity may have sunk deep into his heart; that the iron of envy, selfishness, and ingratitude, may have been driven into his soul; and that he may have felt a stern satisfaction in painting these terrible scenes of judgment and retribution, with all the energy that wounded sensibility and just indignation could supply. We may trace a similar change in the mind of Shakespeare between the Midsummer's Night's Dream and Timon of Athens; and in that of Milton between the morning freshness of Comus and the twilight gloom of Samson Agonistes. The temperament of genius is ever prone to exaggeration, and rarely succeeds in weighing in an impartial balance the good and the evil that are blended in the nature and life of man.

THE STANZE OF RAPHAEL.

In these Stanze we have the imperishable monuments of a gentler and finer, though not a greater genius. The frescoes here contained were the chief occupation of Raphael during the last ten or twelve years of his life. To these he dedicated the maturity of his powers and the ripened fulness of his mind. Whatever he had learned by practice, by observation, by a study of nature and the works of others, by a perception of his own defects, and by the rapid development of his genius, is here stamped in immortal lines and colors. These frescoes form the perfection of painting. It has soared to no loftier heights, and gained no more brilliant or enduring victories. The interval between the hard outlines, stiff attitudes, and somewhat languid beauty of Raphael's earliest works, and the ease, freedom, breadth, fulness, and variety of these frescoes, is amazing, and shows that his industry and self-vigilance must have been equal to his genius.

A detailed account of these frescoes is unnecessary, because engravings, outlines, and descriptions have made them familiar to all who are sufficiently interested in art to take any pleasure in the treatment of such themes.

The School of Athens and the Scourging of Heliodorus, not only represent the culminating point of Raphael's genius, but they are the highest triumphs which painting has achieved or is likely to achieve. In Michael Angelo, we recognise more vigorous drawing; in Titian, a richer tone of color; in Correggio, more magical effects of light and shade; but in these frescoes, while none of the above excellences are wanting, we find the highest attributes of painting in their utmost perfection; invention, composition, sentiment, and expression.

The School of Athens is marked by dignity and grandeur. Of the fifty-two figures which compose it, no one seems to be in another's way, and no one appears in a studied attitude. The charm of animation is blended with the charm of repose. In the perfect art of the composition, nothing artificial is left to offend. The Scourging of Heliodorus is full of energy, power, and movement. The horse and his rider are irresistible, and the scourging youths, terrible as embodied lightning: mortal weapons and mortal muscles are powerless as infancy before such supernatural energies. Like flax before the flame — like leaves before the storm — the strong man and his attendants are consumed and borne away. These two works of Raphael, had all the rest perished, would have vindicated his claim to the title of prince of painters. It may, indeed, well be doubted whether he would ever have surpassed these works, had he lived longer. His rapid progress and early maturity in art seemed to necessitate a brief career. So exquisite an organization must have felt, before its time, the touch of natural decay. If life be estimated by what is done, suffered, and felt, neither Raphael, Mozart, Burns, nor Byron, can be said to have died young, though no one of them lived to see his thirty-eighth birthday.

In the Parnassus — so called from its being a representation of the mountain of that name, with Apollo, the Nine Muses, and a company of the Greek, Latin, and Italian Poets — the central figure, Apollo, is playing upon a violin: a curious circumstance, as showing the different associations connected in those days with that instrument, from those awakened by it at the present time. It is not uncommon in Italy to see angels, in pictures, playing upon violins, but an artist would now as soon think of painting an angel with an umbrella in his hand. How does it happen that an instrument of such capacity, with such boundless variety of expression, upon which such triumphs of execution have been won, should have become linked to such degrading, or, at least, prosaic associations?

In the Miracle of Bolsena, Raphael appears as the rival of Titian, and glows with the rich coloring of the Venetian school. In the Deliverance of St. Peter, he has achieved those triumphs of light and shade which shed their fascinations over the canvas of Correggio. In the Incendio del Borgo, there is a single figure — the naked youth escaping from the fire by a wall, and sustaining his whole weight by his hands — which, for powerful drawing and anatomical knowledge, is worthy of Michael Angelo.

In these frescoes there are two or three variations of, essentially, the same female figure. We see it in the kneeling woman in front of the pope, in the Scourging of Heliodorus; in the two women carrying water, in the Incendio del Borgo; in the female who stands with her back to the spectator, on the left hand of Apollo, in the Parnassus. The same type of form appears in many of his works, and is the nearest approach to mannerism which we can find in this most inventive of painters. It is to be seen in the female who has charge of the demoniac in the Transfiguration, and in the woman leading a child, in the cartoon of the Healing of the Lame Man. The character of all these figures cannot be better expressed than by the hackneyed word, repose. They show how largely Raphael had profited by the study of Greek art. The turn of the head, the braided hair, the serenity of the attitudes, and the broad folds of the draperies, have the purity and tranquillity of sculpture: while, at the same time, they are instinct with the life and the animation of painting.

In the Hall of Constantine, so called, is an enormous fresco, designed by Raphael and executed by Giulio Romano, representing the fight between Constantine and Maxentius, at the Ponte Molle, near Rome. This is the only work of Raphael's which I should not be glad to see again; though it is a picture wonderful for the skill with which it is so treated, as to present the highest animation and rapidity of movement, without the least confusion in the details. But, in regard to battle-pieces, the peace society is in the right. A battle, as described by Homer or Scott, has succession and continuity of interest; and the work is crowned by victory or defeat. but a painter can take but one moment. There stand forever fixed, the uplifted hand, the inflamed countenance, the dying youth, the weeping father. It is a stereotyped page of horror and struggle. Passions, as fleeting as they are fierce, are arrested and made permanent. So, too, the judgment to be passed upon war depends upon its motives and its objects. It may be a stern necessity or an imperative duty. But the painter cannot put upon his canvas that moral element which threw its light upon the brows of those who fought at Marathon and Bunker Hill. He has nothing but the eye to speak to. The death of Leonidas, and a fight between smugglers and revenue officers, can differ only in costume and scenery.

THE TAPESTRIES.

These hang upon the walls of a gallery adjoining the Stanze. The colors are faded, and the fabric shows in many ways the injuries of time and of the various casualties to which they have been exposed. A passing glance is the only tribute which most travellers offer them. But among them are some of Raphael's finest designs. Seven of the cartoons, from which these tapestries were wrought, are at Hampton Court in England; and, from the many engravings which have been made from them, are among the most generally known of all the artist's compositions. Deriving no attractions from coloring, and but little from light and shade, they address the mind solely through the medium of form, and are the least sensuous and most intellectual efforts of the art of painting. They are to the frescoes what the style of Aristotle is to that of Plato. There is nothing here to fix a wandering eye, or to gratify a superficial sense of beauty. They are tributes to that ideal and celestial loveliness, which borrows nothing from mortal colors or the glow of earthly passions; and he, whose soul has been steeped in the languid delights of meretricious art, can no more feel their elevated character than a selfish voluptuary can comprehend the language in which Dante speaks of Beatrice, or be touched by the depth and tenderness of Burns's 'Mary in Heaven.'

THE LOGGIE.

The Loggie are galleries running round three sides of an open court of the palace of the Vatican. They are upon three stories, and the gallery on one side of the second story, which has been for many years closed with glass, is decorated with paintings executed from Raphael's designs and under his directions. The roof of this gallery is divided into thirteen cupolas, each of which contains four frescoes, from subjects taken from the Old Testament. The whole series is thus fifty-two in number, and is popularly known by the name of 'Raphael's Bible.' As they were the work of his pupils, they are of various merit in point of execution; but the genius of the great master is always perceptible. The several subjects are invariably treated in an appropriate manner. The simplicity of the patriarchal times is carefully preserved, but there is nowhere to be seen the slightest intrusion of coarseness or irreverence. We see the same purity of design, the same flowing breadth of drapery, the same ease of movement, and the same expressive character of head and face, visible alike through the various degrees of merit in point of execution, and the defacing influences of time and neglect.

The side wall and the pilasters between the windows are covered with arabesque ornaments, in which fruits, flowers, animals, and vines are blended in innumerable airy and graceful combinations. With these are interspersed decorations in stucco, consisting of heads, reliefs, figures, and groups. The whole are from the designs of Raphael. They are much impaired by time, and restoration, and are but the wreck and shadow of what they once were; but enough is left to vindicate the enthusiastic admiration which they awakened in their prime.

These lovely and sportive creations of beauty, which, in their number and variety, remind us of the luxuriance of tropical vegetation, bear somewhat the same relation to the rest of Raphael's works, as the fairy mythology of the Midsummer's Night's Dream, to the other products of Shakespeare's genius. There is the same surrender of the mind to the frolic impulses of an exuberant fancy; the same lavish expenditure of creative power flowing from an equal consciousness of inexhaustible resources. The artist must have turned from his graver labors to these playful tasks, with a grateful sense of exhilaration and release. In the former, his genius moved in certain prescribed paths, and was constrained within fixed barriers; but, in the latter, it was at liberty to move and wind and disport itself 'at its own sweet will;' and the eagle let loose from the ark did not try his long-imprisoned wings with a more exulting sense of power, or trace upon the blue sky finer or more varied lines of beauty. That ideality, which was a presiding trait in Raphael's mind, is here found in combination, not with solemn or tragic themes, but with those which are playful, engaging, and familiar — the growth of the common earth and the life of every day.

THE LIBRARY OF THE VATICAN.

In entering this, the oldest and the most celebrated library in Europe, every one who has the slightest tinge of literary enthusiasm must be conscious of a peculiar feeling of reverence. But this first emotion is soon displaced by blank astonishment, from the fact that no books are any where to be seen. The visitor is conducted into a noble hall of splendid architectural proportions and embellishments, surrounded by an immense double gallery — the whole adorned with frescoes, busts, statues, and columns, but the books and manuscripts are shut up in cabinets of painted wood, and hidden from vulgar gaze, like the beauties of an eastern harem. The scholar is thus obliged to forego that tantalizing pleasure of glancing at the titles of books as he passes along, and of pausing for a moment to contemplate and admire a tall copy, an Elzevir, or an Aldus. Indeed, the number of printed books is not very large; probably not more than thirty or forty thousand; but the collection of manuscripts is the finest in Europe, and is said to amount to upwards of twenty-five thousand. As a general rule, these manuscripts are not open to examination, and no eager inquirer after knowledge disturbs their venerable dust, or traces the lore that is hidden in their dim and fading lines. The discoveries of Cardinal Mai are a proof of what may be gathered by the hardy pioneers who shall have the courage to penetrate into that wilderness of parchment, but the Germans seem to be the only people left in these stirring times who have the patience and endurance necessary for such enterprises.

Nothing can be more unsatisfactory than a visit to a large library, without such an introduction to some person in authority as will ensure peculiar attention. The ordinary run of visitors are usually committed to the tender mercies of some ignorant subordinate, anxious to earn his fee at the least possible expenditure of time and trouble — and who manifests his impatience at any interruptions occasioned by an impertinent and unseasonable love of knowledge, in such a way as soon to check the most resolute advances. Or if the honors of the library are done by a man of taste and learning, he must be so annoyed by the gaping and vacant curiosity of ignorant visitors, and the constant repetition of the same questions, as to make the nearest possible approach to silence the best safeguard of his self-control. Thus, of the treasures of the Vatican, I can give but small report from personal observation. I saw the famous manuscript of Virgil, of the date of the fourth or fifth century, adorned with fifty miniature designs, which are curious, not merely as illustrations of the work, but as specimens of early art; hard and stiff in outline, guiltless of perspective or of the mysteries of light and shade, but vivid in coloring, and often powerful in expression. There is also a curious manuscript of Terence, of the ninth century, adorned in the same manner. I looked with peculiar interest upon the palimpsest in which Cardinal Mai found the treatise of Cicero de Republica, hidden under a version of St. Augustin's Commentary on the Psalms. A manuscript of Dante, in the handwriting of Boccaccio, and sent by him to Petrarch, with notes said to be in the handwriting of the latter, shines with a light thus thrown upon it from three illustrious names in literature. There is also a large amount of prose and poetry in the handwriting of Tasso, and of Petrarch; including a sketch of the first three cantos of the 'Gerusalemme' of the former, and the 'Rime' of the latter; a sight to drive a collector of autographs frantic. Here, too, strangely misplaced in an ecclesiastical library, are seventeen love-letters addressed by Henry VIII. to Anne Boleyn, nine in French and eight in English. Few of the waifs and strays which have floated down to us upon the stream of the past are more curious and interesting than these letters. It seems odd enough that time, which has consumed so many grave documents, solemn treaties, and weighty records, should have spared these airy trifles — these momentary effusions of feeling — addressed to one eye and one heart, and so little significant to any other. They are silent memorials of a sad tale of passion and cruelty; of selfish appetite on the one side, and of vanity and giddiness on the other; and when I thought of the end of it all — of the fierce hatred which expelled the fierce love in the royal voluptuary's breast, and of the cruel wrongs which, so meekly endured, give to the character of Anne Boleyn all of the interest which dignifies it in the eyes of posterity — a visible shadow seemed to darken over the paper and the words to be written in blood.

The only printed book examined was a copy of Henry VIII.'s work against Luther, a presentation copy to Pope Leo X., printed on vellum, with a dedicatory inscription in Latin, on the fly-leaf, in the handwriting of the royal author. When a nobleman appears in print, said Dr. Johnson, his merits should be handsomely acknowledged: but what shall we say if it be a king? What epithet can express the height and depth of the acknowledgment which is due from the uncrowned multitude? I believe that this treatise of Henry VIII. is not without merit. To one at all touched with that disease of bibliomania, of which Dr. Dibdin writes in a vein of such pleasant exaggeration, the volume was an interesting object of contemplation, as being one of the rarest books in the world; of that class for which rich collectors struggle, and poor collectors sigh in vain.

CHAPTER X.

The Capitol — Ruins in Rome — The Forum — The Palace of the Cæsars — The Colosseum — The Baths of Caracalla — The Pantheon — Arches — Mamertine Prison and Tarpeian Rock.

THE CAPITOL.

No language contains a word of more expression and significance than the Capitol, nor is there a spot on earth more full of historical interest. It was at once a fortress and a temple; the head of the Roman state and the shrine of their religion. Here was the seed and source of Rome, the germ of that mighty power which, planted here, overshadowed the earth. The Capitol was the symbol of ancient Rome, as St. Peter's and the Vatican are the symbols of the modern and mediæval city. Our visions of such a spot are shaped in an heroic mould and inspired by the spirit of Roman history. We paint to ourselves the massive bulk of some castellated rock, whose commanding proportions and rugged grandeur admit of no material modification from the labors of man, and retain the same essential features through all the changes of time: throwing its broad shield of protection alike over the infancy, the maturity, and the decline of the imperial city.

But how disappointing is the touch of reality! After traversing nearly the entire length of the Corso, the traveller turns to the right, and in a few moments finds himself at the foot of a gently inclined ascent, of artificial construction, something between a staircase and a plane; the feet being aided by longitudinal ridges of stone placed at regular intervals. On arriving at the top, he stands in a square of moderate extent, occupied by three buildings, one facing him and one on either hand. Although designed by Michael Angelo, the architecture is neither sublime nor beautiful; and the whole effect is the reverse of imposing. It looks as if three rich noblemen, who wished to live near each other, had bought a piece of ground, and commissioned an architect to build them three houses on a uniform plan: and this trumpery square, these inexpressive façades, this clipped and rounded and diminished hill — are all that modern Rome has to show for the Capitol. The unreverend hand of change has taken the lion by the beard, and put its hook into the jaw of the behemoth. It has filled up the valleys and cut down the heights and smoothed the roughnesses, till the Campidoglio is as little like the Capitol, as the Rome of to-day is like the Rome of Cato the Censor. There is nothing here that recalls the magnificence of the temple of Jupiter Capitolinus, or the venerable associations which belonged to the cottage of Romulus — that modest structure of reeds and straw, which, whether it were genuine or not, so long served to kindle and sustain the spirit of reverence in the Roman people.

In the centre of the piazza or square is the bronze equestrian statue of Marcus Aurelius — the only equestrian statue of that material which has come down to us from antiquity, and the finest work of the kind in the world. The proportions of the horse are not such as would satisfy a Newmarket jockey, but the animation and spirit of the attitude, and the air of life which informs the limbs, and seems actually to distend the nostrils, cannot be too much praised. The face and figure of the rider are worthy of the noble animal on which he is seated, and worthy of the good name which he has left in history. The attitude and expression are dignified, but not haughty, and intimate a disposition more prone to conciliate than to command.

The central building in front is called the Palace of the Senator, for there is still a Roman senator, a harmless puppet created by the pope, and resembling one of his namesakes of antiquity, as a chattering cicerone resembles Cicero. The palace is not his place of residence, but where he sometimes comes to amuse himself and the public by holding a court. In this building, poets and artists were once crowned with laurel by the hands of the senator, occasions to which the presence of rank, learning, and beauty, strains of music, and recitations in prose and verse lent their attractions. The reader of 'Corinne' will remember, that it is on such a ceremonial, that we are first introduced to that splendid vision of genius and beauty.* The building,

* The honor of a coronation at the capitol, enjoyed by Petrarch and in preparation for Tasso at the time of his death, has been bestowed upon a female. On the 31st August, 1766, Maria Madelena Morelli, who had been previously received into the Arcadian Academy, under the name of Corilla Olympica, by

both externally and internally, is without interest. The interior has an air of faded gentility, but not of faded beauty. But for the central tower, it would hardly be worth the trouble of a visit. From that, a scene of varied and magnificent beauty unfolds itself to the eye, in which the natural features, grand and striking as they are, are lost in that magic charm of association, which gives a richer verdure to the plain, a deeper purple to the hill, a finer blue to the sky, and bathes every roof in spiritual light. The history and literature of Rome are lying at our feet, and the living landscape is a page, on which is written one half of all that we have learned at school and at college.

The building on the south side of the square, to the right as we face the Palace of the Senator, is called the Palace of the Conservatori.* In the court-yard and the adjacent arcade are some striking works in sculpture; among them, a colossal statue of Julius Cæsar, a

which she was afterwards generally known, was crowned there with great ceremony. She was a native of Pistoia, and attracted much attention by her talents as a poet and an improvisatrice. Madame de Staël probably borrowed from this scene the incident of Corinne's coronation, as well as her name. The wits of Rome, Pasquin especially, launched many sarcasms upon the occasion; so that the Abbe Pizzi, who, in his capacity of director of the Arcadian Academy, presided over the ceremonial, said, that the crown of Corilla had been to him a crown of thorns. I am afraid that Corilla was not so beautiful as Corinne; she was certainly not so young, having been nearly forty at the time of her coronation.

* The Conservatori were, originally, administrative officers; the senator being a judicial magistrate. Their functions have long since become merely nominal; being little more than walking in a procession, or taking part in a ceremonial.

statue of Augustus, a fine colossal head of Domitian, and a noble group of a lion attacking a horse — all in marble.

In this palace are eight rooms belonging to the Arcadian Academy, in one of which it still meets. In these rooms are a great number of busts of the illustrious men of Italy — artists and men of letters — many by the hand of Canova, but few of conspicuous merit. The requisites for possession of a niche in this temple of fame are carefully defined by a decree of Pius VII., and the claims of the candidates (who must have been dead a certain number of years) are patiently discussed by magistrates and learned bodies; the pope himself being sometimes called upon to decide, in case of conflicting judgments. Such proceedings have an air of solemn trifling, easily open to ridicule; and the satirist may sneer at an atttempt to give immortality to names which do not deserve it, or to withhold it from those which do; but the purpose itself is so commendable — a collection of busts of the great men of a country by competent artists is so valuable a possession — that we will not quarrel with any agency which calls it into existence.

In this palace is one of the most interesting objects in Rome — the celebrated Bronze Wolf of the Capitol — generally believed to be the very group alluded to by Cicero in one of his harangues against Catiline, and commemorated by Virgil in his well-known lines. In such controversies, the wish is father to the faith, and we cannot listen to the arguments in an impartial spirit. The sceptic has as ungracious an office as the devil's attorney, who is heard against the claims of a saint proposed to be canonized. The wolf is a gaunt and grim image, of antique workmanship, and with none of the amenities of Greek art. The infants seem disproportionately small.

The gallery of pictures which is in this palace has very little of first-rate excellence. The Persian Sibyl, by Guercino, and the Cumæan Sibyl, by Domenichino, are no more than pleasing. Much the most impressive work in the collection is the Sta. Petronilla of Guercino. It is a picture of colossal size, with a double subject, as is often the case in Catholic countries; the lower part representing the burial of the saint, and the upper, her reception into paradise. Guercino is deficient in purity of taste, in tenderness and depth of feeling, and in imaginative simplicity. He delights in the contrasts of strong lights and inky shadows. But his great merit is expression; and in this he has hardly any superior. The Sta. Petronilla shews his characteristic excellences and defects, and more of the former than of the latter. Its powerful drawing and sombre depth of color make it a very impressive work, but we look in vain for the ideal grace with which Raphael would have invested such a subject.

On the opposite wall hangs a very different picture, full of joyous life and vernal coloring — the Rape of Europa, by Paul Veronese. In point of keeping and dramatic propriety, it is daringly absurd. Europa is no slender nymph, but a splendid Venetian woman in the prime of life, richly dressed, and of proportions ample enough to make the task of the noble animal on which she is seated no sinecure. She has just stepped out — not from the woods of Phœnicia, but from a palace on the Grand Canal, and her bull ought to be a gondola. But what gorgeous coloring — what depth and fulness of life in the eyes, the cheeks, and the luxuriant form! What a flush of exuberant power is flung over the whole canvas! How impossible to do any thing but admire! It is like seeing Garrick playing Macbeth in a red coat and bag-wig — the power of genius preventing a single smile at the incongruity of the costume. Works of the Venetian school are not common in Rome, and this picture is in consequence the more striking.

The building on the north side of the square contains the Museum of the Capitol, comprising a collection of works in sculpture of considerable extent, among which are some specimens of great excellence. On account of their inferior accommodations, they are seen to far less advantage than those in the Vatican. They are crowded into apartments of moderate size and no architectural pretensions, and look as if they were exposed in a warehouse for sale, rather than arranged in a palace for exhibition. The eye asks in vain for those noble spaces and splendid embellishments of the Vatican, which enhance the merits of fine specimens and shield the defects of inferior works.

The Hall of the Vase derives its name from a fine vase of white marble in the middle of the room. Here is also the Iliac Table, a series of bas-reliefs illustrating the Iliad of Homer; and, perhaps, the most celebrated mosaic in the world, called 'Pliny's Doves,' * representing four doves drinking from a basin, surrounded by a border. The design is simple and pleasing, and the

* It is so called, because it is supposed to be that described by Pliny in the thirty-fifth book of his Natural History.

workmanship beautiful. The revolutions of two thousand years have not changed the eye or the taste of man; this graceful composition is still popular, and constantly repeated by the mosaic workers of Rome, in diminished proportions.

On the walls of the Hall of the Emperors are two of the most beautiful bas-reliefs which have come down to us from antiquity; one representing Perseus rescuing Andromeda, and the other, Endymion sleeping, with his dog by his side. In the centre of the room is a female statue in marble, seated, called by the name of Agrippina, remarkable for the dignified ease of the position, and the minute folds and elaborate carving of the drapery. Around the room are arranged more than seventy busts of Roman emperors and empresses, a collection of much interest, as many of them are unquestionably authentic portraits; and the physiognomist and the phrenologist may amuse themselves in reading their virtues and their crimes, in these, their marble presentments. There are among them some most forbidding countenances; although we may suppose that the court sculptor did his best to soften the harsh lines of cruelty and sensuality.

In the saloon are two statues of centaurs, in nero antico, one young and one in mature life, both of excellent workmanship and full of spirit; a colossal statue of the infant Hercules, in green basalt, and a statue of Æsculapius in nero antico. In this room is also a statue, most unattractive in its subject, but curious as an illustration of the ideas of the ancients as to the limits of art. It represents a woman in extreme old age and painfully ugly. Some suppose her to be a Sibyl, some a Prefica, or hired mourner at Roman funerals, while Winckelman believes it to be a Hecuba. The head is stretched forward, the body is bent in one direction, and the face turned in another. The head is covered with a cloth. It is a work in all respects the reverse of ideal. There is not the slightest attempt to veil or soften the most repulsive features of old age. The artist has aimed only at truth, and in this he has succeeded perfectly. The execution is wonderful. The expression of the face is that of stony despair, and the figure is a wreck battered by time and sorrow.

The last room into which the traveller passes contains several works of the highest excellence, and above all, the Dying Gladiator. A statue of such surpassing merit as this should have a room by itself, for in its presence it is difficult to look at any thing else. It is now admitted by the best authorities, that the statue is a dying Gaul and not a gladiator, but to the popular mind the old appellation will cling forever. Byron's immortal stanza — an exquisite creation of genius, equal to the theme which inspired it — is alone enough to fasten it there with associations that can never be severed. But there is no work of art respecting which such discussions are more intrusive or unnecessary. We do not ask whom it represents, because we are so wholly absorbed with what it is. Its power and pathos are independent of time, place, and condition.

What is it that we see before us? A man dying; nothing more. It is that which happens to all men; the only inevitable fact in every life. Nor is it a marked or conspicuous person. He is not a hero or a poet or an orator. The form is not ideal, the head is not intellectual, the lips are not refined. The shadows of great thoughts never darkened that commonplace brow, nor did the touch of beauty ever thrill along those coarse fibres. But the charm and power of the statue consist in the amazing truth with which the two great elements of humanity and mortality are delineated. A vigorous animal life is suddenly stopped by the touch of death, and the 'sensible warm motion' becomes a 'kneaded clod' before our eyes. The artist gives us all the pathos and the tragedy of death without its ghastliness and horror. The dying man is no longer a trivial person, stained with coarse employments and vulgar associations, but an immortal spirit breaking through its walls of clay. The rags of life fall away from him, and he puts on the dignity and grandeur of death. We feel ourselves in the presence of that awful power, before whose icy sceptre all mortal distinctions are levelled. Life and death are all that for a time we can admit into the mind.

As the sentiment and expression of this statue are admirable, so is the mechanical execution of the highest merit. The skill with which the physical effects of death upon the human frame are represented is most strongly felt by those whose professional training and experience make their judgment upon such points the most valuable. The hair short and crisp and matted by the sweat of the death-struggle, the wrinkled brow, the drooping lid, the lips distended with pain, and the sinking languor of the whole frame, give proof of a patient eye and a skilful hand. No statue was ever more marked by simplicity, or more free from any thing like extravagance or caricature. Such a subject presents many temptations, and unless an artist's taste and judgment were equal to his genius, he would hardly have escaped falling into the weakness of overdoing the tragic elément, and of laying such a weight upon our sympathies that they would have given way under the pressure. But here nothing has been done for effect. No vulgar applause is courted, and the decency and dignity of truth are scrupulously observed.

If it be right to judge of works of art subjectively and not objectively — that is, exclusively by the effect which they leave upon the individual who contemplates them — I should put this work at the head of all the statues in the world. To me, none others were so expressive, so significant, so full of deep meaning. At each successive visit it seemed to be a new work — to reveal something which before had been unspoken — to awaken echoes which before had been silent. Though a solitary figure, taken in and comprehended by the eye at a single glance, it involves a broad circle of experience and suggestion. Such is ever the case with the creations which genius gives us when it walks in the way of truth, and, disdaining the morbid, the fantastic, and the grotesque, gives shape to our common visions, and reality to the universal dream.

This statue is indissolubly associated with Byron's immortal stanza, which, familiar as it is, can no more become hackneyed, than the relations of husband and father on which it is founded. From lines like these, which every body reads and every body remembers — especially when connected with objects of permanent and general interest — we learn how much we owe to the poets. Who, that has ever seen snow falling upon water, has not had a distinct pleasure in the sight, from the fine illustration of the brief duration of sensual pleasures, which Burns has drawn from it? * Who, that has ever beheld a scarlet maple in our autumn woods, has not felt that a new charm was given to it by the lovely image which it suggested to Bryant? † So, we, who look upon the statue since the stanza was written, see it by a finer light than ever shone upon it before. For us alone the rude hut by the Danube is reared, and those young barbarians are sporting upon its banks. We may form some notion of our obligations, by imagining what would have been the emotions of a man of cultivation and sensibility, if the poet had suddenly put the lines into his hands, while he was standing before the statue. Would not something like the miracle of Pygmalion have taken place before his eyes? Would not the marble breast have appeared to heave with emotion, and the drooping brow, to be darkened with suffering?

In the same apartment with the Dying Gladiator are several works of great merit; which, in justice to the spectator and themselves, should be rescued from a presence so trying. In a room of moderate size, the central and prominent statue should be the flower, and the others only act as leaves and buds.

* 'Or like the snow-fall in the river,
A moment white — then melts forever.'

† 'But 'neath yon crimson tree,
Lover to listening maid might breathe his flame,
Nor mark, within its roseate canopy,
Her blush of maiden shame.'

The statue of Antinous is not merely beautiful, but it is beauty itself. Like all his busts and statues, the expression is that of 'Elysian beauty, melancholy grace.' He has the air of a man ever looking into his own grave. The limbs, the figure, the turn of the head, which droops as if with a weight of unshed tears, are so admirable that they can only be praised in superlatives. The contrast between his form and aspect and that of the Dying Gladiator is very striking. The former is a soft flower; the latter, a sturdy weed. The former, born with a fine organization, was reared in the sheltered air of luxury and splendor, and shielded from every blast of trial or trouble: the latter was thrown upon the rocks of life, to struggle over them with toil and pain, and escape by a violent and bloody death. The Gladiator gives the impression of a manly nature, though coarse, who had acted according to his small light so long as he lived, and met his fate without flinching, from pride and courage and not from weariness of life. But the Antinous wears an air of languor and satiety, as if he were weary of the sunshine in which he basked, and felt the serpent's sting under the flowers. Unlike as they were in their lives and fortunes, the magic of art has given them an identity of interest as levelling as the grave itself.

RUINS IN ROME.

The traveller who visits Rome with a mind at all inhabited by images from books, especially if he come from a country like ours, where all is new, enters it with certain vague and magnificent expectations on the subject of ruins, which are pretty sure to end in disappointment. The very name of a ruin paints a picture upon the fancy. We construct at once an airy fabric which shall satisfy all the claims of the imaginative eye. We build it of such material that every fragment shall have a beauty of its own. We shatter it with such graceful desolation that all the lines shall be picturesque, and every broken outline traced upon the sky shall at once charm and sadden the eye. We wreathe it with a becoming drapery of ivy, and crown its battlements with long grass, which gives a voice to the wind that waves it to and fro. We set it in a becoming position, relieve it with some appropriate background, and touch it with soft, melancholy light — with the mellow hues of a deepening twilight, or, better still, with the moon's idealizing rays.

In Rome, such visions, if they exist in the mind, are rudely dispelled by the touch of reality. Many of the ruins in Rome are not happily placed for effect upon the eye and mind. They do not stand apart in solitary grandeur, forming a shrine for memory and thought, and envolving an atmosphere of their own. They are often in unfavorable positions, and bear the shadow of disenchanting proximities. The tide of population flows now in different channels from those of antiquity, and in far less volume; but Rome still continues a large capital, and we can nowhere escape from the debasing associations of actual life. The trail of the present is every where over the past. The Forum is a cattle-market, strewn with wisps of hay, and animated with bucolical figures that never played upon the pipe of Tityrus, nor taught the woods to repeat the name of Amaryllis. The pert villa of an English gentleman has intruded itself into the palace of the Cæsars — as discordant an object to a sensitive idealist as the pink parasol of a lady's maid which put to flight the reveries of some romantic traveller, under the shadow of the great pyramid. The Temple of Antoninus Pius is turned into the custom-house. The Mausoleum of Augustus is encrusted with paltry houses, like an antique coin embedded in lava, and cannot even be discovered without the help of a guide. The beautiful columns of the Theatre of Marcellus — Virgil's Marcellus — are stuck upon the walls of the Orsini Palace, and defaced by dirty shops at the base. Ancient grandeur is degraded to sordid modern uses. 'Mummy is become merchandise; Mizraim cures wounds, and Pharaoh is sold for balsams.'

To most men, ruins are merely phenomena; or, at most, the moral of a tale; but to the antiquary they are texts. They have a secondary interest, founded upon the employment they have given to the mind and the learning they have called forth. We value every thing in proportion as it awakens our faculties, and supplies us with an end and an aim. The scholar, who finds in a bath or a temple a nucleus for his vague and divergent reading to gather around, feels for it something like gratitude as well as attachment; for though it was merely a point of departure, yet, without it, the glow and ardor of the chase would not have quickened his languid energies into life. Scott, in his introduction to the Monastery, has described, with much truth as well as humor, the manner in which Capt. Clutterbuck became interested in the ruins of Kennaqhair

— how they supplied him with an object in life, and how his health of body and mind improved, the moment he had something to read about, think about, and talk about. Every ruin in Rome has had such devoted and admiring students, and many of these shapeless and mouldering fabrics have been the battle-grounds of antiquarian controversy, in which the real points at issue have been lost in the learned dust which the combatants have raised. The books which have been written upon the antiquities of Rome would make a large library; but when we walk down, on a sunny morning, to look at the Basilica of Constantine, or the Temple of Nerva, we do not think of the folios which are slumbering in the archives of the Vatican, but only of the objects before us.

THE FORUM.

Ancient Rome contained no less than nineteen fora of importance. This will not seem strange when we remember, that under that designation were included the modern market-place, court of justice, town-hall, and exchange. Among the Romans, as among the modern Italians, much more of the business of life, both public and private, was transacted out of doors than the climate of a northern latitude will allow. The forum, in its primitive idea and original signification, was merely an open space surrounded by buildings and porticoes.

The piece of ground between the Capitoline and Palatine Hills, irregular in its outline, and comprising some seventy or eighty thousand square feet in extent, bore the proud name of 'Forum Romanum' — *the* Forum of Rome. No spot on earth is more imposing, for it is overshadowed with the power and majesty of the Roman people. Here was laid the foundations of that wonderful political system, which lasted so long and worked so well : which was strong enough to hold the whole world in its grasp, and wise enough to exercise a controlling influence over the legislation and jurisprudence of the civilized world down to the present day. It is a place illustrated equally by the wisdom of great statesmen and the eloquence of great orators. Here was trained that unrivalled power of constructive legislation, which was the great redeeming feature in the Roman mind, and which has transmitted to posterity that precious bequest, the Roman law, a gift quite equal in value to the splendid legacy of Greek literature. Who, that has the least sense of what the present owes to the past, can approach such a spot without reverence and enthusiasm? Especially, what member of the legal profession, unless his heart be dry as parchment, and worn as the steps of a court-house, can fail to do homage to the genius of a place where jurisprudence was reared into a perfect system, while Druids were yet cutting the misletoe on the site of Westminster Hall! The Roman Forum is indeed the Mecca of the law; and when I stood upon it, I felt that the ground was as holy as merely secular interest and associations could make it.

No one, unless forewarned by books and engravings, can have any conception of the change and desolation which have come over this illustrious spot. An unsightly piece of ground, disfeatured with filth and neglect, with a few ruins scattered over it, and two formal rows of trees running through it, is all that we see with the eye of the body. A few peasants wrapped in their mud-colored cloaks, a donkey or two, a yoke of the fine gray oxen of Italy, or perhaps, a solitary, wild-eyed buffalo, are the only living forms in a scene once peopled with wisdom, valor, and eloquence. Nothing gives a stronger impression of the shattering blows which have fallen upon the Eternal City, than the present condition of the Forum. Mr. Cockerell, an English architect, has published a print which he calls the Restoration of the Forum — a crowded assemblage of temples, porticoes, and public structures, of rich and showy architecture; but on the spot I never could recall the past, or see the natural relation between his architectural creation and the forlorn waste around me.

The reader of Virgil will remember the visit which Æneas makes to Evander, as described in the eighth book of the Æneid; one of those quiet and pastoral pictures so congenial to the graceful and tender genius of the poet. Evander is represented as occupying the very spot which was afterwards Rome, and while doing the honors of hospitality to his distinguished guest, he conducts him to the Tarpeian Rock and the Capitoline Hill, then brown with woods and overrun with bushes, and in the course of their walk, we are told in lines which must have been read with peculiar pleasure by his contemporaries, that they saw herds of cattle wandering over the Forum and the splendid streets in its neighborhood.

'Talibus inter se dictis ad tecta subibant,
Pauperis Evandri, passimque armenta videbant,
Romanoque Foro et lautis mugire Carinis.'

ÆNEID, viii. 359.

The whirl of time has brought round changes of which Virgil little dreamed, and given to his fanciful picture the stern lines of truth. Flocks and herds now wander over the solitude of the Forum, and crop their food from the very heart of ancient Rome.

In the Forum, every foot of ground has been the field of antiquarian controversy. Every ruin has changed its name two or three times. Indeed, it is a matter of controversy as to which was the direction of the length and which of the breadth of the Forum; the Italian antiquaries taking one view, and the Germans, backed by the great name of Niebuhr, another. The reason of this confusion and ignorance is to be found in two circumstances; one, that the buildings were very numerous in proportion to the small space which they occupied; and the other, that the original surface has been covered, to the depth of twelve or fifteen feet, by the accumulated soil of ages, so that the foundations of the structures are no longer to be seen. The removal of this deposit, and the entire clearing out of the Forum, were among the plans of improvement projected by the French, during the occupation of Rome in the time of Napoleon; and, in this instance, actually begun. At a later period, some further excavations were made under the direction of Cardinal Gonsalvi, the only man with any life in him that has been stirring in the papal states for the last century; but nothing has been done for many years, nor is there any hope for the immediate future. Annoying as this must be to the antiquary, with whom truth is the first and only consideration, yet the general sentiment of the place is not affected by the twilight of ignorance which still broods over it. To nine travellers out of ten, of what consequence is it whether a particular ruin is called by the name of the Temple of Fortune or the Temple of Vespasian, the Temple of Peace or the Basilica of Constantine? In all cases, indeed, accurate knowledge is not a gain. There is a solitary column in the Forum, which Byron calls 'the nameless column with a buried base,' the history and origin of which were long unknown. Recent excavations have shown it to have been erected by the ex-arch Smaragdus to the Emperor Phocas — the venal offering of a servile courtier to one of the most unmitigated monsters that ever stained the pages of history. Has not the column lost something of its charm? Before, there was a beauty and a mystery around it; there was room for conjecture and food for fancy; it was a voice that sounded from a dim and distant past, and therefore all the more impressive. But now the ideal light is vanished, and the column loses half its grace, since it speaks to us of the wickedness of tyrants and the weakness of slaves.

I shall not attempt to describe the Forum, nor to enumerate the several fragments of buildings which it contains. Descriptions of ruins are more unsatisfactory, even, than descriptions of pictures and statues; and he who seeks information on these points will find it in learned works expressly written for the purpose. The sentiment and spirit of the place can never be communicated or carried away. They are too volatile for language — too ideal for picture — too separate, local, and unique for comparison or illustration. All engravings and pictures of the Forum which I have seen, are too fine. They do not honestly reproduce the slovenly neglect and the unsightly features of the scene. They make the desolation more picturesque than the reality. The Forum is not like the ruins of Pæstum or Palmyra, in which decay is solemnized and idealized by solitude, and the tragic element is not impaired by the touch of any thing vulgar or degrading; but it more resembles some ancient palace which, in the changes of time, has come to be occupied by beggars and paupers; in which the eye is pained by jarring incongruities at every turn; antique splendor overborne by squalid poverty; rags fluttering from stately windows; the plaster dropping from frescoed walls; gilded cornices blackened with smoke and filth; a desolation which is not beautiful; a ruin which is not picturesque.

Those who can remember the Forum as it was at the beginning of the present century, before any excavations had been made, are now but few in number; but the changes caused by these excavations were looked upon, at the time, with no favor by artists; and this feeling was shared with them by the common people in Rome. What was gained to knowledge, say they, was lost to beauty. Formerly, there was a certain unity and harmony in the whole scene. The mantle of earth, which for centuries had been slowly gathering around the ruins, had become a graceful and appropriate garb. Trees and vines and green turf had concealed the rents and chasms of time; and a natural relation had been established between the youth of nature and the decay of art. But the antiquarians had come, and with their pickaxes and shovels had hacked and mangled the touching landscape as surgeons dissect a dead body. They had turned up the turf and cut down the vines and dug unsightly holes and opened deforming trenches. The beauty of the Forum had vanished forever. No more would peasants come here to dance the saltarello; nor artists, to sketch. The antiquarians had felled the tree that they might learn its age by counting the rings in the trunk. They had destroyed, that they might interrogate.

In words like these, the artists and sentimentalists of forty years since lamented what they called the desecration of the Forum. They were not all right; nor yet wholly wrong. Each one will judge of their regrets by his own taste and temperament. Time has since done much to repair the disfigurement of which they then complained.*

THE PALACE OF THE CÆSARS.

Imagine a hill, upwards of a mile in circuit, and less than two hundred feet high, strewn with shapeless ruins and yawning with excavations, to such an extent that the original soil is almost displaced by fragments of brick and mortar; intersperse it with kitchen gardens, for the growing of such matter-of-fact vegetables, as cauliflower, artichokes, and lettuce; throw in occasionally the vine, the laurel, the cypress, and the ivy;

* See Mueller: Rom, Rœmer, und Rœmerinnen. Vol. II. p. 164.

overshadow it with here and there a stately oak; and crown the whole with a smart, modern villa; and you will have some notion of the Palace of the Cæsars. The luxuriance of nature, in this soft climate and upon a fertile soil, has so successfully struggled with the decay of the works of man, and so veiled it with foliage and verdure, that one hardly knows whether to call the scene a landscape or a ruin. It is a labyrinth of vaults, arches, broken walls, and fragments of columns: a mighty maze of desolation without a plan. Portions of stucco, mosaic, and fresco, are still found in many places to attest the imperial splendor of a former age. There is no unity, and the mind brings away no distinct and uniform impression; but in the course of a half day's ramble many noticeable details may be observed, and some food for reflection gathered. In many places, the climbing and trailing plants have so blended themselves with the ruined fragments, as to present those happy combinations of form and color which the painter loves and the thoughtful poet does not shun.

The Villa Spada, the comfortable residence of an English gentleman, is shown to strangers, but I did not avail myself of the privilege. Valery's remarks upon this villa — considering that he was a Frenchman and a scholar — are very creditable to his good temper and kindliness of disposition, better travelling companions than sensitiveness and fastidiousness. He speaks of the roses growing in the garden. Surely, roses springing from such soil must be very unworthy of their privileges, if they do not put on a bloom and fragrance, beyond those which are the gift of the common earth.

THE COLOSSEUM.

The venerable Bede, who lived in the eighth century, is the first person who is known to have given to the Flavian amphitheatre its comparatively modern, and now universal designation of the Colosseum; though the name, derived from a colossal statue of the emperor Nero which stood near it, was probably then familiar to men's ears, as we may infer from his so calling it without explanation or remark. The splendid passage in which Gibbon describes the extent and architecture of this amphitheatre, and the magnificence of the spectacles which were exhibited in it, has become one of the commonplaces of literature; combining, as it does, those two qualities, for which that great historian is so remarkable, rhetorical pomp of diction and careful accuracy of statement. When in its perfect state, the exterior, with its costly ornaments in marble, and its forest of columns, lost the merit of simplicity without gaining that of grandeur. The eye was teased with a multitude of details, not in themselves good; the same defects were repeated in each story, and the real height was diminished by the projecting and ungraceful cornices. The interior arrangements were admirable; and modern architects cannot sufficiently commend the skill with which eighty thousand spectators were accommodated with seats; or the ingenious contrivances, by which, through the help of spacious corridors, multiplied passages, and staircases, every person went directly to his place, and immense audiences were dispersed in less time than is required for a thousand persons to squeeze through the entries of a modern concert-room. Vast as the structure was, it was not too great for the wants of Rome. At the time of its erection it was the only amphitheatre there; nor had any one previously been built of so durable a material as stone. No similar building was subsequently erected, for none was found necessary.

The population of ancient Rome is variously estimated, and is only a matter of conjecture; but, allowing half of the whole number to have been slaves, we may safely say, that in the age of Vespasian there were at least six hundred thousand persons who had a right, in their turn, to witness the games of the amphitheatre. In one of our modern cities, it is probable that not more than five per cent. of the population are ever found, on any one evening, in attendance upon theatres, concerts, and other places of public amusements. But in building the Flavian amphitheatre, it was requisite to provide accommodations for about fifteen per cent. of the people, and that, too, although the performances were always in the day-time, continuing many hours, and often through several days. This difference arose from the fact, which explains many things in Roman history, that the number of persons in Rome, especially under the emperors, who had nothing to do, was far greater in proportion to the whole population, than in any modern, certainly any American capitol. The want of books and newspapers was also another cause of the greater comparative attendance upon places of public amusement.

The interior of the Colosseum was decorated with great splendor. The principal seats were of marble, and covered with cushions. Gilded gratings, ornaments of gold, ivory, and amber, and mosaics of precious stones, displayed the generosity of the emperors, and gratified the taste of the people. This substantial magnificence was rendered in some sort necessary by the disenchanting presence of sunshine. 'Truth,' says Lord Bacon, with great beauty, 'is a naked and open day-light, that doth not shew the masks and mummeries and triumphs of the world, half so stately and daintily as candle-lights.' Thanks to these 'candle-lights,' we want nothing but stucco, gilded wood, and painted canvas to produce all the illusions of the drama; to transport us in the shifting of a scene, to Rome, to Venice, or to Athens — to give to copper and glass the lustre of gold and diamonds, and make the roses of Pæstum out of green paper and pink gauze.

The history of the Colosseum would form a work of much interest, reflecting the character of the successive periods through which it has passed. Its form, presenting every where a solid shield to the assaults of time, was of that kind which most ensures durability; and for many centuries it remained very little changed. After Christianity had banished the barbarous spectacles of paganism, it was still used as the scene of more innocent entertainments. Bunsen remarks, that the Emperor Charlemagne, who was crowned in Rome in the year 800, probably saw the building in its original magnitude and splendor. In the civil commotions of Rome, during the following centuries, it was used as a fortress. Situated as it is in a sort of valley, and commanded by at least three elevations, it would be quite unsuited for such a purpose in our times, but, before the invention of artillery, its massive walls must have easily dashed aside the tide of assault. In 1332, a splendid bull-fight was exhibited in the arena, for the amusement of the Romans, of which Gibbon has given an adequate description near the close of his great work.

How, or at what period, the work of ruin first began, does not distinctly appear. An earthquake may have first shattered its ponderous arches, and thus made an opening for the destructive scythe of time. There can be no doubt that it suffered violence from the hands of civil and foreign war. But more destructive agencies than those of earthquake, conflagration, or war, were let loose upon it. Its massive stones, fitted to each other with such nice adaptation, presented a strong temptation to the cupidity of wealthy nobles and cardinals, with whom building was a ruling passion; and, for many ages, the Colosseum became a quarry. The Palazzo della Cancelleria, the Palazzo Barberini, the Palazzo Farnese, and the Palazzo Veneziano were all built mainly from the plunder of the Colosseum; and meaner robbers emulated the rapacity of their betters, by burning into lime the fragments not available for architectural purposes.

After one pope had endeavored to degrade it into a woollen manufactory, and another, into a manufactory for salt-petre, Benedict XIV., in the middle of the last century, threw over it the protecting mantle of religion, and consecrated it to the memory of the Christian martyrs who had perished in it. The work of restoration, begun by Pius VII., has been continued by his successors, and we have only to hope that it may not be carried so far as to impair the peculiar and unique character of the edifice. It is now watched over by the government as it should be. A sentinel is always on guard to see that no mischief is done, but the visitor is never annoyed by impertinent or intrusive supervision, and 'any thing in reason' is permitted. Lady Morgan relates, that at the time of her visit in Rome it was no unusual circumstance for parties of gay young people, after a ball in the palace of the Princess Borghese, or the Duchess of Devonshire, to adjourn to the Colosseum, and there, under the beams of the moon, and in the soft air of a Roman night, finish the quadrille which had been begun in the blaze of an illuminated saloon. To turn the Colosseum into a ball-room seems putting it to a strange use. The thoughts which it awakens have music in them, but by no means of that kind which inspires dancing. But the English do what they please at Rome, and Italian remonstrance rarely goes beyond an expressive shrug of the shoulders.

If as a building the Colosseum was open to criticism, as a ruin it is perfect. The work of decay has stopped short at the exact point required by taste and sentiment. The monotonous ring of the outer wall is broken, and instead of formal curves and perpendicular lines, the eye rests upon those interruptions and unexpected turns, which are the essential elements of the picturesque, as distinguished from the beautiful and the sublime; and yet so much of the original structure is left, that the fancy can without effort piece out the rents and chasms of time, and line the interior with living forms. When a building is abandoned to decay, it is given over to the dominion of Nature, whose works are never uniform. When the Colosseum was complete, vast as it was, it must have left upon the mind a monotonous impression of sameness, from the architectural repetitions which its plan included; but now that it is a vast ruin, it has all that variety of form and outline which we admire in a Gothic cathedral. Not by rule and measure have the huge stones been clipped and broken. No contriving mind has told what masses should be loosened from the wall, or where they should lie when fallen. No hand of man has trained the climbing plants in the way they should go. All has been left to the will of time and chance, and the result is, that though there is every where resemblance, there is nowhere identity. A little more or a little less of decay — a chasm more or less deep — a fissure more or less prolonged — a drapery of verdure more or less flowing — give to each square yard of the Colosseum its own peculiar expression. It is a wilderness of ruin in which no two fragments are exactly alike.

The material of which the Colosseum was built is exactly fitted to the purposes of a great ruin. It is travertine, of a rich, dark, warm color, deepened and mellowed by time. There is nothing glaring, harsh, or abrupt in the harmony of tints. The blue sky above, and the green earth beneath, are in unison with a tone of coloring not unlike the brown of one of our own early winter landscapes. The travertine is also of a coarse grain and porous texture, not splintering into points and edges, but gradually corroding by natural decay. Stone of such a texture every where opens laps and nooks for the reception and formation of soil.

Every grain of dust that is borne through the air by the lazy breeze of summer, instead of sliding from a glassy surface, is held where it falls. The rocks themselves crumble and decompose, and thus turn into a fertile mould. Thus, the Colosseum is throughout crowned and draped with a covering of earth, in many places of considerable depth. Trailing plants clasp the stones with arms of verdure: wild flowers bloom in their seasons, and long grass nods and waves on the airy battlements. Life has everywhere sprouted from the trunk of death. Insects hum and sport in the sunshine: the burnished lizard darts like a tongue of green flame along the walls, and birds make the hollow quarry overflow with their songs. There is something beautiful and impressive in the contrast between luxuriant life and the rigid skeleton upon which it rests. Nature seems to have been busy in binding up with gentle hand the wounds and bruises of time. She has covered the rents and chasms of decay with that drapery which the touch of every spring renews. She has peopled the solitude with forms and the silence with voices. She has clothed the nakedness of desolation, and crowned the majesty of ruin. She has softened the stern aspect of the scene with the hues of undying youth, and brightened the shadows of dead centuries with the living light of vines and flowers.

As a matter of course, every body goes to see the Colosseum by moonlight. The great charm of the ruin under this condition is, that the imagination is substituted for sight; and the mind, for the eye. The essential character of moonlight is hard rather than soft. The line between light and shadow is sharply defined, and there is no gradation of color. Blocks and walls of silver are bordered by, and spring out of chasms of blackness. But moonlight shrouds the Colosseum in mystery. It opens deep vaults of gloom where the eye meets only an ebon wall, but upon which the fancy paints innumerable pictures in solemn, splendid, and tragic colors. Shadowy forms of emperor and lictor and vestal virgin and gladiator and martyr come out of the darkness, and pass before us in long and silent procession. The breezes which blow through the broken arches are changed into voices, and recall the shouts and cries of a vast audience. By day the Colosseum is an impressive fact; by night, it is a stately vision. By day, it is a lifeless form; by night, a vital thought.

The Colosseum should by all means be seen by a bright starlight, or under the growing sickle of a young moon. The fainter ray and deeper gloom bring out more strongly its visionary and ideal character. When the full moon has blotted out the stars, it fills the vast gulf of the building with a flood of spectral light, which falls with a chilling touch upon the spirit; for then the ruin is like a 'corpse in its shroud of snow,' and the moon is a pale watcher by its side. But when the walls, veiled in deep shadow, seem a part of the darkness in which they are lost — when the stars are seen through their chasms and breaks, and sparkle along the broken line of the battlements — the scene becomes another, though the same; more indistinct, yet not so mournful; contracting the sphere of sight, but enlarging that of thought; less burdening, but more suggestive.

It was my fortune to see the Colosseum, on one occasion, under lights which were neither of night nor day. Arrangements were made by a party of German artists to illuminate it with artificial flames of blue, red, and green. The evening was propitious for the object, being dark and still, and nearly all the idlers in Rome attended. Every thing was managed with taste and skill, and the experiment was entirely successful. It was quite startling to see the darkness suddenly dispelled by these weird lights, revealing a dense mass of animated countenances, and hanging a broad sheet of green or crimson upon the wall. The magic change was a sort of epigram to the eye. But from the association of such things with the illusions of the stage, the spectacle suggested debasing comparisons. It seemed a theatrical exhibition unworthy of the dignity and majesty of the Colosseum. It was like seeing a faded countenance repaired with artificial roses, or a venerable form clothed in some quaint and motley disguise, suited only to the bloom and freshness of youth. Such lights, far more than sunshine, 'gild but to flout the ruin gray.'

But under all aspects, in the blaze of noon, at sunset, by the light of the moon or stars — the Colosseum stands alone and unapproached. It is the monarch of ruins. It is a great tragedy in stone, and it softens and subdues the mind like a drama of Æschylus or Shakespeare. It is a colossal type of those struggles of humanity against an irresistible destiny, in which the tragic poet finds the elements of his art. The calamities which crushed the house of Atreus are symbolized in its broken arches and shattered walls. Built of the most durable materials, and seemingly for eternity—of a size, material, and form to defy the 'strong hours' which conquer all, it has bowed its head to their touch, and passed into the inevitable cycle of decay. 'And this too shall pass away'—which the Eastern monarch engraved upon his signet-ring—is carved upon these Cyclopean blocks. The stones of the Colosseum were once water; and they are now turning into dust. Such is ever the circle of nature. The solid is changing into the fluid, and the fluid into the solid; and that which is unseen is alone indestructible. He does not see the Colosseum aright, who carries away from it no other impressions than those of form, size, and hue. It speaks an intelligible language to the wiser mind. It rebukes the peevish and consoles the patient. It teaches us that there are misfortunes which are clothed with dignity, and sorrows that are crowned with grandeur. As the same blue sky smiles upon the ruin which smiled upon the perfect structure, so the same beneficent Providence bends over our shattered hopes and our answered prayers.

THE BATHS OF CARACALLA.

The heat of the climate, the general use of woollen clothing, and the wearing of sandals on the naked feet, made frequent bathing more a necessity than a luxury with the ancient Romans: but the magnificent baths erected by so many of the emperors, were structures unknown to the simplicity of the republic. The Tiber, whose yellow waters present no very tempting aspect, answered for many generations all the purposes of health and exercise; and the iron muscles which subdued the Samnites, and defeated Pyrrhus, had been braced by frequent struggles with its arrowy stream. As the city increased in size, especially after the aqueducts had begun to distribute the pure element drawn from the veins of the distant hills, public bathing-places were erected; at first, little more than reservoirs of cold water, which served merely for the purposes of ablution. But, with the rapidly increasing population, and more luxurious habits of the empire, arose those splendid establishments which are among the most remarkable facts in Roman civilization.

We are constantly liable to make mistakes in regard to the past, by not adverting to the changes of language. Our word bath no more represents the thermæ or balnea of the Romans, than the word market-place is a fit translation of forum. As with the Romans the forum was the representative of business, government, and legislation, so the bath, under the emperors, included all forms of amusement and entertainment, whether bodily or mental. The Roman thermæ were no more exclusively devoted to the act of bathing than is a modern coffee-house to the drinking of coffee. They comprised the modern club-room, billiard-table, card-room, racket-court, public garden, concert hall, and lecture room. Here musicians played, philosophers discoursed, and poets recited. Here were shady groves for the contemplative, libraries for the studious, and gymnasiums for the athletic. The finest statues, the richest frescoes, and the costliest mosaics were lavished upon them. Within the enclosure embraced by their outer wall, every taste could find gratification.

there was companionship for the sociable, and solitude for the moody; there were books and teachers for the lover of knowledge, and the noblest works of art for the lover of beauty; there was gossip for the vacant mind, and refreshment for the overtasked brain.

Upon the eastern slope of the Aventine — in a spot of congenial seclusion — stand the extensive ruins of the Baths of Caracalla, occupying an area of a mile in circuit, and more resembling the remains of a city than of a single pile of buildings. These ruins present a very different aspect from the shattered ring of the Colosseum. The latter is a great panorama, taken in at a glance: the former, a book of sketches, of which the leaves must be turned over, one by one. In the Baths of Caracalla there is no unity of impression; a mass of details is heaped up like rubbish shot from a cart. They are a town-meeting of ruins without a moderator. The eyes of antiquaries, which make what they do not find, are able to trace in this maze of decay all the complicated arrangements of the ancient thermæ, with as much certainty as Scott's Antiquary could find the intrenchments of a Roman camp in the Kaim of Kinprunes; but to common vision much of it is as indistinct as the ditch was to the observation of Lovell. There is so great an extent of space, occupied with such a variety of objects, that a wide field is open to speculation and conjecture. In many places the walls are standing, and the lines of spacious apartments can be distinctly traced. Floors encumbered with huge fragments of the falling ceiling, masses of brick-work, patches of mosaic, vaults half filled with rubbish, enormous blocks of stone and marble, attest, like the bones of a buried mastodon, the colossal nature of the original structure.

A considerable portion of the roof is still remaining, and may be reached by a narrow staircase in the wall. The soil has here so much accumulated, that it looks more like a neglected garden than the top of a building. It is as if some volcanic force had thrown up a portion of the plain beneath, and by some mysterious power it had been arrested and fixed in the air. We seem to be walking upon one of the terraces of that hanging garden which the king of Babylon reared for the gratification of his Median bride, who pined for the breezy mountain slopes of her native land. The turf beneath our feet is fresh and elastic, and flowers and trailing plants grow in abundance and veil all the rents and scars of time. The view from this spot is one of the finest in Rome, embracing a great number of beautiful and impressive objects, and none that are disenchanting or unsightly. The hour before sunset is the best for this landscape; when the air is quiet, and the shadows are lengthening, and the day lies in the past, like the life of the scene on which we gaze. Stretched upon the luxuriant grass, and looking out upon a landscape made up of nature and art — mountains dotted with towns and hamlets, plains striped and spanned by aqueducts, silent ruins, gardens, vineyards, and the churches and palaces of a populous city — the traveller will feel the great vision of antiquity pass before his face. He may leave his books and his friends at home, and find nobler companionship in that silent but inspiring Egeria, who smiles upon him from the sky, and whispers to him in the breeze. If his moments drag heavily along — if the visionary nymph have no power to charm or stay — there is no Rome for him: to him the great enchantress will not unveil her countenance.

A number of men were occupied in excavating these ruins while I was in Rome, but their labor was rather a rehearsal of work, than work itself. Their inefficiency was at once pitiable and ludicrous. They moved like flies that crawl about in the faint beams of a November sun. I have never seen a more forlorn set of human beings. They were like wrecks and waifs of humanity, for the iron years had pressed all heart and hope out of them, and left nothing but the husk and shell of man. They did not look even dangerous, and evidently had not energy enough to do wrong. They were sadder ruins than those in the shadow of which they moved. Most of them were wrapped in a loose, cumbrous, woollen cloak — a legitimate descendant of the Roman toga — and each one was provided with a wheelbarrow, primitive enough in its construction to have gone out to Mons. Sacer with the seceding populace, in the days of Menenius Agrippa.

THE PANTHEON.

The best preserved monument of ancient Rome, and one of the most beautiful buildings of the modern city, is unhappily placed. The Pantheon stands in a narrow and dirty piazza, and is shouldered and elbowed by a mob of vulgar houses. There is no breathing-space around, which it might penetrate with the light of its own serene beauty. Its harmonious proportions can be seen only in front, and it has on that side the disadvantage of being approached from a point higher than that on which it stands. On one side is a market, and the space before the matchless portico is strewn with fish-bones, decayed vegetables, and offal.

Forsyth, the sternest and most fastidious of architectural critics, has only 'large draughts of unqualified praise' for the Pantheon; and where he finds nothing to censure, who will venture to do any thing but commend? The character of the architecture, and the sense of satisfaction which it leaves upon the mind, are proofs of the enduring charm of simplicity. The portico is perfectly beautiful. It is one hundred and ten feet long and forty-four deep, and rests upon sixteen columns of the Corinthian order, the shafts being of granite and the capitals of marble. Eight of these are in front, and of these eight, there are four (including the two on the extreme right and left) which have two others behind them: the portico being thus divided into three portions, like the nave and side aisles of a cathedral; the middle space, leading to the door, being wider than the others. The granite of the shafts is partly gray and partly rose-colored, but in the shadow in which they stand, the difference of hue is hardly perceptible. The proportions of these columns are faultless, and their massive shafts and richly-carved capitals produce the effect, at once, of beauty and sublimity. The pediment above is now a bald front of ragged stone, but it was once adorned with bas-reliefs in bronze; and the holes made by the rivets with which they were fastened, are still to be seen.

The aisles of the portico were once vaulted with

bronze, and massive beams or slabs of the same metal stretched across the whole structure; but this was removed by Urban VIII. and melted into a baldachino to deface St. Peter's, and cannon to defend the castle of St. Angelo; and, not content with this, he has added insult to injury, and commemorated his robbery in a Latin inscription, in which he claims to be commended as for a praiseworthy act. But even this is not the heaviest weight resting on the memory of that vandal pope. He shares with Bernini the reproach of having added those hideous belfries which now rise above each end of the vestibule; as wanton and unprovoked an offence against good taste as ever was committed. A cocked hat upon the statue of Demosthenes in the Vatican, would not be a more discordant addition. The artist should have gone to the stake, before giving his hand to such a piece of disfigurement.

The cell, or main portion of the building to which the portico is attached, is a simple structure, circular in form, and built of brick. It was formerly encrusted with marble. The cell and the portico stand to each other in the most harmonious relation, although it seems to be admitted that the latter was an addition, not contemplated when the cell was built. But in the combination there is nothing forced or unnatural, and they seem as necessary and as preordained complements, one to the other, as a fine face and a fine head. The cell is a type of masculine dignity, and the portico, of feminine grace; and the result is a perfect architectural union.

The interior — a rotunda, surmounted by a dome — is converted into a Christian church, a purpose to which its form and structure are not well adapted, and the altars and their accessories are not improvements in an architectural point of view. But in spite of this — in spite of all that it has suffered at the hands of rapacity and bad taste — though the panels of the majestic dome have been stripped of their bronze, and the whole has been daubed over with a glaring coat of whitewash — the interior still remains, with all its rare beauty essentially unimpaired. And the reason of this is, that this charm is the result of form and proportion, and cannot be lost except by entire destruction. The only light which the temple receives is from a circular opening of twenty-eight feet in diameter at the top, and falling, as it does, directly from the sky, it fills the whole space with the purity of the heavens themselves. The magical effect of this kind of illumination it is impossible to describe. Sweep away the altars with their tawdry decorations, erase the tasteless ornaments of the cornice, restore their plundered bronze to the panels of the dome, or at least paint them of an appropriate color, dispose a few statues and busts, of fitting excellence, around the wall, and the result would be absolute perfection.

The pavement of the Pantheon, composed of porphyry, pavonazzetto, and giallo antico, though constantly overflowed by the Tiber, and drenched by the rains which fall upon it from the roof, is the finest in Rome. There is an opening in the centre, through which the water entering by the dome is carried off into a reservoir.

The Pantheon has a peculiar interest in the history of art, as the burial-place of Raphael. His grave was opened in 1833, and the remains found to be lying in the spot which Vasari had pointed out. Annibal Caracci and Cardinal Gonsalvi were also buried here.

ARCHES.

Triumphal arches were obvious offerings to the vanity of a living emperor, and equally available as expressions of gratitude and respect reared to the memory of those who had so lived as to be regretted after death. In their form and structure, the resources both of architecture and sculpture were called into exercise, and the decline of art was marked by multiplicity of details and redundancy of ornament. In its original destination, the arch was meant to do honor to a successful general; and it was so contrived that every man of the victorious army should pass under it, and for a moment dwell in the shadow of a monument which his own merit had helped to call into existence. That the form of the arch, caught from the covering heaven above, is the expression of a universal instinct, the experience of to-day shews in those fragile structures of wood or canvas with which we do honor to our governors and presidents. They spring from the same impulse as the massive and marble piles of Rome.

The Arch of Constantine is the most imposing and the best preserved of these structures. When this was reared, the pernicious habit had already begun of piecing out new buildings with patches torn from old ones, and the fragments of earlier works are wrought into this. Its general architectural design, in common to a greater or less degree with all the Roman arches, is open to the objection that the columns on each front have nothing to support, and are merely ornamental appendages, which columns should never be. The sculptural details are numerous, and not of uniform merit, the earlier portions — supposed to have been taken from a demolished arch of Trajan — being much superior to the works of Constantine's own age.*

The arch of Titus is the most graceful in its form of all the Roman arches. The great interest which attaches to it arises from the representations which its bas-reliefs contain of the spoils of the temple at Jerusalem — the golden table, the seven-branched candlestick, and the silver trumpet of the jubilee. The Jews to this day, it is said, never pass under this arch; avoiding the sight of this mournful record of the downfall of their country, and the desecration of their religion.

The Arch of Janus Quadrifrons was probably not a

* It was under this Arch of Constantine that the Emperor Charles V. made his entry into Rome, April 6, 1536. Although his visit was not particularly welcome to the pope, he was received with a degree of splendor proportioned to the power which he wielded and the terror which he inspired. Rabelais, who was then in Rome in the suite of Cardinal du Bellai, states that two or three hundred houses and three or four churches were levelled to the ground, in order to widen the streets through which the imperial procession was to pass, and that no compensation was paid to the owners of these houses. There is probably some exaggeration in this account. Robertson, as usual, takes refuge in flowing generalities, and tells us that it was 'found necessary to remove the ruins of an ancient temple of peace, in order to widen one of the streets through which the cavalcade was to pass.'

votive offering or memorial, but a mere structure of convenience. It is an immense cube, with an arch on each side, forming a vault in the centre. It is built of blocks of marble, scooped out into niches and stuck over with paltry columns, shewing a period of very indifferent taste in art. In the middle ages this arch was turned into a fortress, and occupied by the Frangipani family; and the top is still defaced by the ruins of the building they added.

The Cloaca Maxima is carried along near the Arch of Janus, and opens into the Tiber. Modern scepticism, which has overturned so much of the old faith, has not laid its withering touch upon this venerable monument. Romulus and Numa have been changed into thin shadows — the twilight ghosts of tradition that disappear before the dawn of history — but the stones of the Cloaca are still alive to speak of an antiquity of at least twenty-four hundred years. In Egypt, a monument no older would be esteemed a mere babe; but in Europe, twenty-four centuries seems a good old age. The structure of the Cloaca bears witness to two things. In the first place, it shows much mechanical skill and considerable knowledge of masonry. It is composed of immense blocks of stones, nicely fitted together, and without cement. The material used is not the travertine limestone, so common in Rome, nor yet the piperino, of which the tomb of the Scipios is built, but a coarse, volcanic compound, which was doubtless found on the spot. The solidity and faithfulness of its construction are shown by the fact, that neither floods nor earthquakes have done it any perceptible injury; and, old as it is, it is quite as likely to be in at the death of Rome, as any thing that has since been built by the hand of man. In the next place, it shows that whatever might have been the form of government in Rome at the time, it was a government enlightened enough to project a work of great public utility, and strong enough to enforce its execution upon the people. The conception and completion of such a work presuppose the elements of a state in a considerable degree of development — the relations of law — gradations of rank and subordination of classes — a legislative head, an executive arm, and an obedient body.

Opposite the Arch of Janus Quadrifrons — at the extremity of a low passage which leads to the Cloaca Maxima — issuing from beneath an arch of brick-work — is a spring of the purest water, translucent as air, still flowing with every beat of the pulse of nature, as it has flowed for thousands of years. Neither time nor flood, nor earthquake nor the crash of falling ruins have broken this silver vein that runs back to the deep heart of the hills. Vaulted and embedded in antiquity, this living stream shares in the youth of the sunbeams that shine upon a ruin, and the breezes that blow over it; and its brow is as unwrinkled as when the thirsty laborer upon the Cloaca stooped to drink of its wave. This spring was to me one of the pleasantest objects in Rome; partly because I had never heard of it, and, coming upon it unexpectedly, felt something of the satisfaction of a first discoverer; and partly from the wonderful clearness and purity of the water, which was never stained by dust or falling leaves or the feet of animals. It is a mistake to suppose that the beauty of water depends upon its being presented in large masses.

Where it is muddy and turbid, as is the case generally with the rivers in Italy, it requires bulk, form, and movement to make us forget the want of clearness and sparkle; for a small quantity of dirty water, if flowing, is a ditch; if stagnant, is a puddle. But a spring of pure water, however small, has a gem-like value; and a slender stream, sauntering and singing through a meadow, is a constant pleasure both to the eye and the ear.

To this spring the Nausicaas of modern Rome resort for the same object as that for which the daughter of Alcinous drove out from her father's palace, on the day when she met the many-wandering Ulysses. Mrs. Barbauld has written a very pleasant mock-heroic poem on washing-days, and with our associations, resting upon our in-door life, this useful domestic ceremony will bear no other treatment; but in southern Europe, where washing is done in the open air, by fountains and running streams, and enlivened with chat, laughter, and singing; it may be fairly said to have as much of the poetical and artistic element as is accorded to such occupations as hop-picking or hay-making. I have certainly seen groups around a fountain in Italy, which an artist need not have disdained to transfer to his sketck-book, and I presume a Spanish or an Italian scholar reads the episode in the Odyssey, to which I have alluded, without any sense of its incongruity and unfitness for poetical purposes.

MAMERTINE PRISON AND TARPEIAN ROCK.

There are so few things in Rome that carry us back to the days of the kings, that a peculiar interest attaches itself to two objects, one artificial and one natural, simply because of the venerable associations that belong to them; and these are the Mamertine Prison and the Tarpeian Rock.

The Mamertine Prison is a hideous vault, divided into an upper and lower portion, scooped out of the solid rock, on the declivity of the Capitoline, and lined with massive blocks in the Etruscan style of architecture; the very appearance of which vouches for their great antiquity. A more heart-breaking place of confinement it is not easy to imagine. According to the traditions of the church, St. Peter was imprisoned here by the order of Nero, and the pillar to which he was bound, and a fountain which sprang up miraculously to furnish the water of baptism to his gaolers whom he converted, are shown to the visitor. Whatever might have been my doubts, I did not make them known to my conductor: respecting his convictions, if I did not subscribe to them. I needed no other impressions to solemnize my thoughts than those derived from classical history. There is no reason to doubt that Jugurtha was starved to death in these pitiless vaults. What a death for a soldier who had passed half his life on horseback on the burning plains of Africa! Here, too, the companions of Catiline were strangled. It is a curious fact, that the chances of literature and history should have carved two such names as those of Sallust and Cicero on these Cyclopean walls. The upper room is now fitted up as a church, or oratory.

The Tarpeian Rock is on the southern side of the Capitoline Hill, and is covered with a thick growth of shabby houses, and gardens which are not exactly 'trim.' The soil has gathered round the base in considerable quantities, so that the formidable impressions derived from Roman writers are not confirmed by the sight. But a very respectable precipice may still be seen, and a traitor who should now leap from the top would probably be as harmless, ever after, as Clodius or Catiline.

On the banks of the Tiber, near the spot where the Cloaca Maxima empties into the river, stands the circular building, called the Temple of Vesta, though many antiquaries insist that this is a misnomer. Its form is simple, consisting of a circular core surrounded by a peristyle of columns, originally twenty in number, of which nineteen yet remain. The columns are of marble, of the Corinthian order, and fluted. The entablature is gone, and a very ugly roof of red tiles is crushed down directly upon the capitals of the columns. It is a pretty toy of a building; too small, to borrow an expression of Horace Walpole's, to live in, and too large to hang at one's watch-chain. Its form and features are multiplied in an immense progeny of bronze models and inkstands, to which it has given birth.

CHAPTER XI.

Basilicas and Churches — St. John Lateran — Sta. Maria Maggiore — Sta. Maria degli Angeli — San Pietro in Vincoli — Ara Cœli — San Clemente — San Pietro in Montorio — Trinità de' Monti — San Onofrio — Sta. Maria della Pace — San Agostino — San Gregorio — Sta. Maria sopra Minerva — Sta. Maria del Popolo — Sta. Agnese — Sta. Cecilia in Trastevere.

THE process by which Christianity supplanted Paganism in the Roman empire was, of course, gradual. The new religion found an old faith rooted in the popular mind, supported by wealth and power, hallowed by the traditions of a dim antiquity, and graced with the finest attributes of poetry and architecture. Christianity could not destroy, without at the same time reconstructing. The instinct of reverence, already formed, was to be diverted to higher and purer objects. The links of association, already woven, were not to be rudely snapped, but to be gently unwound, and attached to new forms. Christianity addressed, with more authoritative voice and higher sanctions, the religious principle — the sentiment of worship — in the heart of man; but to this, paganism had also appealed, and upon this it had rested. The errand of the new faith was not one of extermination, but of exaltation and purification. It was obliged to accept and recognise existing ideas and existing forms. The exquisite skill with which the apostle Paul, in his address to the Athenians, availed himself of the religious instincts of his hearers, as a foundation on which to rear the nobler faith which he brought; and the tact with which he made these instincts a starting point from which to soar to a purer region — have been often noticed with admiration. Thus, the early preachers of Christianity were obliged to use a persuasive and conciliatory tone, whenever they approached a polished and intellectual community, and to admit that God had not, in times past, utterly hidden his face from his children. These obvious considerations should modify the extreme severity of tone into which Protestant writers are apt to fall, whenever they notice any resemblance between the ceremonies of the Church of Rome and the rites of Paganism.

The temples in Rome were not adapted to the uses of Christian worship. With the ancients, worship was a ceremony addressed to the eye, in which the priest was the performer, and the people were the spectators. Hence, in the ancient temples the architectural splendor is on the exterior, and the interior is simple and unadorned. Sacrifices, also, formed a large part of religious observances among the ancients, and these consisted principally of burnt meats: an opening at the top was therefore necessary that the powerful odor might not be too offensive. This is undoubtedly the explanation of the open dome of the Pantheon. But Christian worship is spiritual in its character, and social in its form. The sermon or exhortation, the prayer, and the hymn require a place favorable to hearing rather than seeing. Thus, when Christianity became the dominant faith, and large audiences began to gather round its teachers, the old temples were found not to be suited for the purposes of churches. But there was a class of buildings which, in their plan and construction, were admirably adapted to the requisitions of Christian worship; and these were the basilicas.

Without going into the learning, historical or architectural, of this subject, it is enough to say, that a basilica, in its primitive sense, was that part of a royal residence in which the monarch, either in person or by deputy, transacted the business of his office. It was — to compare great things with small — like the hall in which an English country gentleman and justice of the peace hears complaints against vagrants and poachers. In Rome, this appellation was applied to those buildings erected, usually in the forum, for the transaction of judicial business; in which the prætor heard causes and received complaints; and for this purpose its plan and proportions were admirably adapted. The form of the basilica is, indeed, one of the natural and inevitable results of architecture. As the problem how to dispose of a crowd in such a way, that the greatest number of persons possible may see the same thing at the same time, is solved by the amphitheatre; so the arrangements of a basilica are precisely those which will best enable the magistrates forming a court of justice to hear causes, to deliberate upon them, to pronounce their decision, and at the same time give to suitors, advocates, and the public, their fair share of accommodation. A rectangular space was marked out by two rows of columns, which supported a roof. Outside of, and on either hand of these columns, a wall was reared, of inferior height, and attached to the columns by a lean-to roof, and leaving a space above for air and light to enter between the capitals of the columns. These side structures were divided into an upper and lower part. At the end of the rectangle, opposite the entrance, was the tribunal for the magistrates, rectangular or circular, sometimes on the same level with the general floor, and sometimes raised above it. Thus, we have seats for presiding magistrates, an open space in front for parties and their advocates, a gallery for the accommodation of the public, and side passages to pass in and out. A portico was generally added in front.

The early Christian churches, borrowing the name of the basilica, imitated with very little change its form and arrangements, putting the altar in the place occupied by the tribunal. By some writers it has been surmised that this was because the bishops and priests were regarded as clothed with the power of administering spiritual justice in the form of rebuke or penance, but the fact is sufficiently explained by the fitness of the basilica for the purposes of public worship, without going in search of any more recondite motives. Though the old basilicas themselves were not used as churches, yet their sites were often selected as the spots on which to build them, in order that the reverence which had gradually gathered round the soil, as devoted to the administration of justice, might be transferred to the new structure. The modern basilicas have undergone considerable changes, but they retain the essential features of the altar, the nave, and the side aisles, to vindicate their origin and descent.

There are seven basilicas in Rome,* and upwards of three hundred churches. It is commonly stated, and perhaps, without exaggeration, that the Pope might say mass every day during the year in a different church. The foundation of many of these goes back to a very early period in the history of Christianity, but, in consequence of the restorations and additions made necessary by natural decay and the hand of violence, all of them, with hardly an exception, have lost the stamp of antiquity and become, substantially, modern edifices. Those which are the least changed, and on that account among the most interesting, are St. Clemente, St. Lorenzo, and Sta. Agnese, (the two last without the walls), Sta. Maria in Trastevere, and St. Georgio in Velabro. The round form of the pagan temple is pre-

* These are, within the walls, St. Peter's, St. John Lateran, Sta. Maria Maggiore, and Sta. Croce in Gerusalemme ; beyond the walls, St. Paul's, St. Sebastian, and St. Lorenzo. Five of these, St. Peter's, St. John Lateran, Sta. Maria Maggiore, St. Paul's, and St. Lorenzo are also called patriarchal churches. The Christian world was originally divided into five patriarchates. The first and most important was that of Rome, comprising Europe, Africa, and afterwards America. The others were of Constantinople, Alexandria, Antioch, and Jerusalem. The jurisdiction of the Pope, as patriarch of Rome, was confined within the limits of his patriarchate; but, as sovereign pontiff and successor of St. Peter, it extended over the whole Christian world. The eastern patriarchs have long since disappeared, but their memory is preserved in Rome, in these patriarchal churches.

The churches of San Marcello, Santi Apostoli, and Sta. Agnese are sometimes, on account of their antiquity, considered as basilicas. — GAUME. Les Trois Rome, tom. i. p. 260.

served in St. Stefano Rotondo, St. Bernardo, and Sta. Costanza. The simple plan of the basilica was variously modified in the course of time. The transept was added, forming a Latin or Greek cross, according as it divided the nave into unequal or equal portions; piers were substituted for columns; the roof was vaulted, and the whole crowned with a dome. Nothing recalling the sublime cathedrals of Germany, France, and England is to be found in Rome. The only specimen of Gothic architecture — and that an indifferent specimen — is the Church of Sta. Maria sopra Minerva.

It need hardly be said that the churches in Rome will furnish constant interest and occupation to the traveller, and contribute in large measure to the stock of recollections which he carries home. Whether devotional feeling, love of art, or the study of history and antiquities be the ruling passion of the mind, he will find in these churches and their contents a world of matter, not to be exhausted in the term of an ordinary life. Tombs and monuments of illustrious men; pictures painted, and statues carved by hands that trembled with devotional fervor; rich chapels decked with gold, marble, and gems; mosaics, venerable from antiquity or exquisite from workmanship, present their boundless attractions to those who are drawn to them by merely secular tastes. Nor can even a Protestant and a layman be insensible to the spirit which hangs over them all, and is felt by every one who crosses the threshold of the humblest and plainest, unless he be the lightest of scoffers or the sourest of Puritans. They are open at all times, spreading out their benignant arms of invitation, and, in the spirit of the Saviour, bidding all who are weary and heavy-laden to come to them and seek rest. No surly official stands at the entrance to scowl away the poor Christian that does not wear the wedding-garment of respectability. The interior is not cut up into pews, protected by doors that are slow to open, and often guarded by countenances that are slow to expand into a look of invitation. The deep stillness, felt like a palpable presence, falls with a hushing power upon worldly emotions, and permits whispers, unheard in the roar of common life, to become audible. The few persons who are present are either kneeling in silence, or moving about with noiseless steps. In the windless air, the very flames of the tapers do not tremble, but burn like painted flames upon painted candles. If there be a touch of worldly thrift in the covering of a picture by a curtain which is withdrawn only by the touch of a fee; if tawdry ornaments offend the taste, or even the sense of propriety; if tinsel, spangles, and artificial flowers sometimes recall a milliner's shop rather than a church — who will not consent, in the spirit of candor which is the spirit of wisdom, to overlook these discordant appendages and say, 'What is the chaff to the wheat?' Of those who have spent any considerable time in Rome, at least, of those who have lived long enough to feel the dangers and duties of life, there are but few, I think, who will not be disposed to thank the churches of Rome for something more than mere gratifications of the taste; for influences, transitory, perhaps, but beneficent while they last; for momentary glimpses of things spiritually discerned; for a presence that calms and a power that elevates. Protestant ideas and convictions are, in my opinion, not weakened by a residence in Rome; but Protestants, in aiming at the reverse of wrong, have not always hit upon the right. The Romish Church, especially, is wiser in providing so much more liberally for that instinct of worship which is a deep thirst of the human soul. I envy not the head or the heart of that man who, when he sees the pavement of a Catholic church sprinkled with kneeling forms, rapt with devotional fervor, is conscious of no other emotion than a sneering protest against the mummeries of superstition. We walk in darkness, among pitfalls and snares, and the riddle of the life that is around us can only be solved by looking above us. If the swinging of a censer and the tinkling of a bell can help men to lift their thoughts from the dust of earthly passions, let their aid be accepted, and let the end consecrate the means.

As I have no purpose of writing either a guide-book or a history, I shall pass lightly over the churches of Rome, and record only such points of interest as were set down at the time, or as are recalled by an unforced effort of memory.

In studying the plan of Rome from the tower of the capitol, (which should be done the first fair day after the traveller's arrival), an imposing mass of buildings is seen towards the south-east, over the wall of the Colosseum, marking the extreme boundary of the Cælian Hill. These are the basilica of St. John Lateran, with its cloisters, baptistery, and Scala Santa, and the Lateran Palace. They form nearly an equilateral triangle with the Colosseum and the Baths of Caracalla. Their situation is beautiful, but it is the beauty of desolation. The tide of population has ebbed away from them, and left them surrounded with the silent and open spaces of the country.

The basilica of St. John Lateran is held in peculiar reverence from its venerable antiquity, and from its having been long regarded as the mother church of Christendom. The original edifice, founded by Constantine, was greatly injured by fire in the fourteenth century; and it has since been so altered and enlarged that hardly a stone of the old fabric remains; but, as there has never been a total demolition and reconstruction, the chain of association remains unbroken, and the reverend form of the first Christian emperor, whose statue stands in the vestibule, is still the presiding genius of the place. The façade is of a style of architecture kindred to that of St. Peter's, but superior in beauty and simplicity; the perpendicular of the columns and pilasters, which support the massive entablature, being broken only by the horizontal line of the balconies, running across nearly in the middle. The interior is rich and imposing, though not in the purest taste. The features of the basilica have disappeared; as the columns which once separated the nave from the aisles are imprisoned in piers, patched over with ornaments in stucco and marble. Twelve colossal statues of the apostles in marble — six on either hand — occupy niches scooped out of these piers. The execution of these works fell upon evil days in art, and they are characterized by flutter and extravagance. The draperies look as if the wearers had been out in a high wind and suddenly stiffened into stone: and their attitudes are painful to the eye, for they seem to be maintained by muscular effort. But they show great skill and mechanical cleverness. They are in art what Darwin's Botanic Garden is in poetry; and in making this comparison, I recognise the merits both of the statues and the poem.

The high altar, of gilded bronze, resting on four columns of granite, resembling the diminished spire of a cathedral, recalls those Gothic forms so rarely seen in Rome. The venerable mosaics of the tribune, executed by a contemporary of Cimabue, shew in the attitude and expression of the figures the gleams of the new dawn of art, but they are not in harmony with the objects around them.*

The basilica of Santa Maria Maggiore has little to be commended, externally; but the interior, through all the changes which it has undergone, still retains the features of the basilica essentially unimpaired; and a single glance at its noble and harmonious proportions vindicates the taste and judgment of those who adapted that form to the purposes of Christian worship. An immense nave is divided from the side aisles by a row of thirty-six marble columns, of the Ionic order, supporting a simple entablature, on which rests the upper

* Pope Sylvester II. who died in 1003, was buried in this church. When the church was repaired, or rebuilt, in 1648, his tomb was opened, and the remains of the venerable pontiff appeared unchanged; the features distinct and the arms crossed upon the breast. But at the approach of the air the figure melted away, and in a few moments nothing was left but a handful of dust. Mrs. Gray relates a similar occurrence as having happened at the opening of an Etruscan tomb.

wall of the nave, where alternate windows and niches are separated by pilasters. The flat roof, covered with sunken panels, is elaborately carved, and blazes with gilding. There is no confusion of details, no incongruity of parts, no crowd of tasteless ornaments. The lines and surfaces are not crossed and entangled, but all breathe the air of simplicity. The great extent of the inclosed space gives the impression of sublimity, while the separate features are all beautiful.

The church of Santa Maria degli Angeli has a magnificent interior, of which the shell was once the great hall of the Baths of Diocletian. The form is a Greek cross, with a vestibule in a circular form. The original adaptation of the hall to the purposes of a church was by Michael Angelo; and the changes and additions by subsequent architects are not deemed improvements. The pavement, though raised several feet by reason of the dampness of the soil — to the great disfigurement of the columns, the bases of which are buried out of sight — is still quite low. Standing at the central point, where the lines of the nave and the transept cross each other, the effect is incomparably fine. The four radiating arms which here meet and blend, leave the impression of simplicity and regularity, without formal monotony, and typify the spirit of Christianity, which binds together the four corners of the globe by the ties of a common love and a common faith.

Attached to the church is the convent of the Certosa, with its spacious cloisters running round four sides of a square, and enclosing an open space of considerable extent. These cloisters are among the things for which we have reason to envy the old world. They are merely arcades, or piazzas, round a quadrangle, and seem to have been designed for the benefit of monastic institutions in hot climates; so that their inmates might have the advantage of air and exercise, without exposure to the sun. They are a proof of how much may be done in architecture by adherence to simplicity and loyalty to nature. Milton, whose exquisite tastes were never allowed to triumph over his stern convictions of duty, says, in a well-known passage of his Il Penseroso,

'But let my due feet never fail,
To walk the studious cloister's pale.'

To a man of scholarly habits and imaginative temperament, these walks would be a constant source of refreshment and inspiration. The roof, the pavement, the wall, and the open arches, which look out into the quadrangle, afford ample scope to architectural invention; and the quadrangle itself may be a flower-garden, or a patch of green turf with a fountain in the centre. These cloisters blend together the beauty of art and the beauty of nature; the solemn monotony of stone and marble with the bloom and verdure which the touch of every spring renews. As the musing dreamer paces along, the enclosed landscape which he sees through the arched loopholes of his retreat assumes every moment a new aspect, and prevents the sense of sight from becoming torpid and unobservant by constantly falling upon the same combination of objects.

In the centre of the square around which the cloisters of this church are built, is a fountain; and, overshadowing the fountain, is a group of three cypresses, which are said to have been planted by the hands of Michael

Angelo. There were originally four, but one has been destroyed by lightning. They are of immense size, and strikingly picturesque; all the more so from the fact that they begin to show, in their broken outlines and in the gaps made in their verdurous bulk, the marks of time and decay. Dark, solitary, and motionless, they are vegetable monuments carved in green. The breeze does not bend their spiry tops, and they have no share in the life that beats in the pulses of the mountain pine. They look like a group of monks standing in bodily proximity, but mental isolation.

San Pietro in Vincoli is one of the noblest churches in Rome, comprising a nave separated from two aisles, by fluted marble columns of the Doric order. Here is the celebrated statue of Moses, by Michael Angelo, about which so much has been written, and which is viewed in so different a spirit by different observers. In criticising a work of art, reference should always be had to the objects which the artist had in view in executing it. This statue was originally intended to form a part of an immense monumental structure, designed by Pope Julius II. for himself, and urged on with characteristic ardor and impatience. But death called him away before his colossal mausoleum was ready for his reception; and his costly project was never carried into execution by his successors. The plan proposed was a massive parallelogram of marble, of some forty feet by twenty, adorned with niches, pilasters, and emblematic statues, and surmounted by a cornice. Above the cornice, at each of the corners, a colossal statue was to have been placed. The Moses was to have been one of these. A smaller parallelogam was to have rested upon the larger, and the whole was to have been crowned by two figures, representing Heaven and Earth, supporting a sarcophagus. A plan like this, carried out by the genius of Michael Angelo, would have resulted in the most magnificent combination of sculpture and architecture that the world has ever seen; but if the pope had lived, it is probable that the clashing of his own character with that of the artist would have prevented its completion. They were too much alike to act together in harmony. Both were haughty and impatient; the one, too ready to command, and the other, not always willing to obey. The pope's pride of place was opposed to the artist's pride of genius; and there meeting, like that of flint and steel, broke into angry sparks of controversy.

Thus, the statue of Moses was meant to have been raised considerably above the eye of the spectator, and to have been a single object in a colossal structure of architecture and sculpture, which would have had a foreground and a background, and been crowned with a mass at once dome-like and pyramidal. Torn, as it is, from its proper place; divorced from its proportionate companionship; stuck against the wall of a church; and brought face to face with the observer — what wonder that so many of those who see it, turn away with no other impressions than those of caricature and exaggeration! But who, that can appreciate the sublime in art, will fail to bow down before it as embodied in this wonderful statue? The majestic character of the head, the prodigious muscles of the chest and arms, and the beard that flows like a torrent to the waist, represent a being of more than mortal port and power, speaking with the authority, and frowning with the sanctions of incarnate law. The drapery of the lower part of the figure is inferior to the anatomy of the upper part. Remarkable as the execution of the statue is, the expression is yet more so; for, notwithstanding its colossal proportions, its prominent characteristic is the embodiment of intellectual power. It is the great leader and lawgiver of his people that we see, whose voice was command, and whose outstretched arm sustained a nation's infant steps. He looks as if he might control the energies of nature as well as shape the mould in which the character of his people should be formed. That any one should stand before this statue in a scoffing mood, is to me perfectly inexplicable. My own emotions were more nearly akin to absolute bodily fear. At an irreverent word, I should have expected the brow to contract into a darker frown, and the marble lips to unclose in rebuke.*

In the sacristy are an indifferent picture by Domenichino, the Deliverance of St. Peter; and a female head, with eyes upturned, by Guido, to which the name of Speranza, or Hope, is given; though it is probably an

* This statue, as is well known, has the hair so disposed in front as to resemble the horns projecting from the top of the forehead. This was a common representation of Moses in early and mediæval art, and was founded upon an erroneous translation in the Vulgate Bible of the twenty-ninth verse of the thirty-fourth chapter of Exodus. In the Vulgate it reads, 'Ignorabat quod cornuta esset facies sua,' 'He knew not that his face was horned.' The received version, 'He wist not that the skin of his face shone,' is the correct translation of the passage. See Sir Thomas Browne's observations upon the subject, in his 'Inquiry into Vulgar and Common Errors.'

idealized portrait. This is a very pleasing work; superficial and sentimental, and therefore popular. There were several copies, in various stages of progress, in different parts of the room, all very bad. The sacristan, who seemed to have a quiet sense of humor, as well as a sort of personal pride in the picture, appeared to take much satisfaction in exhibiting these unsuccessful copies, and in comparing them with the original. He would bring one and show it to me, and after a while, produce another, with an expression in his face which seemed to say, 'You think that is as bad as it can be, but here is one a great deal worse.'

On approaching the Capitol, a flight of one hundred and twenty-four steps of marble leads, on the left, to the church of Ara Cœli, one of the oldest and the ugliest in Rome. But no one is held in greater reverence by the people, and none is more frequented by throngs of worshippers. This is mainly owing to its possessing a miraculous wooden image of the infant Saviour, which is reputed to be of great efficacy in the healing of diseases. The pillars and walls of the church are covered with little votive pictures, commemorating escapes from accident and illness — a practice which the classical student may trace back to the custom of suspending similar tablets in the temple of Neptune, by those who had been rescued from the perils of shipwreck. On the twelfth day after Christmas, a curious and characteristic spectacle is presented at this church. A kind of stage is erected behind a curtain, which, slowly rising, reveals a group of figures as large as life, of wood or pasteboard, of the Holy Family and the Adoration of the Magi. The Virgin, with pink cheeks and a very fine gown, holds the miraculous Bambino on her lap. St. Joseph is looking on: the three magi kneel or bow in attitudes of reverence and worship. The disposition of the group and the arrangement of the lights are managed with considerable skill. On this occasion, the church is always thronged, especially by peasants from the country, who testify the liveliest admiration, and the most unquestioning faith in what they see.

In this church reposes the dust of Pietro della Valle, the oriental traveller of the seventeenth century, one of those enterprising and adventurous spirits, that, from time to time, break out of Europe to breathe the freer air, and expatiate in the broader fields of the east. From his twenty-eighth to his fortieth year, his life was as restless as a wave. After running over Turkey, Asia Minor, and Egypt, he travelled across the desert to Aleppo and Bagdad. At the latter place, he fell in love with and married Sitti Maani Gioerida, a young Georgian lady, in whom he found a congenial spirit. With a man's endurance and a woman's love, she followed him in all his subsequent wanderings, shrinking neither from toil nor danger. He entered into the service of the Shah of Persia, and fought in his armies against the Turks; his faithful companion never leaving his side. But this rough life of peril was too much for the delicate frame which enclosed her brave spirit and loving heart, and she died after a union of five years. Her inconsolable husband could not prevail upon himself to part with the remains of one he had so fondly loved. He caused them to be embalmed, and they attended him in all his subsequent wanderings, which extended over the peninsula of India; whence he returned over the desert to Aleppo, and after visiting Cyprus, Malta, Sicily, and Naples, he reached Rome, his native place, on the 28th of March, 1626. He some time after deposited the remains of his wife in the Church of Ara Cœli, and pronounced a funeral oration in her honor. In Rome, Della Valle became a lion of the first magnitude, and was presented to the pope, who gave him an office about his person. The wild habits of the East still clung to him, for in a fit of rage he killed a coachman who had offended him, in the piazza of St. Peter's, at the very moment of the papal benediction; for which, no harsher punishment than a temporary banishment from Rome was awarded to him. Truth compels me to add, that, like many inconsolable husbands, he lighted the nuptial torch a second time; marrying a young lady, a relation of his deceased wife, whom he had brought with him into Italy. Upon his death-bed he requested that he might be laid by the side of his first love, and here they both sleep, and a modest tomb marks the spot of their repose.

In a street which leads from Saint John Lateran to the Colosseum is the church of San Clemente, one of the most curious and venerable in Rome, and perhaps, more than any other, carrying us back to the early ages of the church. Though we may reject the tradition which dates its foundation from the first century, there is no doubt that it is at least as old as the beginning of the fifth. Through a small porch or vestibule, a court, or atrium, is entered, with a portico running round it. Through this, the church is approached.

The interior consists of a nave and two side aisles, without a transept. The altar, crowned by a tabernacle resting upon four columns of violet-colored marble, and the ambones or reading pulpits of white, are raised above the floor of the nave by steps, and enclosed by a low wall of marble sculptured with crowns, crosses, and other Christian symbols. At the end, opposite the entrance, is the absis or tribune, of a semicircular form, containing the ancient altar and the bishop's throne. This tribune is raised above the floor of the nave, and shut off from it by two gates. The vault is adorned with curious old mosaics.

Every part of this church had originally its meaning or significance. The external court was for those who, by a course of penance, were washing away the sins of guilt or unbelief; and they were in the habit of entreating to be remembered in the prayers of those who were privileged to enter the church. In the interior, the two aisles were appropriated to those who had been baptized, or were in preparation for that holy rite; one being occupied by men, and the other, by women. The bishop and priests sat on seats in the absis. The enclosed space in the centre was filled by the acolyths, or subordinate ecclesiastical officers, who read or chanted the gospels and the epistles from the two ambones.

The church of San Pietro in Montorio, or Monte Aureo,* was erected to mark the spot where, according to the traditions of the church, St. Peter suffered

* Monte Aureo, or Mons Aureus, so called from the golden yellow of its gravelly soil.

martyrdom. There is nothing in the architecture, external or internal, to attract attention, unless it be the circular rose window of the façade, a Gothic embellishment which is a rare exotic in Rome. The chief interest of this church is derived from the paintings by Sebastian del Piombo, contained in the first lateral chapel on the right hand. The principal subjects are the Transfiguration and the Flagellation — the latter, one of those painful representations, to which no amount of reverence or skill in the artist can ever reconcile us. They are painted by laying the oil colors upon stone, after a manner said to have been invented by Sebastian del Piombo himself. The designs were furnished in whole, or in part, by Michael Angelo — Sebastian del Piombo being a Venetian, and a great master in color, in which Michael Angelo felt himself to be weak. It is said that this combination was formed in the hope that the result of their labors might impair the popularity of Raphael, at that time the favorite of the pope and the delight of the people. In the figure of the Saviour, in the Flagellation, connoisseurs detect the powerful drawing and profound knowledge of anatomy of the great Florentine. In these pictures the shadows are blackened by time, and, as the chapel is not strongly lighted, the whole effect is sombre and dingy; and though their power as works of art is readily acknowledged, they are not attractive.

A door, on the right hand side of the nave, leads into the cloister belonging to a Franciscan convent attached to this church. In the centre of the area, marking the exact spot of the apostle's martyrdom, is a small circular temple of travertine, surrounded by sixteen granite columns of the Doric order, supporting an entablature, upon which rests a dome crowned by a cross. It was designed by Bramante, and is generally esteemed a very elegant building; but it seems to me to have been overpraised. The plan is simple, the proportions are harmonious, and there is always something in a circular entablature, supported by columns, which attracts and contents the eye. But the dimensions are so small, that it looks like an architectural toy, too pretty and finical for a church, and better adapted for a summer-house; and even suggesting to a profane eye those structures of sugar which are designed by inspired confectioners for central ornaments to supper-tables.*

The Trinità de' Monti is familiar to all visitors in Rome, from its conspicuous position, crowning the magnificent staircase of travertine, leading from the Piazza di Spagna to the Pincian Hill, which most travellers ascend, once every day at least during their residence in Rome. This church, formerly belonging to the Franciscan monks, suffered severely from the destructive propensities of the French soldiers who were quartered in the adjoining convent, during the

* Raphael has introduced this temple of Bramante into his cartoon of Paul preaching at Athens. His eye, formed upon the study of the antique, had a peculiar predilection for circular forms. See the round temple in the cartoon of Paul and Barnabas at Lystra, and the beautiful architectural design in the background of the Sposalizio at Milan. I fear the great painter would not have looked upon the pointed arches, the slender columns, and the lancet windows of York Minster or Strasburg Cathedral, with proper admiration.

French occupation of Rome, in the first revolution. Many of the pictures were destroyed, or irreparably injured, and the building itself was abandoned and closed from 1798 to 1816, when it was restored by Louis XVIII., after the designs of a French architect. The old pictures which had disappeared were replaced by new ones, painted by students of the French academy in Rome; a compensation which will remind the classical reader of the old joke of Lucius Mummius.

Since 1827, this church and convent have been in the possession of nuns of the French order of 'Les dames du sacré cœur,' who devote themselves to the education of girls. It is only opened on Sunday, during matins and vespers, and, on account of the music, which is performed by the nuns, it is a good deal resorted to on those occasions by strangers. The public are admitted at a side door, opened by a demure-looking female, who was instructed (so the story ran) to exclude all gentlemen who were young and handsome. The interior is a single nave, with three wide and deep chapels on either hand. Above the entrance is a gallery, with an organ, and here the music is performed by the nuns, who are concealed behind a curtain. Their voices are sweet and pleasing, and the music selected is usually simple and appropriate; but the highest effects of church music can by no means be reached by female voices alone. The transept and choir are divided from the nave by a lofty iron railing, through which the pupils of the convent are indistinctly seen in attendance upon the services. Their dress is simple but not unbecoming—a gown of dark color and a white veil. As they come in by twos and threes, gliding with noiseless steps over the pavement, in the dim, religious light which revealed only the common elements of youth and womanhood, without any individual traits, there was something in the sight which touched both the imagination and the heart. The vague, romantic interest which clings to the monastic dress, the floating veil, and the iron grating — of which that cunning magician, Mrs. Radcliffe, has so skilfully availed herself — was enough for those who were sufficiently young and untried to look upon the whole thing as a mere piece of poetry; while those who were older and more versed in the ways of life found in the simple facts — the plain prose — of the case, the cue for sympathy and interest. The sentiments which Mrs. Hemans has embodied in her very beautiful poem, entitled 'Evening Prayer at a Girl's School,' were always in my mind on those occasions. That man lives to little purpose, in my judgment, who does not gather, from increasing years and enlarged observation, a stronger sense of the peculiar perils to which woman is exposed — of her unequal chances in the lottery of happiness, and of the sterner sentence passed upon her wrong-doings. In thoughts like these there was a power that lifted the heart above the atmosphere of sect, and I never omitted to offer a silent prayer that these fair young creatures might be shielded from the snares that every where lurk in the path of woman, and, if they failed of happiness, might, at least, not part with peace.

This church contains one of the most celebrated pictures in Rome, the Descent from the Cross, by Daniele da Volterra, a work of great power and deep feeling. The composition is animated and expressive, and the drawing hardly inferior to that of Michael Angelo.*

Upon the Janiculum, about half way up the slope, stand the church and convent of San Onofrio, at right angles to each other, and with a portico common to both. Upon the wall, under the portico attached to the convent, are three frescoes by Domenichino, carefully protected by a covering of glass, representing the Baptism, Flagellation, and Temptation of St. Jerome. But the great and absorbing interest of this church and convent is derived from their association with Tasso. The great poet, in the spring of the year 1595, was attacked by an illness which he felt would be fatal, and he desired that his last breath might be drawn in the sacred retreats of this convent. He brought with him a frame prematurely old, and a heart broken by the weight of the burden of life, and his greeting to the monks who helped him from his carriage was comprised in the simple words, 'I am come to die among you.' He lingered but a few weeks, soothed by friendly offices and nursed with tender care, his time principally occupied in those devotional exercises always so congenial to his religious sensibility. The close of his life of struggle and sorrow was tranquil and peaceful. The clouds were lifted up at sunset, and this great 'orb of song' sank to his rest in unshadowed glory. A small slab,

* The picture exhibited is an oil copy of the original fresco, which was detached from the wall some years since and removed into the sacristy, and is not now usually shown.

set into the pavement of the church, near the entrance, and containing a brief Latin inscription, marks the spot where his remains were laid. And what need is there of any thing more? Why lavish the luxury of architecture and sculpture upon a name which is its own monument? Can the costly cenotaph which is said to be erecting for him ever have the interest of the simple stone which designates his dust? In the library are some interesting memorials of him; a mask in wax, moulded from a plaster-cast taken after death — the features sunken and wasted, but the brow noble and intellectual — an autograph letter, an ink-stand, a girdle, and a sort of vase which once belonged to him. The windows of the room in which he died were also pointed out.

The garden in the rear is a spacious enclosure, planted with oaks and cypresses; with plots and beds of homelier vegetables. In one corner is a semicircular range of seats, cut in the living turf, where the Arcadian Academy sometimes held their sessions, and where, occasionally, I believe, a religious fraternity still meets. A more attractive place of gathering can hardly be imagined, for it commands an enchanting view, fitted either to suggest poetical images or awaken devotional feeling. Near it was once a venerable oak, known all over Rome as Tasso's oak, and held in due honor accordingly. It was blown down a few years ago, but not entirely destroyed; for, when I saw it, there were some vigorous shoots growing out of the shattered stump.

Many of the Roman churches are visited by strangers exclusively for the works of art which they contain. In Sta. Maria della Pace, in the first chapel on the right, is a celebrated fresco by Raphael — the Cumæan, Persian, Phrygian, and Tiburtine Sibyls, represented in the fervor of inspiration, and surrounded by angels holding tablets on which to record the glowing words of poetry and prophecy. It is a composition of great beauty and dignity. The figures are of colossal size, painted upon the wall below the cornice and above the arched recess of the chapel, and they are disposed with much judgment and skill. In expression and arrangement, in the character of the heads, and the simple flow of the draperies, they are stamped with the finest impress of Raphael's genius; but the original coloring has been impaired. About the middle of the seventeenth century, in the time of Pope Alexander VII., some rash hand undertook to retouch and restore it with oil colors. From these it was skilfully cleansed in 1816, but, between the two processes, the fresco unavoidedly suffered some wrong.*

* These frescoes were painted at the expense of Agostino Chigi, the founder of the Chigi family; one of those princely bankers and merchants of the middle ages, like the Medici in Florence and the Fuggers in Augsburg, who did business in that lordly way which, in these days of competition and five per cent. commissions, we can form hardly a conception of. His annual income was estimated at seventy thousand ducats of gold. The ducat was in actual value about equivalent to a Spanish dollar, but at that time, its exchangeable value was much greater. Raphael had received five hundred scudi for these frescoes, but made a demand upon Chigi's cashier for a further sum, which he maintained to be due to him therefor. The cashier — probably a dry man of business who thought the

In the church of San Agostino is also a fresco by Raphael, the prophet Isaiah between two angels. The prophet holds a roll in his hand, and the angels, a tablet; both containing inscriptions. This is not considered one of Raphael's happiest works. The shadow of Michael Angelo's genius was upon him at the time, and in endeavoring to catch the peculiar style of his illustrious rival, he gave up some of his own characteristic traits without gaining a proper equivalent in return. He ceased, in some measure, to be Raphael, but did not succeed in becoming Michael Angelo. That Raphael should have been greatly struck with the grandeur and sublimity of the prophets in the Sistine Chapel — that he should have felt the value of such a revelation in art, and endeavored to heighten his own style by a study and even imitation of them — is honorable to both artists, and perfectly in keeping with that many-sided pursuit of excellence which was so marked a trait in Raphael. This fresco has also suffered much from restoration.

In one of the chapels of the church of San Gregorio are the two celebrated frescoes, so well known in the history of art, painted by Domenichino and Guido, in rivalry with each other; the former representing the Flagellation of St. Andrew, and the latter, the same

whole thing a most absurd waste of money — refused to honor the painter's draft; and thereupon the matter was referred to Michael Angelo as arbitrator. When he had looked at the figures, he remarked that for the heads alone Raphael ought to be paid a hundred scudi a-piece. Chigi, on hearing this, directed his cashier to pay the whole sum demanded, without any further demur; adding that he should have become bankrupt, if Michael Angelo had gone on to value the draperies.

saint adoring the cross as he is led to execution. The circumstances under which these works were painted have given them a reputation beyond their intrinsic merits. As between the two, the superiority of Domenichino in power and correctness of drawing, and dramatic truth of expression, is very obvious; but he is inferior to his rival, certainly in coloring, and perhaps in fancy. Neither of them can be called imaginative. In this work of Domenichino's, as in many others, the merit of the subordinate parts is greater than that of the principal subject. A group of women in the foreground thrust back by soldiers, and a frightened child hiding his face in his mother's lap, are especially admired.

This church was founded by Gregory the Great in the seventh century, and he was for many years a monk in the convent attached to it. The late pope, Gregory XVI., was also for many years abbot of this same convent; a fact no otherwise noticeable than as showing in how many ways, in this wonderful Rome, the past is linked to the present; and how a space of more than a thousand years is spanned by a bridge of which every arch is perfect.

The churches of Rome are not rich in works of sculpture of a high order. Christian art has not manifested itself to any great extent in marble, and for reasons inseparable from the nature of the material. The spiritual element in Christianity speaks through expression, but sculpture can never emancipate itself from tyranny of form. When a statue becomes too expressive, it ceases to be statuesque and begins to be picturesque. Before the idea of the Saviour, or even of the Virgin, sculpture drops, or ought to drop its chisel in reverential awe. The venerable forms of saints and martyrs are not ideal enough for its purposes. And as for angels, the wings present great difficulties. Cut out of marble, and stuck upon the shoulders where there are no muscles to move or support them, they become unsightly excrescences. The angels of our visions float, and speed on their errands of blessing by their power of will alone, without mechanism or muscle.

In the church of Sta. Maria sopra Minerva is a full-length statue of Christ by Michael Angelo; a work, admirable so far as the handling of the marble is concerned, but by no means successful in overcoming the essential difficulties of the subject.

In the church of Sta. Maria del Popolo is a work in marble, which has a rare and peculiar interest — a statue of Jonah sitting upon a whale — designed by Raphael, and probably, also, executed by him. The whale is hardly larger than the man: a disproportion explained by the fact that the subject was early chosen by Christian artists as a type of the resurrection, and was meant to be a symbol, and not a representation. For the same reason, the prophet appears in the bloom of youth. Its merit as a work of art is more than respectable. The block from which the statue is carved, is said to have fallen from the so-called temple of Jupiter Stator, in the Forum.

In Sta. Agnese, in the Piazza Navona, the chapels are decorated with elaborate bas-reliefs instead of paintings, and another work of the same kind but of higher pretensions, by Algardi, is in the subterranean chapel.

The same criticism may be passed upon all of them, that they overstep the modesty of sculpture. They aim at the illusions of perspective, and light and shade. In short, they try to be pictures and cannot; and form a sort of hybrid in art between sculpture and wax-work.

In the church of Sta. Cecilia, in Trastevere, is one of the most beautiful and interesting statues in Rome, that of the saint to whom the church is dedicated, who suffered martyrdom in the third century. It was her dying request that the house in which she dwelt might be converted into a place of worship for Christians; which was accordingly done. Upon the decay of the house, a church was built on the site in the ninth century. It was renewed and repaired in 1725; at which time many of its interesting antiquities and works of art were removed or destroyed. Further changes in the interior were made during the reign of the late Pope Gregory XVI.

The remains of the saint were deposited in this church in the year 820, and exhumed in 1599. They were found in a coffin of cypress-wood, cased in a sarcophagus of marble, lying on the right side, and covered with a simple drapery. The wooden coffin was enclosed in silver, and recommitted to its resting-place with great solemnity. Stefano Maderno, a sculptor and architect, was commissioned by Cardinal Sfondrato to execute a statue which should preserve the attitude in which the saint was found; a work which he performed with great skill, delicacy, and feeling. It lies in a sarcophagus, adorned with agate, lapis lazuli, and gilded bronze, in a very costly but very tasteless manner ; the side next the spectator being open to the view. It is reclining on the right side, the position natural, and modest. The arms are extended, and the hands marked by delicacy and refinement. The person is entirely covered in simple and beautifully wrought drapery. The head, enveloped with a cloth, rests upon the forehead, and is therefore so turned that the side face only is seen. A gold band round the neck marks the wound of the executioner's axe. The whole air of the figure represents death and not sleep. The feminine delicacy and purity, the tenderness of feeling and depth of sentiment which breathe through it, are in the highest degree admirable, and make it one of the most touching and beautiful works of modern sculpture. It is a subject of wonder that an artist, capable of conceiving and executing such a statue, should have left no other conspicuous monument of his genius, and should be remembered only by this solitary creation.

CHAPTER XII.

Palaces: Borghese — Barberini — Colonna — Doria-Pamphili — Farnese — Farnesini — Spada — Rospigliosi — Sciarra. Villas: Ludovisi — Borghese — Albani — Pamphili-Doria — Madama — Melini — Magliana — Torlonia.

PALACES AND VILLAS.

'There is a soul of goodness in things evil,' says Shakespeare. This is only another form of expressing that principle of compensation which runs through the world and its works. Viewing the Romish Church as an instrument, or an assemblage of instruments, to accomplish certain ends, without reference to the nature of those ends, or to the effect produced upon the individual instruments themselves, it may be pronounced the most perfect institution the world has ever known. Nothing was ever so admirably devised to cause the energies of its members to work together to accomplish a great common object. The citizen, in Sparta, was not so much absorbed by the state as the individual — be he priest, bishop, or cardinal — is by the church. The church is the stream, and the individual members are but drops that swell its tide and increase its current. No one can deny that there is something grand, as well as terrible, in this universal self-annihilation;

and the commanding position of the Romish Church at this moment is a proof of the prodigious power which it gives.

To produce this result — to secure to the Church the undivided energies of its children — the celibacy of the clergy was an essential condition precedent. It was only by annihilating the natural ambition of founding a family, that the church could monopolize all those impulses and affections which in ordinary cases flow out upon a man's children and flow no further. And this great distinction between the Catholic and the Protestant clergy is shown in the different ways in which the wealth drawn by both from the revenues of the Church is expended. The great ambition of an English bishop, commonly springing from the middle classes, and whose descendants will return to them, is to lay up money for his children and bequeath them wealth if not rank. Thus, he lives far within his means, eats the bread of carefulness, and gives nothing to luxury or splendor; and the records of Doctors-Commons show that there is no class of persons who leave fortunes so large, in proportion to their incomes and the time they have enjoyed them, as bishops. On the other hand, a Roman prelate, having no sons to establish in life, and no daughters to portion, seeks to link his fleeting existence with the enduring creations of genius. He builds a chapel, and adorns it with gems and marble; he repairs a church, he orders pictures and statues, and bestows them upon the public. If he be a cardinal and very rich, his ambition soars higher. He founds a palace or a villa; fills it with works of art and precious remains of antiquity; designing it to be not only his abode while living, but his monument when dead.

Thus, without the celibacy of the Roman clergy, we could not have had the palaces and villas of Rome and its vicinity, for most of them were built by cardinals or popes, and from the revenues of the church. They form marked points of interest and attraction, and are among the peculiar and characteristic features of the Eternal City. The distinction between a palace and a villa does not depend upon situation, for though there are no palaces without the walls, yet there are villas within them. A villa is a palace with a garden. A palace is a villa without a garden.

The Roman palaces, mostly of later date than those of Florence, are of a more showy style of architecture; and they differ more among themselves. The Palazzo Veneziano, the oldest of them, built in the latter half of the fifteenth century, is the only one which, by its simple façade, its small windows, and its heavy cornice, recalls the massive structures of Florence. This palace marks the starting-point from simplicity in the history of Roman palatial architecture. The style, as it goes on, becomes more rich and gay. The period of its highest excellence, at which we see invention under the control of good taste, may be placed during the first part of the sixteenth century, when Bramante, Peruzzi, and San Gallo were lawgivers in architecture. The Palazzo della Cancellaria, the Palazzo Giraud, the Palazzo Sora, all by Bramante; the Palazzo Sacchetti, and the Palazzo Farnese, by San Gallo; the Palazzo Massimo and the Farnesina, by Peruzzi, are the best specimens of their class — offering the most to admiration and the least to criticism.

From the middle of the sixteenth century, civil architecture in Rome begins gradually to decline. New palaces are built, in which the taste of powerful patrons demands the attractions of novelty, Architects like Ammanati and Pitro Ligorio, confident in themselves, and unwilling to move in paths which others had opened, aimed at more showy effects and more striking combinations. In their designs, however, there is so much genius and inventive power, that the results which they produce are worthy of great praise ; and faults in detail are overlooked in the dazzling effectiveness of the whole. It would have been well if architecture could have stopped here; but that law of progress, or rather of movement, which will not allow an enduring pause at the point where beauty and simplicity meet, is an ever propelling impulse when the downward path of decline has once been taken. In the middle of the seventeenth century, architecture had reached its lowest stage of degeneracy, under the corrupting influence of Borromini, a man of inventive power, but of wayward and fantastic taste — whose fancy ran riot in frivolous details and grotesque embellishments — who had an antipathy to right angles and straight lines, and delighted in curves, twists, and spirals — who decorated his fronts in the style of a jeweller or confectioner, and gave to stone and marble the flimsy and unsubstantial look of stucco. The side of the Doria Palace facing the Corso, the work of Valvasori, represents, in its vicious style and puerile ornaments, the marked defects of this school of architecture. It is of immense extent, but so overloaded with details which have no character, and embellishments which have no grace, that there is nothing of massiveness or grandeur in the effect. The line of the cornice is so broken and interrupted, that the building seems to rest upon a yielding foundation, or to have been strained by an earthquake. In the eighteenth century, so few works were constructed that no distinct character in architecture can be assigned to it. The Consulta and Corsini Palaces, built by Fuga, were improvements upon some of their predecessors, and the Palazzo Braschi, the newest of all, erected at the close of the last century, has the finest staircase in Rome.

Of late years, so far as can be judged from the little that has been done, architecture seems to have been under the guidance of a better taste. Classical models especially, have been much studied under the influence of Canina, a practical architect, profoundly versed in the learning of his profession; and there is a growing disposition to return to the regularity of classical forms. But there is a want of vital power and inventive genius. Architecture, in its present aspect, resembles the painting of Camucini. We recognise the study of good models; we find little to object to; but we do not look at the pictures or the buildings a second time.

The palaces of Rome, which have been estimated to be seventy-five in number, though differing in details, in the extent of ground which they occupy, and in the splendor of their decorations, have certain features in common. They are usually built of stone, of a style of architecture showy and effective, if not always in good taste; blending the characteristics of a fortress and a dwelling-place. Their form is generally that of a quadrangle, built round a cortile or court-yard, into which a staircase of stone or marble opens. The apartments of each floor, which are often of immense size, communicate with each other, and are now frequently occupied by persons of widely different pursuits and social rank. The lower floor is perhaps a sculptor's studio, or a stable, or a furniture warehouse. An English or American family takes a suite of rooms in the upper part, or a German or French painter revels in the luxuries of light and space, in apartments where acres of canvas can be displayed without crowding. The staircase is the only thing in common, and that is often as filthy as the street itself, and ladies who would preserve the purity of their drapery intact, must walk circumspectly, and show themselves magnanimous in the matter of ankles.

Though these palaces make fine pictures, yet, to a northern taste, at least, few of them would be comfortable residences. They wear an air of dreary splendor and desolate magnificence. The immense apartments have but little furniture, and that generally of an inferior description. The floors of marble or brick are with out carpets, and no cheerful fireplace displays its hospitable and domestic blaze, though in winter the rooms are often deadly cold and damp. The marble columns chill the eye, and the gilded cornice mocks the shivering visitor like the play of the morning sun upon a field of ice. Many, perhaps a large proportion, of the owners of these stately structures have become greatly reduced in their fortunes, and hide their faded grandeur in some corner of their lordly mansion, like the snail in the lobster's shell. In such cases, a melancholy air of decay and neglect hangs over the scene. Broken windows, dilapidated furniture, tarnished gilding, niches without statues, spaces on the wall where once were pictures, betrays to the hasty glance the forlorn condition of the impoverished nobleman. In the ante-chamber, perhaps a throne and canopy of velvet and gold attest the high rank of the family, but its splendor is over-dusted and be-cobwebbed, and from its rickety appearance it looks as if a single vigorous kick would bring it down in a mass of ruin. The custode who shows the apartments is probably an ancient servant of the house — perhaps a faithful Caleb Balderstone — whose faded livery and subdued manner tell a tale of changed fortunes as forcibly as the aspect of the palace itself. This is a form of ruin, not uncommon in Rome, more saddening than fallen columns, broken arches, and shattered pediments. These last are out of the pale of human sympathy, like sarcophagi in an Egyptian pyramid. The men that reared them — that moved about in the buildings of which they formed a part — are mere shadows — hollow names — like Belus, or Ninus, or the brave heroes that lived before Agamemnon. They are nothing to us and we are nothing to them. These ruins of antiquity are no more than pictures, and we judge of them and feel about them as about the ivy that wraps them in its melancholy beauty. It is impossible to waste much compassion on a man who lived two thousand years ago, wore a toga, and had three names ending in *us*. But when a living man is suffering the mortifications of decaying fortune, or the sorrows and annoyances of poverty, whose ancestor two hundred years ago was rich — to see a cobbler mending shoes in rooms where nobles have feasted, and beauty has smiled — beggars taking their stand upon marble staircases — the spider spinning his web upon gilded ceilings — these are ruins which have no compensating or reconciling element. They have neither dignity nor grace: from them neither the poet nor the painter can gather the materials of his art. The sharp compassion which they awaken is unrelieved by glimpses of the heroic or touches of the imaginative.

Many of these palaces contain extensive collections of paintings, arranged usually in show apartments with special reference to exhibition, and the public are admitted to view them, at all reasonable hours, with the utmost liberality, on the payment of a small fee to the custode.

The Palazzo Borghese, a building of immense size, contains the finest private collection of pictures in Rome, upwards of six hundred in number, distributed through nine apartments on the ground-floor. The public are freely admitted, for several hours of every day, to view the collection, and artists are allowed to make copies. In short, every visitor, of decent appearance and decent behavior, can get as much satisfaction out of these pictures as the owner himself. The Borghese family is still rich, and the suite of apartments devoted to the collection is taken good care of. There are some handsome and costly tables of marble distributed through them, and in one of them a little fountain sports and sings — a very pretty plaything for a grown-up child.

Here is a celebrated landscape of Domenichino, the Chase of Diana, well known by Raphael Morghen's engraving. It represents a fine wooded scene with a stream flowing in the foreground. Diana stands in the centre, with hands upraised, holding in one a bow and in the other a quiver, a figure not entirely free from affectation. Of her attendant nymphs, some are sporting in the stream, some are undressing, some are grouped together and shooting their arrows at a bird which is tied to a pole, and one, on the right, a fine, animated figure, is holding back a greyhound by the slip. The composition is studied and skilful, but not always refined, nor in all parts entirely free from academic stiffness. The figures are well drawn, but the draperies, rather mannered. The coloring struck me as very good. The whole air of the picture is fresh, breezy, and joyous, like that of an old English ballad or Chaucer's 'Flower and the Leaf,' and though it can hardly be called an imaginative work, it comes very near being so.

The gem of this collection is the Entombment of Christ, by Raphael, painted by him in his twenty-fourth year. There is considerable difference of opinion as to the merits of this celebrated work. The exclusive admirers of Christian art so called — the disciples of the Pre-Raphaelite school, who value an angular virgin, with limbs that look as if they had been cut out of tin, more than the best forms of Guido or Domenichino — esteem it one of Raphael's highest efforts, and one of the last expressions of his uncorrupted pencil. On the other hand, the more genial and terrestrial critics pronounce it stiff and feeble, at least in comparison with the artist's later works. Rumohr denies to it the merit of pathos, asserts that there is more power and feeling in the original designs preserved at Florence, and doubts whether it was painted entirely by Raphael's hand.* Platner appeals from this harsh sentence with much earnestness, and intimates that it may fairly claim a rank above the Transfiguration or the Madonna di Foligno.† Truth, as usual, will be deemed by the majority of judgments to lie between these extremes. A certain hardness of outline, and a little stiffness in the flow of the drapery, show that in technical skill and mere handling of the pencil, the artist had not reached the full stature of manhood; and there is perhaps some exaggeration in the action. But the figure of the Saviour on the left, borne in the arms of two men, is admirable both in drawing and expression. The fainting Madonna on the right, and the three females who support her, form a touching and pathetic group. The heads and faces are such as Raphael only could have painted; and its combination of dignity with dramatic energy is also peculiarly his own. In the background is a striking landscape, with the Mount of Calvary in the distance.

This picture is painted upon wood, which has been protected on the back by iron sheathing, as it was found to have been gnawed by worms and cracked in two places.

* Italienische Forschungen, Th. iii. p. 60.

† 'Dieses Gemälde gehört unstreitig unter die vortrefflichsten Werke Raphaels; und man könnte geneigt sein ihm den Vorzug vor allen übriger Oelbildern dieses grossen Künstlers in Rom, selbst nicht mit Ausnahme der berühmten Transfiguration und der sogenannten Madonna di Fuligno, zu ertheilen.' — Beschreibung der Stadt Rom. B. iii. Th. 3, p. 285.

In another room is a picture by Titian, whose works are rare in Rome. The subject is allegorical. A fine landscape is bounded on the right by a village and a lake, and, on the left, by a mountain castle. In the foreground is a fountain, near which two female figures are seated, one richly dressed and holding flowers in her gloved hand; the other with only a red scarf over her shoulder, with a cup, or small drinking vessel, in her left hand. Between the two, a young Cupid appears to be reaching after some flowers which have dropped into the fountain. The two female figures are supposed to represent Divine and Earthly Love, but this seems to be by no means a natural or satisfactory explanation, and we should be puzzled to determine which was meant to be the divine, and which, the earthly emblem. Neither of them are celestial in their expression, but both are full of warm, terrestrial life. Whatever be its subject, it has that magic of color so peculiar to Titian, especially in the red scarf and rich carnation tints of the undraped figure, which is also beautiful both in attitude and expression.

In the same room with the Titian is a remarkable portrait, representing a handsome man in the bloom of early manhood, dressed in black, and with a cap and feather also black. It is set down in the catalogue as a portrait of Cæsar Borgia, by Raphael; but probably the artist and the subject are both misnomers. It is certainly not in Raphael's usual style, nor does the face respond to our conceptions of the monster Borgia. It is the face of a handsome, smiling, seductive, unscrupulous man — against whom both men and women would do well to be on their guard — reckless, pleasurable, and inventive — a sort of medieval and Italian Lovelace — but not absolutely a devil incarnate like Cæsar Borgia, the worst character in history, whose name is linked to no virtue and a thousand crimes. It was probably painted by an artist of the Venetian school, perhaps a pupil of Titian, and is an admirable work of art.

The celebrated Danae by Correggio did not please me much. The expression is wanton, the figure lean, and the countenance vapid and simpering. The peculiar fascination of Correggio's manner, his luxurious softness of touch, and his indescribable play of light and shade, are not wanting, but the coloring seems to have been impaired by injudicious cleaning. The two Cupids in front, who are trying the points of their arrows, are charmingly painted.

In the Barberini Palace is the world-renowned portrait of Beatrice Cenci, commonly ascribed to Guido, though on that point, I believe, there is some doubt. At any rate, it is a beautifully painted picture, representing a young and lovely face, wrecked and shattered by storms of suffering. The head-dress is peculiar and rather trying to an artist's power of color, consisting of heavy folds of white cloth wound round the head, from which a few locks of yellowish brown hair escape. There is a deeply touching expression in the eyes, which are large, soft, and lustrous. They look as if they had wept away all their power of tears. The lips are delicate, full of tremulous sensibility; but absolutely rigid and frozen from intense suffering. The outline of the face is fine and the features regular

The portrait represents a young creature of exquisite organization, full of imagination and sensibility, capable of receiving and bestowing happiness in its rarest and finest forms, but out of whom all the life had been pressed by hideous calamity and unspeakable suffering. A sweet, soft, and gentle nature, born to be loved, sheltered, and caressed, is driven to madness, and loses its very essence, from outrage and wrong. It was a lily growing in a garden; an aerolite fell upon it and crushed it to the roots.

The power and pathos of this portrait exceeded my highest expectations. It has been frequently engraved and copied, but no engraving or copy that I have ever seen retains the peculiar character of the original. For many years, no artist has been allowed to copy directly from the picture; and the many transcripts which are found all over the world are but repetitions at second-hand; but, were the rule relaxed, the charm of the original is so delicate and airy as hardly to be brought away by the most skilful pencil.*

* A brief and good account of the Cenci tragedy is contained in the supplement to Michaud's 'Biographie Universelle,' art. CENCI. The character of the father, was more detestable, and his crimes more hideous, than is generally apprehended; but the particular outrage which is supposed to darken his memory was not proved against him. The character of Beatrice was not quite so exalted as, through sympathy with her misfortunes, has been commonly imagined. The motives of the Pope, Clement VIII., have, also, not been fairly stated. He seems to have acted conscientiously, and waited long before signing the fatal sentence; and a part of the family would probably have been pardoned, but that, unhappily, during his deliberations, two cases of parricide

In this palace is also another celebrated picture; a portrait of the Fornarina, by Raphael. It represents a female, naked to the waist, with a turban on her head. The eyes are black and bright, and the countenance has some animal beauty, but an expression the reverse of elevated or intellectual. The arms and bosom are beautifully and carefully painted, but it is not a pleasing work, nor does it represent an attractive person. Some writer has remarked, that a man in choosing his wife should ask himself what are her resources for a rainy day in the country. Judging from her countenance, the Fornarina would seem to be very indifferently supplied with such capacities and accomplishments; in short, an artist's model, a sensual toy, whose power over an intellectual man, if she had any, would be yielded to with something like self-contempt.

In one of the rooms is a magnificent cabinet of wood and carved ivory, of which the central subject is Michael Angelo's Last Judgment, wrought with a minute patience and elaborate skill, which makes the heart ache to look at it. It was the work of two German artists, and is said to have occupied thirty-four years in the execution.

The garden of the Colonna Palace extends along the slope of the Quirinal Hill. It is of moderate extent, planted with ilex, box, and pine, and commanding very pleasing views. Here are many interesting ruins and fragments, especially some vaults of

occurred in the Papal States. This determined him against an act of mercy.

the baths of Constantine now used as granaries, and two enormous masses of marble, belonging to an edifice of the Corinthian order. The building of which they were a part must have been of stupendous magnitude, and have formed a most conspicuous object in so commanding a position, yet nothing is known with certainty upon the subject; and antiquaries can only guess that these colossal fragments fell from the temple of the Sun built by Aurelian.

In the great hall of the Palazzo Colonna, one of the noblest rooms I have ever seen, an amateur concert was given on the fourth day of February, 1848, in aid of the funds of some charitable institution. The prima donna was Mrs. Sartoris, (*neé* Adelaide Kemble), whose voice is fine and rich, and who sang with great taste, feeling, and expression. Two things struck me in her performance. One was the extreme ease of her execution, without the slightest appearance of pulling, straining, or stretching; and the other was the solid good sense of her singing, if I may so apply the phrase. There was not the least nonsense about it. Good sense, if not the foundation of good singing, is an important element in it, and it was as marked a trait in Mrs. Sartoris's singing as it is in her sister, Mrs. Kemble's, reading. None of the other performers were more than respectable. The company, about four hundred in number, was mostly English; a large proportion, ladies, whose fine forms and blooming complexions were well set off by the statues and frescoes of the noble apartment in which they were gathered.

The Palazzo Doria-Pamphili has an immense façade

on the Corso; in which, however, there is nothing to commend but the rich plate-glass in the windows. Here is a very large collection of pictures, but few of first-rate excellence. Two celebrated landscapes of Claude Lorraine are among its most valued treasures. In one, a smiling rural region is depicted, and in the background a stream and a mill; from which it is usually called the Molino. In the other, the sun is reflected from a sea-mirror; in the background, trees are waving; in front and on the right, is a temple into which a procession is passing. When I saw these landscapes, I had not read 'The Modern Painters,' and I admired them heartily and perhaps ignorantly, and though I have since read that most eloquent and original book, I cannot renounce the feeling altogether. Claude's figures are worthless, his foregrounds wanting in distinctness and individuality, and his general transcript of forms incorrect, but the character of his foliage is excellent and his atmospheric effects are matchless. The crisp sparkling and dancing light which he pours over his scenes produces an almost intoxicating effect, and takes away from the eye, for a time at least, the power of perceiving the want of formal accuracy. The author of the 'Modern Painters' is a great writer on art, and when he is wrong, it is often only from pushing right principles to an extreme. His book is a golden book, steeped in the poetry and the religion of art, just in theory and exquisite in spirit, and the young artist should clasp it to his heart and wear it like a phylactery upon his brow, but the author may live to admit that all its vehement and impetuous judgments are not correct.

The Palazzo Farnese, one of the finest palaces in Rome, is a shameless receiver of stolen goods. The stones of which it was built were torn from the Colosseum. The granite basins of the fountains were found in the baths of Caracalla. In the portico of the cortile is a sarcophagus of Parian marble taken from the tomb of Cecilia Metella; a stupid and tasteless act of spoliation, since, in its present condition, it has no appropriateness or significance, but is merely a piece of furniture — a pretty thing to look at; as if the owner of a fine house in Boston should have a monument from Mt. Auburn brought in and put into his entry.

The great hall, or gallery, is painted in fresco by Annibale and Agostino Caracci and their scholars. The subjects are taken from mythology, most of them having reference to the passion of love. The central piece is the Triumph of Bacchus and Ariadne, and among the others are Cephalus and Aurora, Venus and Anchises, Perseus and Andromeda, Hero and Leander, Syrinx and Pan, Polyphemus and Galatea. Eight small subjects over the windows are by Domenichino. About half of Lempriere's Classical Dictionary is painted on the walls and ceiling of the hall; an immense labor which occupied the unbroken toil of eight years, and is said to have been rewarded with the paltry pittance of five hundred scudi! A certain unity and significance are sought to be given to the whole cycle of subjects by four groups at the corners, each of which is composed of two figures, symbolizing celestial and terrestrial Love, represented in various attitudes of struggle, and finally clasped in a reconciling embrace.

These frescoes are very fair representations alike of the powers of the Caracci and of the school of art of which they were the founders. The very name of Eclectic which they adopted, or which was fastened upon them, involves an essential impossibility. Every great and original artist makes use of canvas and colors as instruments to embody certain ideal conceptions. These conceptions are formed according to an innate law of his nature, and they can no more help being what they are than a rose-bush can help bearing roses. To the eye of Michael Angelo, form was the prominent essence of objects; while to that of Titian, the impressions of color superseded all others; and in their paintings each developed his own perceptions. An attempt to combine the form of Michael Angelo with the coloring of Titian, as Tintoretto aspired to do, is simply to aim at an impossibility; like an attempt to combine a man and a horse together and make a centaur. All delineation upon a flat surface, with colors, is an imitation, necessarily more or less imperfect; and if the idea of form is to be so strongly impressed, as is done in the paintings of Michael Angelo, something must be sacrificed in point of color. The artist must make his election, and give up some things, in order to attain others more completely.

The Caracci, living at a period when art had much declined from the height it had attained at the beginning of the sixteenth century, were inspired with a generous ambition to elevate it; and they devoted themselves to this object with great industry and honorable singleness of purpose. But they wanted not only the Promethean touch of genius but also a wide range of general cultivation, and that grace and accomplishment of mind which spring from early liberal training, and the right to mingle freely and on terms of equality with refined and lettered society. Their works, as compared with the works of the best age of art, are like a manufacture as compared with a growth. Their drawing is singularly correct, but wanting in vital power. Raphael seems to have gone about the streets, and whenever he saw a marked and expressive attitude, to have daguerreotyped it upon his brain and reproduced it like a birth. The Caracci appear to have always drawn from an academic model, and not to have improved upon the particular position in which he might have stood. With the former, the idea came first, and forms and groups were used to embody it; but, with the latter, forms and groups were disposed in the hope that out of such a disposition an idea might spring. I have, before, occasionally illustrated painting by literature, and I will here venture to do it again. When we pass from the works of Raphael and Michael Angelo to those of the Caracci, it is like going from Shakespeare's Julius Cæsar to Addison's Cato, or from Spenser's 'Fairie Queene,' and Chaucer's 'Canterbury Tales,' to Wilkie's 'Epigoniad,' or Glover's 'Leonidas.' By this illustration I do not mean to say that there is the same amount of difference in the two cases, for that would be unjust to the Caracci, but merely that the inferiority of the latter is similar in kind.

These observations may be continued further by comparing, for a moment, the subjects of these works with those of the frescoes in the Vatican and Sistine

Chapel. Raphael and Michael Angelo invent such designs as illustrate incidents in religious history, or in the life of the soul, and thus have an unchanging interest to all who have been baptized into the name of Christ. Their works are consequently not merely paintings, but also symbols: they address the soul as well as the eye: they have a vital significance as well as a formal beauty. The Caracci, invited to decorate the residence of a grave ecclesiastic, cover the walls with a profusion of mythological love-stories, which express nothing beyond what they really are. They are not even allegories, but only fables or myths long since dead with the faith that gave them birth. In point of execution, there is certainly great merit in these frescoes: drawing always correct and sometimes powerful, varied grouping, animated movement, and a rich, sober tone of color, neither gay nor sombre. But there is no such grandeur as we bend before in Michael Angelo's prophets, and no such beauty as followed Raphael's inspired pencil. Over the whole, a cold, formal, and academic atmosphere is breathed. We look, we admire, but we turn away and forget. The expression of the heads and faces want individuality. The general character of the groups is meant to express a joyous abandonment to sensuous emotions, but the rich and frolic life which the ancients could put into a bacchanalian procession, sculptured on a frieze, is wanting here. It is a sort of make-believe rapture. Some of the subjects are coarsely treated — Diana and Endymion, for instance. The best thing is the drunken Silenus riding upon an ass, in the Triumph of

Bacchus and Ariadne; and this fact alone, in a composition in which there are so many figures meant to be dignified, and so many meant to be beautiful, involves an emphatic criticism.

The Palazzo Farnesina, the splendid monument of the taste and magnificence of Agostino Chigi, is a pilgrim-shrine in art, because it contains the finest expressions of Raphael's genius when manifesting itself in purely secular forms. It is also a palace well known in what may be called the gossip of history, on account of the luxury and extravagance with which Chigi lived here, during the pontificate of Leo X. The stories which are preserved of his entertainments reveal a sort of insanity of profusion, like the ragout of pearls in the Arabian tale, or the bank-note sandwiches which are said to have been eaten upon wagers. For one of these entertainments, given to the pope and cardinals, an imposing structure, adorned with paintings and other works of art, is said to have been reared in a single night. To grace the board on this occasion, fish were brought alive from France, Spain, and Constantinople, and dishes of parrot's tongues were served up to the guests. And it is even said, that the gold and silver dishes used were carried from the table and thrown into the Tiber, that they might never again be profaned by meaner lips or hands. The madness of this act is lessened, but not its folly, by the testimony of some authorities, who say that nets were carefully spread across the river, so that little of the precious jettison was lost. The building erected for this entertainment was subsequently carried away by an inundation of the Tiber.*

In the large hall of this palace, facing the garden, the ceiling is adorned with frescoes from the story of Cupid and Psyche, designed by Raphael, and executed for the most part by his scholars, under his superintendence. The selection of this most happy subject is a striking proof of the unerring taste and judgment of the great artist. The story, first appearing in the Golden Ass of Apuleius, a writer of the silver age of Roman literature, was not, however, the indigenous growth of the unimaginative Roman mind. Its airy analogies and delicate fancies, without doubt, first grew in the gardens of the East. It is an allegory, typifying, under the form of the love adventures of an immortal god and a mortal maiden, the struggles of the soul in its endeavors to reach spiritual perfection, its conflicts with debasing passions, its purifications by misfortunes, and its final triumph ; but, like the 'Fairie Queene' and the 'Pilgrim's Progress,' the allegory is often forgotten in the narrative, and many incidents are introduced simply for the sake of carrying on the story. Strictly

* These stories are found in Bayle's Dictionary, article 'Chigi,' and in the description of the Farnesina by Platner, in the 'Beschreibung der Stadt Rom.' vol. iii. Th. 3, p. 590, and there the original authorities are given. I confess that such statements seem to me enterprising drafts upon the credulity of posterity, which I, for one, am not disposed to honor. The narrative of this entertainment, as Platner well remarks, is darkened with a tragic interest from its contrast with the horrors to which Rome was soon after exposed through its capture and plunder by the imperial troops.

speaking, it is not so much an allegory, as the record of an allegory. The temptation to illustrate religious sensibility by analogies drawn from the passion of love, is very strong; and religious writers, Catholic as well as Protestant, have often debased their effusions by yielding to it.*

The ceiling of the hall is divided into three kinds of spaces, the flat surface on the top, the curved arches at the sides, and the lunettes between the arches. The flat part of the ceiling is occupied by the two principal compositions completing the cycle of the story; one representing the judgment of the gods, with Jupiter at their head, as to the fate of Psyche, in which Venus and Cupid appear as opposing counsel; and the other, the nuptial feast, after the decision in favor of Psyche, and her reunion with her immortal lover, and when her perishable mortality has been purged away by a draught of nectar. These frescoes have apparent borders, and are seemingly fastened by painted nails, so that the whole has the effect of a piece of tapestry stretched across the ceiling. The arched spaces on the sides are occupied by various incidents in the story. The lunettes between the arches are filled with subjects illustrating the power of love over gods and demigods. Little sportive Cupids, singly or in pairs, carry off in

* An abstract of the story of Cupid and Psyche may be found in Dunlop's History of Fiction, Vol. I. p. 114, (Phil. ed. 1842,) and also in Sir George Head's 'Tour of Many Days in Rome,' Vol. iii. p. 120. It has also been reproduced in various forms by Marino, La Fontaine, Moliere, and Mrs. Tighe.

triumph the thunderbolts of Jupiter, the trident of Neptune, the lance and shield of Mars, the caduceus of Mercury, the club of Hercules, and the hammer of Vulcan. These subjects are enclosed in a graceful framework, composed of flowers, foliage, and fruits.

Raphael's genius, which, in the Vatican, expresses spiritual grandeur and intellectual dignity by ideal forms, in these lovely compositions, arrests and embodies, in forms not less ideal, the most ethereal graces of a poetical mythology. All the fine visions of the golden morning of the world are here, sparkling in their unexhaled dew. They are painted as a Greek might have painted them, who believed in the wonders which he drew. They are no cold transcripts of dead forms: the poetry of Homer is not more vital. The blue sky and luminous air of Greece bend over and idealize every scene and every group. The nymphs that haunted the piny mountains of Arcadia, or danced upon the shores of the whispering Ægean, live once more in the Venus, the Psyche, and the Graces of Raphael. These compositions are remarkable, not only for grace and beauty of design, for truth of expression and for dramatic vivacity, but also for their purity of feeling. No coarse or unhandsome image, like a blot on a fair page, disturbs the satisfaction awakened by such ideal loveliness. This is especially observable in the little *amorini* in the lunettes. They are full of frolic, and seem heartily enjoying the pranks they play and the mischief they do; but their mirth and their movements are both childlike. They dally with the innocence of love, in all the moods and caprices of a sportive fancy.

In technical execution, these compositions are not throughout of uniform excellence. In some portions, critics detect a heaviness of form, which is remarked as characteristic of Giulio Romano. The best groups are, Cupid showing Psyche to the three Graces, which is partly painted by Raphael's own hand; Cupid complaining to Jupiter of the cruelty of his mother, and receiving from him a kiss in token of good will; and Mercury carrying Psyche to Olympus. As to the color of the original composition, no judgment can be formed. As the arcades of the apartment next to the garden were originally open, the frescoes soon began to suffer from the damp occasioned by the proximity of the Tiber, and in the time of Carlo Maratta, they underwent a careful restoration under his directions, in the course of which they were almost entirely repainted. The arcades were then glazed.

In an adjoining apartment is an earlier fresco by Raphael, not inferior in invention and superior in execution, since nearly all of it was painted by his own hand — the Triumph of Galatea. In this charming composition, this daughter of the sea is borne over the waves in a shell drawn by two dolphins, surrounded by tritons and nereids, while *amorini* flutter in the air above her head and look down upon her with beaming smiles. The face of Galatea is one of the most beautiful ever painted. It seems to glow with the delicious emotions of new-born-love, with which the figure appears also to be almost winged. All the subordinate and attendant forms are instinct with the most graceful life and the most jubilant movement. It is a picture made of youth, beauty, sunbeams, and smiles. It is so full of truth and reality, that one almost forgets that it is all a dream, more unsubstantial than the shadow of smoke. We look upon it as if it were the record of an actual transaction; as if that lovely face had been really convulsed with grief over the mangled form of her murdered Acis. Glowing and luxuriant as the tone of the composition is, it is treated with perfect delicacy of feeling, and its sweetness and grace have no taint of the meretricious.

In one of the lunettes of this apartment is a colossal head in charcoal, said to have been struck off at a heat by Michael Angelo. Some traditions report that this great artist, going to call upon Daniele da Volterra, who was at work there, and not finding him, left this sketch as a sort of visiting card; others, that he drew it by way of admonishing Raphael to paint thereafter in a grander and broader style than he had done in the Galatea. Platner, with that inexorable scepticism so characteristic of the Germans, shakes his head in doubt over the whole story — says that the head is not worthy of Michael Angelo's pencil, and that the incident is not mentioned by any contemporary writer. I do not presume either to support or to controvert his judgment as to the merits of the work, but can only say that I recall it as a powerful and expressive head. The tradition may or may not be trustworthy. It is certainly true that there are many floating stories about artists, which are copied without inquiry from one book into another, but which rest upon no authority whatever, and are generally the absolute fabrications of some wonder-monger. It seems to me quite likely that Michael Angelo — supposing the head to be his work

— meant to express the tragical catastrophe of that mythological drama which opened so smilingly in Raphael's fresco, and that this was the grim countenance of Polyphemus scowling upon the beautiful being whose favor he could not win. The two together also represent most happily the contrasted images in the famous passage of Gray. On one side are the fair laughing morn, and the softly blowing zephyrs, the azure realm, the gilded vessel, 'youth on the prow and pleasure at the helm;' and, on the other, the embodied whirlwind, 'that hushed in grim repose expects his evening prey.'

In the Palazzo Spada is a remarkable colossal statue, well known not only for its intrinsic merit as a work of art, but for the controversies to which it has given birth as to whom it represents. It is generally admitted to be a statue of Pompey, and perhaps the very one at the base of which 'great Cæsar fell.' On this last point, the evidence is quite sufficient to allow a willing faith to rest upon it; and in such cases faith is always willing. It is about nine feet high, undraped, with the exception of a short chlamys hanging over the left shoulder and arm. In the extended left hand is a globe, with the remains of a figure, probably a victory, upon it. The right arm is a restoration. The expression of the head and face is stern, but not elevated or intellectual; corresponding to the character of Pompey, a mere soldier, with very questionable claims to the title of Great, bestowed upon him by his countrymen. This statue was found entire, with the exception of the right arm; yet the head had evidently been separated from the trunk, and seems not to have been that which originally belonged to it. During the

French occupation of Rome, Voltaire's tragedy of Brutus was acted in the Colosseum; and this statue was transported there, that the mock Cæsar might fall at the foot of the real statue — though in doing this, it was necessary to saw off the restored right arm * — a piece of dramatic enthusiasm, like that of the London manager who, to give due effect to a melo-drama founded upon the murder of Weare, introduced into one of the scenes the very horse and gig which belonged to him.

In this palace there is also a tolerable collection of pictures. Among them is a beautiful female portrait with a black veil over the head, not noticed in the guide-books, two pretty, laughing heads ascribed to Correggio, and a portrait of Paul III., by Titian, looking like an old monkey. In the cortile is a curious piece of architectural jugglery — a covered portico with Doric columns, gradually diminishing in height, thus enhancing the real effect of the perspective. The success of the experiment is quite complete, for, though only about thirty feet in length, the portico seems to the eye to be at least twice as long; and, after walking through it and ascertaining its exact dimensions, we feel a little as if we had been imposed upon, somewhat in the same mood as when

* Platner relates a curious anecdote in regard to the statue. In 1812, Fea, the antiquary, published a pamphlet in which he maintained that it was a statue of Domitian, and not of Pompey; but there was no doubt that, in point of fact, this was contrary to his real opinion, and put forth to disparage the statue, for the purpose of preventing its threatened removal to Paris. — Beschreibung der Stadt Rom. vol. iii. Th. 3, p. 448.

we learn that our compassion has been roused by a feigned tale of distress.

In the casino of the garden attached to the Palazzo Rospigliosi is the celebrated fresco by Guido, representing Aurora scattering flowers before the chariot of the Sun. This beautiful work is full of life and movement. The forms are carefully drawn, and the character of the heads is soft and graceful, without marked individuality, and sometimes bordering upon insipidity. The figure representing the Sun has a little foppery in the expression, and there is a sort of theatrical strut in the attitude and movements of some of the Hours, which seems to demand our admiration and insist upon it. The color is vivid and brilliant, though the blue, both of the sky and the sea, is rather cold and hard. The distant landscape lying below and slowly struggling out of darkness, is happily conceived. This fresco is much the finest work of Guido out of Bologna, and is quite worthy of his often abused genius in its best mood. It is one of the most popular subjects in art, and has every where been made known by the admirable engraving of Raphael Morghen. It is painted on the ceiling, and though at a moderate height from the floor, cannot be long examined without vigorous remonstrances from certain muscles of the neck called upon to do very unusual work. There were several copies lying about the room, of various sizes, most of which could hardly be called tolerable.

In the adjoining rooms are several pictures in oil, by Domenichino, Ludovico Caracci, Guido, Daniele da Volterra, and others, deserving more attention than they usually receive in so trying a neighborhood. Here is also an antique bust of Scipio Africanus in green basalt, a fine expressive head, admirably wrought and remarkable for having a representation of a scar on the forehead.

What is called the garden of this palace is a small enclosure with a simple fountain in the centre, laid out in flower-beds divided by gravel walks, with trailing plants and lemon-trees along the walls. I was there on a warm sunny day in the latter part of January, and even then the breath of spring was on the breeze. Hardy roses were blooming in the open air, and the mignionette and the early violets had begun to diffuse their modest odors. The bright fountain, the vivid sunshine, and the rich green made up a living picture more glowing even than the Aurora of Guido. In sheltered spots in Rome there is hardly such a thing known as winter. No month is without its flowers — the orange and lemon-trees, the box, the ilex, and the laurel always retain their green life; and every sunny noon calls out the lizards from their retreat.

In the Palazzo Sciarra is an excellent collection of pictures. The most celebrated among them is the portrait by Raphael, known by the name of Il Suonatore, from the bow of a violin, crowned with laurel, held in the hand of the figure. The original is not known. This is one of the best portraits that ever have been painted. There are no masses of pulpy, boneless flesh, no chalky lights and snuffy shadows, no running of one feature into another, no attempt to get a staring likeness by seizing upon one or two prominent characteristics and letting the rest go; but every thing is distinctly rendered, and the whole is animated by a living soul, which looks out of the deep-set eyes, plays round the firm lips, and reposes on the intellectual brow.

Here is also a well-known picture ascribed to Leonardo da Vinci, containing two female figures in half length, and known by the name of Vanity and Modesty, though there seems to be no particular propriety in that appellation. Mrs. Jameson suggests that the subject is 'Mary Magdalene rebuked by her sister Martha for her vanity and luxury.' One of the figures is veiled, and the other has a smiling, unconcerned look. It is very elaborately and delicately painted and richly colored.

Here, too, is one of the many repetitions of Caravaggio's Cheating Gamesters; a picture of much expression and considerable merit in its way. There is great force and character in all the heads, and the coloring is bright and clear, free from the charcoal shadows and chalky lights which so often characterize the works of this grim and sombre artist.

The Villa Ludovisi, though its grounds are a mile in circumference, is within the walls of Rome. Its owner, Prince Piombino, forms an exception to the general rule of Italian liberality; for he does not open his gates to the universal public, but permits his villa to be seen only upon his written permission, not always readily obtained. The principal building, inhabited by the prince, is not shown. A smaller structure, or casino, is appropriated to sculpture; and it contains one of the finest private collections in Rome. Here is the celebrated colossal bust of Juno, one of the noblest works of antiquity. When seen from the proper point of view, the grandeur of the head and the sublimity of the expression are beyond all praise. She is the only goddess I have ever seen. The others of her class are women, some beautiful, some majestic, some graceful, but still, women. There is a tranquil, passionless serenity in the brow and lips — 'the depth and not the tumult of the soul' — which seem brought from a region undisturbed by mortal emotions and mortal changes.

A beautiful group, supposed by Winckelmann to represent Orestes recognised by his sister Electra, belongs to the best age of Grecian art. The expression is that of deep and tender feeling, without extravagance or caricature; quite worthy of the poetry of Sophocles which it illustrates.

In the same collection is a painfully affecting group, in figures of colossal size. A man is represented as stabbing himself with a sword in his right hand, while he supports with his left a woman dying, and sunk down upon her knees. The group has been called by many names, but it probably represents a barbarian killing himself and his wife, to avoid being carried into slavery. Such a subject, if tolerably well executed, has a certain power over the feelings; but as a work of art, the group did not seem to me of very great merit, nor to have been executed in the best periods of sculpture. Indeed, the choice of so harrowing a subject is inconsistent with that calmness and repose which the Greek sculptors regarded as so essential to their art.

A group of Pluto and Proserpine, by Bernini, has the characteristic merits and defects of this artist. Its violent action and theatrical expression are in strong contrast to the works around it.

In a smaller building, in another part of the grounds, upon the ceiling of the ground-floor, is Guercino's fresco of Aurora. The goddess is in a car drawn by two piebald horses. Two winged figures are near her; one holding a wreath, and the other, a basket of flowers. Female forms representing, according to some explanations, the Hours, and according to others, the Stars, appear to flee before her coming. Tithonus behind the car follows its progress with his eyes. It is a very expressive work, remarkable for its bold relief, and for its powerful coloring in Guercino's peculiar style; but it has not the life and charm of Guido's similar composition. In one of the lunettes is Day, or the Dawn, represented as a youth with flowers in one hand and a torch in the other. Opposite is Night, a female figure sleeping, with two sleeping children, and a bat and owl. This last is a beautiful composition, full of the languor and sweetness of a tropical night.

After the powers of attention had been so severely tried by these works of sculpture and painting, it was a great relief to escape into the garden and recreate the exhausted faculties with sunshine, fresh air, fountains, trees, and flowers. The garden itself, however, is a work of art, and is said to have been laid out by Le Notre, by whom the park and grounds of Versailles were designed. It is an admirable specimen of that formal and stately style of gardening which is not without its charm. The long, broad alleys are scrupulously neat, and, overshadowed as they are by magnificent trees, they present those fine, converging lines of perspective, which combine in some measure the beauty of architecture with the beauty of nature. Such walks seem to require living figures appropriate to their peculiar style. A stately lady in full dress should come pacing down them with swan-like step — a greyhound by her side — and a peacock should expand his gorgeous plumage upon a balustrade.

There are many statues scattered over the grounds, which are in excellent condition, and evidently well attended to. There are also a conservatory, a grotto, and a dairy-house. The latter is newly built, but the outside is painted so as to represent ruin and dilapidation; so that at a little distance it looks, on a cursory glance, like a building falling to pieces and gone to decay — an odd and rather poor conceit.

The entrance to the Villa Borghese is just beyond the Porta del Popolo. The grounds, which are three miles in circuit, are thrown open to the public as freely as if they belonged to it. At all times, numerous parties will be found availing themselves of this generous privilege, some in carriages, some on horseback, but mostly on foot; for, as a place of resort, it is more popular with persons of modest condition among the Romans than with the favored classes. This liberality on the part of Prince Borghese is the general rule in Rome, and is one of the many reasons which make that city so delightful a place of residence to strangers. The magic word 'forestiere,' is an 'open sesame' at which all doors fly apart and all bolts are drawn aside. It was pleasant to note that the hospitality of the prince was never abused. Often as I was there, I never saw the smallest act of spoliation or indecorum. Every one seemed to feel that the bounty thus extended involved a corresponding obligation, and comported himself accordingly.

In these extensive grounds, every variety of taste will find its appropriate gratification. They contain many remains of ancient art scattered through them — such as sepulchral monuments, vases, statues whole or broken, and bas-reliefs — a temple, a hippodrome, or circus, a mock ruin, a pretty lake near the entrance, with a mimic waterfall, the delight of children indigenous and exotic, and two or three fountains. The sketcher and the lover of nature will be attracted by the rich masses of oak and laurel, the lines of funereal cypresses, and the broad-spreading canopies of the stone pine. At appropriate hours of the day, especially on Sunday, the middle classes of Rome, the characteristic portion of its population, are largely represented here, and he, who is interested in marking the minute shades of difference which distinguish one portion of Christian and civilized man from another, will here meet with large opportunities for observing the manners and habits of these frank and amiable people. For the recluse and self-withdrawn there are regions of solitude and seclusion where the silence is primeval; broken only by the hum of an insect or the chirp of a bird. As the grounds are so extensive, and as they are also blighted with the curse of malaria, a large portion of them is left undisturbed by the hand of man. The tree grows as it will, the leaves rot where they fall and mingle with the soil, and the grass is thick and matted together; and the American, in the pleasure-grounds of a prince, dim with the shadows of a remote antiquity, is not unfrequently reminded of the untrodden forests of his own land.*

The principal building, or casino, is rich in works of sculpture, and is also well worth visiting from the number and size of the apartments, their fine proportions, and the taste and splendor with which they are embellished. Combining as it does so much beauty with the means of securing coolness in warm weather, such as ample spaces, wide staircases, marble floors, and lofty ceilings, it is unfortunately uninhabitable in summer and autumn from malaria; and is not used except as a show-place or museum, kept up for the benefit of the public. In winter, the apartments, especially those on the first floor, are like an ice-house from dampness and cold, and only to be visited by an invalid with great precaution.

The floor of the principal saloon, or hall, is occupied in part by large pieces of mosaic, found upon an estate belonging to the family, in the neighborhood of Tivoli, in 1835. The drawing and workmanship are inferior, and show it to have been executed in the decaying periods of art. The subjects are fights between men and animals. The names of the combatants are designated by letters. Though of little or no value as a work of art, the mosaic is curious as an illustration of costume and manners. Upon the upper part of the wall, opposite the entrance, is a colossal group in relief, representing Marcus Curtius precipitating himself into the

* This is a description of the grounds as they were. They are now sadly changed, having suffered great injury during the recent French invasion.

gulf in the Forum. In this magnificent room, which is decorated with equal taste and splendor, are many fine statues and busts; among the latter, those of the twelve Cæsars by modern hands. In the gallery, a finely decorated apartment which communicates with the saloon, is a series of busts of Roman emperors, in porphyry, with alabaster draperies, resting on columns of red granite. They are by modern hands and of good workmanship; but the strong contrasts of color which they present degrade sculpture into mere decorative furniture.

In one of the upper rooms is a very remarkable marble group, by Bernini, of Apollo and Daphne. It represents the moment when the flying nymph is seized by the god, and is already beginning to be transformed into a laurel. The upraised hands are terminated by twigs and leaves instead of fingers. The feet are rooted in the ground, and the whole of the lower part of the form is barked about and enveloped in foliage in a manner wonderful to look at and difficult to describe. The face, thrown back, breathes the repose of death. Apollo, a light, graceful figure, is in eager pursuit, with arms outstretched, and drapery flying back from the rapidity of his movement.

In mere technical dexterity and mechanical skill, this group excels any thing of the kind I have ever seen. It is a miracle of manipulation. It is such a work as would, beforehand, have been pronounced an absolute impossibility; and, as it is, we look at it with a sort of incredulous wonder as if there must be some trick about it, and it could not be what it purports to be. The manner in which the flesh passes away into foliage is something quite indescribable, and remains a mystery after careful examination. Such a work would have been esteemed very remarkable if cut out of pine wood, but, wrought as it is in marble, it appears rather the result of magic than of mortal tools and fingers.

In the same apartment are two other works of Bernini, David with a sling, and Æneas carrying Anchises, both of considerable merit. These, and the Apollo and Daphne, were all executed by him between his fifteenth and eighteenth year; an instance of precocity in sculpture quite without parallel, and at least equal to that of Chatterton in poetry. These statues show the natural vigor of his genius, as many of his later works give proof of the false direction which it took under the influence of bad taste and corrupting patronage. Had the path in which his powers moved been as true as their moving impulse was strong, he would have surpassed every name in modern sculpture, except that of Michael Angelo. When we turn from these works of the Villa Borghese to the clumsy fountain in the Piazza Navona, the bronze covering of the chair of St. Peter's, and the vile statue of Sta. Theresa in the Church of Sta. Maria della Vittoria, it is difficult to imagine that they all proceeded from the same mind; still less, that the works done in the green tree should so far surpass those done in the dry.

'Cœpisti melius quam desinis; ultima primis
Cedunt: dissimilis quam hic vir et ille puer.'

In another room of the upper suite, is Canova's celebrated statue of the Princess Pauline Borghese, which has only been shown to the public within a comparatively recent period, and which enjoys a certain factitious interest from its supposed history, beyond that which its intrinsic merits, as a work of art, can claim. The statue is in a recumbent posture, reclining on a couch, which is also sculptured out of marble, and the upper part of the person is supported by marble cushions. The costume, with the exception of a very light scarf, is that of Eve before the fall, and there is a consciousness of nakedness in the air and expression which obtrudes the fact offensively upon the attention. Its merits appeared to me to consist rather in the satin-like softness and polish given to the surface of the marble, than in the grace or proportions of the figure. The subject, too, was of a kind calculated to bring out rather the shadows than the lights of Canova's genius.

The Villa Albani is situated a short distance beyond the Porta Salaria, upon a broad thoroughfare which forms one of the most agreeable promenades in the neighborhood of Rome. The national pride of a Roman would probably select this villa as the one most worthy to be commended to a stranger's admiration, from its combining, in the highest perfection, all the elements most sought and valued in these suburban structures. The principal villa with its portico and wings, the billiard-room, and summer-house, form a group of buildings, beautifully situated upon a gentle eminence, commanding a varied and extensive view of the Campagna and the Sabine Hills; and, though not impervious to criticism in particular details, the whole combination, when seen under the bright illumination of an Italian sun, and relieved by the splendid panorama around it, forms one of the most smiling, airy, and graceful architectural pictures it is possible to look upon. Nor is the enchantment which distance lends dissipated upon a nearer view. Built in the middle of the last century, which is only yesterday in Rome, its whole aspect is youthful and fresh; without disfeature and without decay. Every thing is on a scale of consistent magnificence. An unrivalled collection of works of art is lodged in spacious apartments, richly but not gaudily decorated. The elaborate gardens are not abandoned to neglect, and thus permitted to lose their distinctive character without gaining the unbought charm of the natural landscape. The villa is at once a rich museum and an attractive abode, and presents a combination of splendor and comfort which would meet the different requisitions of an Italian prince and an English nobleman.

The collection of the Villa Albani is confined to works of sculpture, and in number and value ranks next to those of the Vatican and the Capitol. Several of the apartments are ornamented with fresco paintings, which are pleasing specimens of decorative embellishment, but of no great value as works of art. As the statues, busts, vases, and bas-reliefs of this collection are some hundreds in number, and as I never had an opportunity of visiting it but once, and then was hurried through the rooms in company with a numerous party, by an impatient custode, it is quite impossible for me to speak of its treasures except in general terms of admiration. The bas-relief of Antinous crowned with lotus flowers, which Murray calls 'the gem of the collection,' is a very beautiful work — the marble polished almost to metallic brightness, and the face wearing that peculiar expression of voluptuous melancholy, so common in the busts and statues of Antinous. I also remember an admirable statue in bronze, the Apollo Sauroctonos; an exquisite bas-relief, representing the marriage of Peleus and Thetis; a noble statue of Minerva; a curious and lifelike statue of a female satyr in the billiard-room; and a bust of Æsop in the coffee-house, very ugly but very intellectual.

The gardens of the Villa Albani are of moderate extent, but very elaborately laid out with terraces, balustrades, and flights of steps, adorned with busts, statues, and vases, and sparkling with fountains. From the arena in front of the casino a flight of steps leads to the first level, and from this, another flight conducts to the second. Formal beds of flowers are laid out and kept with care; and the usual appendages of such gardens — borders of box, smoothly swept walks, and trees ranged in rectangular rows — are not wanting. As these grounds of the Villa Albani are a favorable specimen of the Italian style of gardening, so called, a few words of explanation on this point may not be out of place.

There are but two styles of laying out gardens, or, more properly, pleasure-grounds; one, English, and one, Italian: whatever changes have been introduced in other countries are but modifications of these two systems. The difference in them is the result mainly of differences in climate, and of consequent diversity of habits and tastes. The Englishman, living in a climate of uniform coolness, is led to form habits of active exercise, and he delights to surround his dwelling-place with as much land as his means will allow, so that his walks and rides may be as extensive as possible. His house becomes only a small part of the landscape, and he brings the greenness and wildness of nature as near as possible to his very door. He disposes of his trees and shrubs in such a way as to banish the idea of formality, and to create the impression that they have been sown by the hand of Nature herself. Living under a gray and overclouded sky, where lights and shadows rapidly alternate, and gleams of watery sunshine fall in broken fragments, he is obliged to forego the sudden contrasts of broad masses of light and shade, and to seek that general effect, the combination of many particulars, which requires a large space to be produced. The moisture of the English climate is also highly favorable to the growth of trees and shrubs, and is the immediate cause of that exquisite verdure which is the great charm of an English landscape. A lawn can only be seen in perfection in England; and it is not surprising that an embellishment so refreshing to the eye, and always so attainable, should form an essential part in English pleasure-grounds. On the other hand, the Italian, living in a hot climate, does not fall into habits of bodily activity. Long walks or rides are not tempting to him, and, for a portion of the year, at least, are quite out of the question. His purpose in laying out his grounds is to enlarge his house. He seeks to be led into the open air by insensible gradations and unobserved intervals. His garden is to a considerable extent an architectural creation. His terraces and balustrades form rooms in the open air, without walls or roof. Not having a certain portion of the day appropriated to exercise, he seeks to secure the power of going into the open air, when the humor may seize him, without being exposed to observation. The powerful sun which burns up his grass creates a necessity for shade, and, instead of distributing his trees in clumps over a lawn, he plants them in rectangular rows, so that by the meeting of their branches they may make a sun-proof canopy. As the light falls in monotonous sheets from a cloudless and dazzling sky, he contrives by salient projections, by walls, vases, balustrades, statues, and by thick-foliaged trees like pines and cypresses, to produce strong shadows, and thus modify the general glare. For the same reason — the prevalence of heat and sunshine — fountains are added — if not to cool the air, to awaken dreams of coolness and refresh the thoughts if not the senses. The English writers upon the subject have not dealt quite fairly with Italian landscape gardening, nor judged of it with reference to the ends proposed to be accomplished by it. Their groves nodding at groves — their fraternal alleys — their formal walls of verdure, are not caricatures of Nature, introduced from a perverse preference of what is quaint and fantastic, but simply such a direction and use of the energies of Nature as shall produce certain results which are required by the climate, and which shall so blend with the features of the palace or villa, as to produce an architectural whole.

The Villa Albani has an interest in the history of art from its association with the name of Winckelmann, who resided there more or less for several years, in the capacity of librarian to Cardinal Albani. The relation between them was honorable to both parties, and is an instance of patronage, extended and received, without unreasonable exactions on the one side, or degrading subserviency on the other. The liberality of the cardinal was directed by the taste and knowledge of Winckelmann, whilst with the command of the cardinal's resources and the sense of security and mental self-possession given by his delicate generosity, the researches of Winckelmann were prosecuted under the most favorable conditions, and led to most successful results. It is a happy combination, when the streams of wealth are thus guided by the hands of genius and taste: they are sure to bring beauty and fertility in their train.

I visited this villa on the twenty-second day of February, with a numerous party, prepared to enjoy and not to criticise. The day was of rare beauty, and the air full of that dreamy softness so characteristic of an Italian spring. The distant hills stood up in the clear air, with their waving outlines distinctly cut against the warm, blue sky. The sunshine turned the spray of the fountains into a substance dazzling as itself. Many flowers were already in bloom, and the day was warm enough to make the shadows attractive to the eye, and the sound of flowing and falling water musical to the ear. All of the party would have frankly confessed, I think, that the charm of the garden outweighed that of the collection. We lingered often and long, sometimes over a knot of violets, sometimes by a fountain, sometimes on the brink of a fairy lake to look at the mimic heaven reflected in its depths, sometimes under a tent-like roof of foliage; and we left the scene with slow steps and oft-reverted glances.

The Villa Pamphili-Doria, beyond the Porta S. Pancrazio, is the most extensive of all the Roman villas; the grounds being nearly six miles in circumference. The principal building I never visited, and I believe it contains nothing very remarkable. The grounds around it form a very attractive place of resort, to which strangers are freely admitted at all reasonable hours. They are laid out with terraces, clipped avenues, walks of box, and formal beds of flowers; but the artificial character gradually disappears, and, in the more distant portions, the growth of bushes and trees is careless and natural. The surface of the soil is irregular, rising into elevations and depressed into valleys. From an open space, at no great distance from the casino, is one of the finest views of St. Peter's and the Vatican. The unsightly façade is on the other side and out of the way: the whole height of the church from the base to the dome, is taken in at a glance; and the dome itself puts on its grandest and sublimest aspect.

Within the grounds is an artificial lake, ornamented by statues and a mimic waterfall. The banks of this lake, on one side at least, are varied in surface and covered with what seems a natural growth of trees and underwood; and a pleasanter spot to dream away an hour in cannot be found in the neighborhood of Rome. The reverie inspired by the genius of the place will rarely be broken by the approach of human footsteps, but the falling water and the rustling foliage will supply sound and movement enough to awaken a sense of companionship, and quicken the flow of thought.

But the finest ornament of these grounds is a noble grove of pines — lofty and venerable — whose spreading tops are so interwoven as to form a plain of sombre verdure high in the air. Beneath, the ground is covered with the fallen spikes of foliage, and, what with the weird aspect of the old trunks, and the brown shadows, dark even in the blaze of noon, it is a ghostly tabernacle, suggesting the gloomy superstitions of the north and the grim rites of Druids, rather than the smiling myths of Greece and Italy. These pines are so high, and the ground on which they stand so elevated, that they form a conspicuous feature in the landscape, visible far and wide, especially from the Monte Pincio.

The Villa Madama, which derives its name from its having been the property of Margaret of Austria, daughter of Charles V., is outside of the walls, on the southern slope of Monte Mario. It was built from the designs of Raphael, and completed by his pupils after his death. In the interior are a frieze and ceiling painted in fresco by Giulio Romano, with representations of mythological subjects. Its finest architectural feature is the loggia, an open portico, with a roof divided into arched compartments and terminated by a semicircular vault, the whole decorated, if I remember right, with fast-fading frescoes of figures and arabesques.

From the Villa Madama to the Villa Melini, which crowns the summit of the hill, there is a woodland path, nearly lost in a tangled growth of shrubbery and underwood. The sturdy branches meet above one's head, and the matted vines and bushes, especially a thorn-bearing creeper, like the smilax, present a wall of resistance not easily overcome. There was nothing that gave any token that man's hand had ever been here, or that his foot had ever passed by the spot. And all this within a mile of St. Peter's!

The Villa Melini is beautifully situated, and commands a fine view of Rome, in some respects the finest that can be seen from any point. The chief ornament of the grounds is a noble walk of venerable cypresses, which look old enough to have bent over the musing steps of Raphael and Michael Angelo.*

About five miles from Rome, on the road to Ostia, is the Villa Magliana, a castellated building of somewhat striking aspect, with battlemented walls and a tower. The court-yard, adorned with a fountain, is entered through an imposing portal. Inscriptions upon the fountains and walls recall the names of Innocent VIII., and of Julius II., by whom the villa was built, and with whom it was a favorite place of resort. Leo X. was also fond of it, and it is said that his death was caused by a cold caught here. In one of the rooms, originally a chapel, are some frescoes by Raphael, or at least ascribed to him, and, so far as their merit can be discerned in their faded and ruined state, not unworthy of his genius. One of them represents God the Father surrounded by a glory of cherubim; and the other, the Martyrdom of Sta. Felicitas.† Through the latter, some inconceivable Vandal has caused a window to be cut.

* A pine-tree in the grounds of the Villa Melini, conspicuous from its size and solitary position, is said to have been saved from the axe to which it was doomed, by the liberality of the late Sir George Beaumont; an incident commemorated by Wordsworth in one of his sonnets.

† Mrs. Jameson says Sta. Cecilia.

This villa, once the luxurious retreat of popes, is fallen from its high estate, and is no more than a humble farm-house. Its spacious rooms were filled with grain and other agricultural produce. Men in the garb of common laborers were lounging about; the court-yard was littered with straw and filth; and barn-door fowls were pecking and scratching around the fountain. Though I was there on a bright morning in spring, nothing could be more unattractive than the whole aspect of the place and its immediate neighborhood. The Tiber flowed near by through a monotonous country, and the dreary plains beyond presented nothing of interest to the eye.*

The Villa Torlonia, about a mile beyond the Porta Pia, belongs to the great banker who taxes all the world that comes to Rome. The casino is a Grecian structure of some architectural pretension, but with the appearance of having been hastily and slightly built. The interior, with a singular disregard of the requisitions of a Roman climate, is cut up into a multitude of small, low rooms, which are lavishly adorned with costly marbles and mosaics, and with frescoes which are not exactly good, but undoubtedly the best that money can buy. Compared with the noble apartments, the spacious corridors, and the stately terraces of the Villa Albani, the general effect is poor and mean. The large hall is a showy room, with marble columns and

* The frescoes of the Villa Magliana have been engraved by Lewis Gruner, an admirable interpreter of the genius of Raphael, who is engaged upon a series of plates from the cartoons at Hampton Court, which will undoubtedly do full justice to these great works, at least more than has yet been done.

a mosaic copied from one at Palestrina, representing an inundation of the Nile. In a building in the garden is a theatre, quite pretty and tasteful in its arrangements, and large enough to accommodate an audience of eight hundred or a thousand persons. In the grounds, which are not very extensive, are a great variety of objects — an artificial ruin, two granite obelisks, a column, fountains, an amphitheatre, a Gothic stable, and a grotto with artificial stalactites. Wealth has been lavished with the most reckless profusion, but the expenditures of good taste have been upon a very parsimonious scale. There is a want of harmony, fitness, and proportion. Discordant objects are huddled together, as in the landscapes of a china teacup ; and the whole effort suggests the combination of the wealth of a millionaire and the tastes of a cockney. The villa is not completed, or was not, at the time of my visit. Many workmen were busy in different parts of the grounds, and the unfinished buildings, and the extensive excavations in the soil, presented an aspect quite rare in the latitude of Rome, where man seems to have given up work, and to have nothing left to do but to fold his hands and look on.

CHAPTER XIII.

Obelisks — Fountains — The Castle of St. Angelo — Historical Houses in Rome — Campana's Museum — The College of the Propaganda — The Protestant Burying-ground—Valley of Egeria.

OBELISKS.

The standard of antiquity is set backward, as the traveller moves towards the east. The scale of France and Germany is fixed at an earlier date than that of England. The mediæval structures of Northern Italy are younger than the classical remains of Rome. These last are of later growth than the ruined temples of Magna Græcia and Sicily. The Parthenon is a birth of yesterday, compared with the Pyramids; and now the Pyramids seem called upon to bow their venerable heads and acknowledge the older claims of Nineveh.

But the remote past — the infancy of the world — has sent its representatives to Rome, that this wonderful city might be wanting in nothing venerable and impressive. Of the eleven Egyptian obelisks which are such conspicuous objects in the scenery of Rome, three, at least, are of an origin prior to the conquest of Egypt by Cambyses. That of the Piazza del Popolo, which is the oldest, is of the age of Moses, and those of Monte Citorio and St. John Lateran are not much younger. The obelisk of the Vatican, though without hieroglyphics, is, according to Champollion, to be referred to the reign of the successor of the great Sesostris, fourteen centuries before Christ.* That before Sta. Maria Maggiore, and that on the Monte Cavallo, are plain shafts, without hieroglyphics, and were probably hewn from the quarries of Egypt while that country was under the Roman rule. The five others, which are covered with hieroglyphics, and stand, respectively, in the Piazza Navona, near the Church of Sta. Maria sopra Minerva, on the Trinità de' Monti, near the Pantheon, and on the Monte Pincio, are supposed to belong to the dynasty of the Ptolemies. All the Roman obelisks are of red granite, a material, both in grain and color, extremely well adapted to such forms. That of St. John Lateran is the largest, the shaft being upwards of a hundred feet high; but it is broken in three pieces. Those of Sta. Maria Maggiore and of the Piazza del Popolo, which are the next largest, are also broken in several places. Of those which are unbroken, that of the Vatican is much the largest. The four last named were all erected by Fontana during the pontificate of Sixtus V.

These obelisks, with hardly a single exception, are well placed, and in harmonious relations with the objects around them.† That of the Vatican and that of the

* Beschreibung der Stadt Rom. B. 2, Th. 1, p. 156.

† To this remark there is at least one exception. The obelisk which is near the Church of Sta. Maria sopra Minerva, is placed on the back of a marble elephant — one of Bernini's offences against good taste.

Piazza del Popolo are the happiest in their position and locality, for each is the central point in an open and level space, — so that the eye can do full justice to its height and proportions. The impression which they make upon the mind is in unity with the gravity and melancholy of Rome itself. Such structures would not suit a merchants' exchange, or a place of gay resort; but in Rome there is neither business nor gaiety. They are architectural pilgrims that speak to us of the wonders of an older land; and the hieroglyphics carved upon them are sermons in an unknown tongue, upon the changes of time and the fleeting character of all things under the sun. Brought from a conquered country to swell the triumphs of the mistress of the earth, they have lived to see the land into which they were borne suffer the same decline, and fall into the same decay, as that from which they came. The power which hewed them from the quarry, and the power which transplanted them, are alike in the past; and their testimony comes enforced with the weight of two experiences.

There is a striking fact about these obelisks, that though by far the oldest structures in Rome, they are not by any means ruins. Their edges are sharp, and the characters carved upon them are as legible as ever. Their form, and the hardness of their material, seem to have defied the destructive agencies alike of nature and of man. No bronze or iron could be extracted from them; they could not be burned into lime, and were not worth breaking up to build into palaces. The circle of architecture began with the pyramids and obelisks of Egypt, and with them it is likely to close. If Rome should ever become what Palmyra now is, a naked and melancholy waste, its obelisks will probably form the most conspicuous objects in the sketches which the accomplished traveller from Australia or New Zealand will carry home for the amusement of his friends.

FOUNTAINS.

In two essential elements of social civilization, the ancient Romans have never been equalled. They constructed the most durable roads, and made the most liberal provisions for a copious supply of water. The nine aqueducts which, in the time of Frontinus, poured their streams into Rome, furnished, according to the calculations of Tournon, an amount of water equal to that which would have been delivered by a river ten metres* in breadth and two in depth, flowing at the rate of thirty (French) inches a second. According to the same authority, the quantity of water supplied by these aqueducts, every twenty-four hours, was one million three hundred and twenty thousand cubic metres,† an amount seven times greater than the Canal de l'Ourcq conducts to the city of Paris. Well might Frontinus, with a just glow of national pride, claim for

* A metre is 3,281 feet.

† 1,320,000 cubic metres are 349,635,000 wine gallons. The daily supply of Cochituate water to the city of Boston, during the year 1852, was 8,126,000 gallons, being about $\frac{1}{43}$ of the amount furnished by the Roman aqueducts. But the lake is able to supply about 17,000,000 gallons daily.

these works of noble utility an emphatic superiority over the pompous pyramids of Egypt, and even the unprofitable elegance of Greek architecture!

The wants of modern Rome are supplied by three aqueducts, the Acqua Vergine, the Acqua Paola, and the Acqua Felice. The Acqua Vergine, the source of which is near the Anio, a few miles from Rome, yields sixty-six thousand cubic metres of water every twenty-four hours, and furnishes thirteen large fountains and thirty-seven smaller ones. Among the former are the Fontana Trevi, the fountains of the Piazza Navona and the Barcaccia of the Piazza di Spagna. Its water is the best in Rome.

The Acqua Paola, which is brought from the Lake of Bracciano, about twenty-five miles from Rome, yields nearly four thousand cubic metres every twenty-four hours. The fountains of St. Peter's are supplied from this aqueduct.

The Acqua Felice, the source of which is near the ruins of Gabii, on the road to Palestrina, about twelve miles from Rome, yields twenty thousand five hundred and thirty-seven cubic metres every twenty-four hours, and supplies twenty-seven public fountains. The waters of this aqueduct, drawn from a marshy source, are inferior to those of the other two.

There are one hundred and eight public fountains in Rome. The private ones are much more numerous, and all are most copiously supplied with water by these three aqueducts. No city in Christendom is so bountifully furnished in this respect as Rome. Tournon calculates that the amount, in proportion to the population, is forty times greater than that enjoyed by Paris.*

The fountains in Rome are among its most delightful features: the stranger is never out of the sound of their dash and play. In the blaze of noon, they charm the eye with their silver spray and feathery foam, and, in the stillness of night, they soothe the ear with their

* I am sorry to say that the Romans do not avail themselves of their water privileges as they ought to do. Their streets are disgracefully dirty, and their persons do not show a very intimate acquaintance with the product of their fountains. Edward Lear, the artist, in the entertaining letter-press journal which accompanies his 'Illustrated Excursion in Italy,' relates that he heard, among the inhabitants of a town in the Abruzzi, of an Englishman who had been there many years before, and who was pronounced universally to have been insane, and on four distinct grounds; he often drank water instead of wine; he more than once paid more money for an article than it was worth; he persisted in walking even when he had hired a horse, and he always washed himself, sometimes even twice a day! Consistent and uniform cleanliness is, indeed, an almost exclusively English grace. Pure hands, pure teeth, and linen without reproach, are rather the exception than the rule on the continent.

It may be here remarked that the water in Rome is not distributed over the houses by pipes, but is drawn up from the fountain, or reservoir, in the court by a peculiar contrivance. A rope or wire extends diagonally from the window of the apartment to be supplied, to the fountain: along this rope a bucket descends, which, when filled, is drawn up by another rope passing through a pulley fastened above the window. This piece of rigging is one of the first objects which the traveller sees on looking out of the window in the morning, and, unless he be forewarned, he will be somewhat puzzled to make out its meaning and purpose.

monotonous music, that fills and overflows the silent streets and deserted squares. They bring the life of the country into the hot and dusty city; and the heart of the hills from which their waters are drawn seems to throb through their pulse-like flow. They present an image of perpetual youth, the more striking from its contrast with the venerable antiquity that is around them. By that law of association which is founded upon opposition, they are especially linked to the obelisks, as they are often brought together in local proximity. The obelisks are the oldest works of men's hands, but the fountains that play and murmur at their feet are expressions of that immortal youth which painters represent in their bodiless cherubs. The obelisks are heavy with the weight of forty centuries; but the fountains are a perpetual present — born with the upward jet and dying with the downward plunge.

In an architectural point of view, many of these fountains are in questionable taste: and, perhaps, most of them are open to the general criticism that the water is overborne by the stone, marble, or bronze, through or over which it flows. The frame is disproportioned to the picture. As I have remarked in another place, the fountains of St. Peter's are an exception to this general rule. In them, the architectural framework is comparatively simple, and performs no more than its proper function of displaying the water. On this account, these fountains, less striking at first than some of their more ambitious brethren, constantly gain in favor, and are in time preferred to all others, simplicity and good taste being sure to vindicate their claims in the long run.

Of all the fountains, the Fontana Paolina and the Fontana di Trevi are the most striking and the best known. The Fontana Paolina is on the Janiculum, in a conspicuous position, commanding a fine and extensive view. It is an imposing though not altogether tasteful architectural structure, resembling the gable of a church. Six Ionic columns support an entablature, and between the columns are five arches, the three central ones being of the same height as the entablature, while the two on either side are of smaller dimensions. Above the entablature is an attic with an inscription, surmounted by the papal arms in bas-relief, crowned with a cross between two blazing urns. Through each of the large arches, an exulting and magnificent stream of water leaps into a wide and deep reservoir in front; while in each of the smaller ones, a smaller jet descends through a carved dragon's head. The whole effect is very grand. The rushing streams of water are full of the untamed strength of the mountains. They bound and roar through the arches like young lions springing upon their prey. They form an image of boundless, vivid and unworn energies; while the broad, deep pool into which they fall, is equally expressive of tranquil and mellowed power. A considerable stream flows from the reservoir, which empties into the Tiber, furnishing moving power in its course to several small manufacturing establishments.

The Fontana di Trevi is in the heart of Rome. A mass of rocks is tumbled together at the base of the façade of an immense palace. In a large niche, in the centre of the façade, is a statue of Neptune in his car, the horses of which, with their attendant tritons, are pawing and sprawling among the rocks. On either side of Neptune, in a smaller niche, is an allegorical statue, and above the head of each of the statues is a bas-relief. All this is in bad taste, — an incongruous blending of fact and fable, chilled by the coldest of allegories; but it sounds worse in description than it looks to the eye. The water gushes up in sparkling and copious masses from the crevices between the rocks, spouts from the nostrils of the horses and the conchs of the tritons, and gives to the whole scene its own dancing and glittering beauty. The figures, human and animal, seem to be no more than men and horses enjoying their bath, and having a frolic at the same time. As we look, we begin with criticism, but we end with admiration. The several streams and jets are united, and, forming a fine cascade, flow over into a spacious basin, which is below the level of the piazza. This is the scene of the moonlight interview between Corinna and Oswald, as described in the sixth chapter of the fourth book of the novel; and, to this day, whenever the moon has touched the trembling waters with her silver rod, the mind's eye sees the shadows of the lovers resting upon the stream.

THE CASTLE OF ST. ANGELO.

The castle of St. Angelo — originally the Mausoleum of Hadrian — the Pantheon, and the tomb of Cecilia Metella, are the best preserved monuments of ancient Rome; and this is mainly due to the circular form which is common to them all. This form presents no salient point, either to the elements or the hand of violence, and offers no sharp corners for the teeth of time to nibble upon.

In nothing does the mind of to-day more differ from the mind of antiquity, than in the feeling in regard to the disposal of the dead. The emperor Hadrian, with the resources of a world at his command, erects a costly palace for his tomb, and lavishes upon it all the luxuries of sculpture and architecture. Such was the taste of those times. The Roman tombs were houses for the dead, ranged along the sides of travelled thoroughfares, as if the tide of life that rolled through them might be felt by the mute clay on either hand. The Roman clung to the substantial satisfactions of the earth. To be weary of the sun is a modern disease. To be buried in a place of rural seclusion seemed to add a new pang to the sting of separation, and deepen the loneliness of the realm of shadows. But, in our days, our dreams and wishes in regard to our final resting-place rarely take the form of architectural splendor. We seek to lie down upon the lap of the common earth, and not be thrust from her gentle embrace by stone or marble. We wish the shadow of silence to rest upon our graves, and that our own dust may pass into the life of nature and revolve in her cycles of renewal and decay.

The most familiar view of Rome embraces the castle and bridge of St. Angelo and the church of St. Peter's. A thousand times had I seen it in engravings, and it was with a feeling — half recognition and half surprise — that I beheld the real group in the smokeless air of a Roman December. The combination is so happy and picturesque, that they appear to have arranged themselves for the especial benefit of artists, and to be good-naturedly standing, like models, to be sketched. They make a picture inevitable.

The Mausoleum has undergone many changes, and a considerable portion of the upper part has been added in modern times; but its primitive appearance and original form were so remarkable, that it probably presents much the same aspect to the eye as on the day when the remains of the master of the world were committed to its trust. At first, it was merely a magnificent sarcophagus, devoted to no object but to honor the imperial dust that slept in its rocky core; but in the stormy centuries that swept over Rome, it played many parts and was dedicated to many services. With the first lowering of the clouds of war over the doomed city, it was turned into a fortress — a character which it has never since lost. No building in the world has probably lived through a more eventful existence, and none, if there were tongues in stones, could tell a tale of more varied interest. Before the modern improvements in artillery, its position and structure made it a place of so much strength, that its gain or loss often decided the fate of a civil contest. About the beginning of the sixteenth century, the covered gallery was built which leads from the palace of the Vatican, and in the middle of the seventeenth, Urban VIII. added a mound, ditch, and bastion, and a battery of a hundred cannon, cast from the bronze of the Pantheon.

For a long period, the castle of St. Angelo was the principal state prison of the papal government. Here, in the year 1537, was brought and confined the fiery-hearted Benvenuto Cellini, whose autobiographical memoirs contain not only a most amusing account of his own life, but present a curious and instructive picture of the times in which he lived. After narrating the circumstances of his arrest, he tells us — as if it were rather a noticeable circumstance — that this was the first time that he had known the inside of a prison, and that he was then in his thirty-seventh year; and, considering h's stormy temper, and that by his own showing he had committed at least one homicide, besides having been frequently engaged in duels and desperate brawls, we may well share in his surprise. His adventures in the castle, his account of the hypochondriac governor who imagined himself to be a bat, the courage and address he showed in making his escape, his unhappy accident in breaking his leg just as liberty was within his grasp, his reconsignment to prison, and his final deliverance — are all set down in his memoirs, in 'very choice Italian,' and done into very fair English by Mr. Roscoe.

To see the interior of the castle, it is necessary to have the permission of the governor. I went over it with a party of friends on a fine morning in January. We were received in a sort of guard-room, and committed to the charge of an inferior officer, who conducted us over the building with much civility. By torch-light, and through narrow passages which looked like shafts cut through a mountain of rock, we were led into the sepulchral vault, which is dimly lighted by two windows pierced in the massive wall. The masonry is of the most admirable description, and the blocks are like a solid, unbroken surface of rock. In passing to the top of the building, we were conducted through a spacious and handsomely furnished saloon, or drawing-room. A lady was there, engaged in some feminine occupation, and a nice little girl was practising upon the piano. Such a piece of domestic life was in agreeable contrast with the grim monotony and solemn gloom of the regions from which we had emerged. It was pleasant to think that a family heart was beating within those iron walls, and that children were romping over spots so long associated with crime, violence, and death. I did not omit to ask for the cell in which Cellini was confined, and it was duly pointed out to me. It was a small and dark apartment, neither better nor worse than most places of imprisonment.

The top of the castle commands a beautiful view of Rome; and especially of St. Peter's, which nowhere else appears to better advantage. The colossal statue of the archangel Michael, in bronze, which is so conspicuous an object from below, is the work of a Flemish sculptor, and was placed there about the middle of the last century, by Benedict XIV. He is represented in the act of sheathing a sword. The idea of a warrior-angel, even as presented to the mind in the magnificent poetry of Milton, is not exactly to our taste; but when we see this conception set forth in bronze, and magnified to twice the size of life, the incongruity of the two elements is strongly forced upon us. Nor is there any peculiar merit in the statue, as a work of art, to plead for the discord of the conception. And yet, for all this, there is no person who has ever been to Rome, who would not be sorry to hear that it had been thrown down by a stroke of lightning. It is so familiar an object — for it is visible from nearly all points, and one can hardly lift his eyes without seeing it—that it forms a part of our aggregate image of Rome; and the improvement would not be worth the change. It is like an ugly weathercock which we have been accustomed to look at every day in boyhood and youth; and, though in maturity or decline we recognise its ugliness, we protest against its removal.*

HISTORICAL HOUSES IN ROME.

There are many historical houses in Rome, and in spite of the changes which several of them have undergone, they are still objects of peculiar interest. In the Via delle Quattro Fontane, at the corner made by the street which leads from the Quirinal Palace to the Porta Pia, stands an unpretending house, conspicuous among its neighbors for the many green blinds with which the front is adorned. This, tradition points out

* The angel of the castle of St. Angelo reminds me of a singular trait—shall I say national, or personal?—in M. Beyle, the author, under the assumed name of Stendhal, of 'Promenades dans Rome.' In speaking of the angel and its attitude, he says that it suggested a fine reply to the French officer who was in command of the fortress at the downfall of Napoleon, and who, when summoned to surrender, said that he would do so when the angel on the top had sheathed his sword. All this is very grand; but mark the result. He did surrender, and the angel did not sheathe his sword. Interpreted by the event, this fine speech becomes a mere piece of vaporing bravado, which, one would think, a French writer would take particular care not to record. But M. Beyle is so taken with this mouth-filling gasconade, that the practical bathos of the conclusion quite drops out of his mind, and he accepts the brass-gilt sublime for the true metal.

as the house in which Milton was received and entertained by Cardinal Barberini, and where he heard Leonora Baroni sing; who, then enjoying the reputation of one of the first singers in Europe, little thought that her name would be immortalized by an unknown youth, from a remote region, a stranger and a heretic, from whose exquisite genius her voice called forth echoes sweeter than itself.

Sir Walter Scott, during his brief residence in Rome, had apartments in the Casa Bernini, in a street not far from the Piazza di Spagna, a house otherwise interesting as having been the residence of the artist whose name it bears.

In the Via Sistina, near the head of the splendid flight of steps leading from the Piazza di Spagna to the Trinità de' Monti, at a short distance from each other, are three houses which were occupied, respectively, by Salvator Rosa, Claude Lorraine, and Nicholas Poussin. A finer situation for an artist's residence can hardly be found than this spot affords, commanding, as it does, fine views of Rome, and with the best advantages of light and air. Poussin, especially, could never have looked from his window without seeing a varied and glowing picture.

The house which stands at the point where the Via Sistina and the Via Gregoriana unite their converging lines was built and occupied by the brothers Zuccari. It is a spacious dwelling, beautifully situated, and at this moment one of the most desirable habitations in Rome. It is also known by the name of the Casa Bartholdi, the Prussian Consul General of that name having lived there some years since. Under his direction, one of the rooms in the second story was painted in fresco by four distinguished German artists, Cornelius, Veit, Overbeck, and Schadow — the subjects being taken from the history of Joseph. They may be regarded as the first steps of that school of modern German art, which has reached so large a development in the frescoes at Munich; and, on this account, though the positive merit is not great, they will always be examined with interest, as being among the earliest works which breathe a purity and elevation of feeling, that makes us tolerant towards hardness in drawing and coldness of coloring. Upon the ground-floor — neglected and rarely seen — are some decorations in fresco by Federigo Zuccari.*

The great name of Raphael is identified with two houses; one in the Via Coronari, a street which runs in a westerly direction from a point just north of the Piazza Navona. Here he resided for many years, but

* This house is said by Mr. Dennistoun, in his learned and interesting 'Memoirs of the Dukes of Urbino,' to be still in the possession of the descendants of the Zuccari. It will always be recalled by me with peculiar satisfaction, as having been the residence, at the time of my visit in Rome, of a valued friend and countryman — a young man who, resisting the temptations of an ample fortune, devoted himself to the arts of painting and music with a perseverance and industry which could have been sustained only by high taste and sincere love of the occupation. His genial and graceful hospitalities will always be remembered with grateful pleasure by those who had the privilege of sharing in them — commended, as they were, by intelligent conversation in three languages, by the best of music, and that simple and cordial welcome which bound all his guests in a chain of common sympathy.

removed before his death to a beautiful palace, built by Bramante, in the street leading from the Castle of St. Angelo to St. Peter's, which is still standing. The house in the Via Coronari is abandoned to neglect, and left to take its chance of occupants, in a way that shows a strange insensibility among the people of Rome to the memory of that illustrious artist, who has done more than any one man that ever lived to make their city a place of attraction to strangers.

CAMPANA'S MUSEUM.

The museum of the Cavaliere Campana is full of interest and instruction to all those who are attracted to the subject of Etruscan antiquities. A large portion of its contents has been gathered from excavations made with great sagacity and perseverance by the Cav. Campana, upon his own estates. It is arranged in a suite of several rooms, and is, on certain days, shown to the public and explained either by the accomplished owner himself, or by some other competent person. The collection consists of vases, bas-reliefs, glass vessels, gold ornaments, household and military utensils, coins, statues, and sarcophagi. The glass vessels have been in some cases covered with brilliant prismatic colors by the decomposition of their elements, through time or some chemical agency. Some of the bas-reliefs are very fine, especially a series representing the labors of Hercules, showing evident marks of the influence of Greek art. Some of the works in stone are very rude, and have a family resemblance to those of Egypt. The household implements are curious. Among them is a pair of scales like the modern, with bronze animals for weights. There were also bronze strigils for the use of bathers, and metal mirrors, beautifully fashioned, turning on a pivot. The collection of vases was, as might be expected, large and curious: some of them embellished with designs of much beauty. The gold ornaments, which are arranged in glass cases, formed the most generally attractive portion of the museum. They consisted of head-bands, necklaces, chains, bracelets, rings, and broaches. The workmanship was very good, but not of such rare excellence as I had been led to expect. The gold seemed to be entirely pure, without any mixture of alloy. The whole collection was like a leaf torn out of a lost book of history. An Etruscan bracelet made for an arm that has been dust for thirty centuries, viewed by an American, in a Roman house built, perhaps, before his country was discovered! What a cycle, embracing the past, the present, and the future, does this statement include? Etruria had reached a venerable antiquity before Rome was born. Rome is to us what Etruria was to Rome — a monument and a memorial. Will there be for us a past as there is a present and a future? Will our civilization exhaust itself? Will the wild grape grow over the arches of the Croton aqueduct, and antiquaries dispute over the ruins of the Girard College?

THE COLLEGE OF THE PROPAGANDA.

This celebrated establishment was founded and liberally endowed by Gregory XV. in 1622, for the purpose of educating youths, born in heathen or heretic countries, in the principles of the Catholic faith, and sending them back as missionaries to their native homes. The death of Gregory followed within a year after, but his plans were zealously embraced by his successor Urban VIII. and the brother of the latter, Cardinal Antonio Barberini, by whom ample funds were bestowed upon the college. The building occupied by the institution in the Piazza di Spagna, a capricious and irregular piece of architecture, was erected by Urban VIII. from the plans partly of Bernini and partly of Boromini. It includes the palace once occupied by Vives, a Spanish prelate and ambassador, who bequeathed his whole fortune to the establishment.

At the breaking out of the French Revolution, this foundation, enriched by the bounty of devout Catholics all over Christendom, was one of the most powerful and wealthy in Europe. It enjoyed an annual income of three hundred thousand Roman crowns. It appealed to the unconverted by the written as well as the spoken word. Its printing-office was one of the finest in the world, and had the means of publishing books in twenty-seven different languages. But before the storm which uprooted so many venerable institutions, this college also bowed its head. Its property was diverted to other objects, by the government of republican France, after its armies had taken possession of Rome.* Its types were carried to Paris. Its pupils were scattered, and its doors remained closed for many years. The shepherd was smitten and the sheep dispersed.

* My authority for this statement is a French writer, M. Poujoulat, 'Toscane et Rome,' p. 281.

After the restoration of the Bourbons in 1818, the college was re-opened under the patronage and auspices of Pius VII. and Cardinals Gonsalvi and de la Somaglia. Some fragments of its former possessions were found and restored to it, and fresh contributions were gathered in various parts of Europe. Its resources are still inadequate to the expenses, and the deficiency is made up by assistance derived from similar institutions in other countries. It has now about sixty pupils at a time, upon an average, within its walls, gathered from all parts of the world. They wear a uniform dress, a long, black robe, or cassock, edged with red, and a red girdle. Two bands, like broad ribbons, depend from the shoulders behind, representing leading-strings, and typifying a state of pupilage. The scholars are not obliged to be at any expense; the institution paying the charge of their journey to Rome, of their entire support while there, and of their return to their native country. No one is admitted who is over twenty years old, and each one is obliged to give a pledge that he will devote his life to the dissemination of Catholic doctrines among his own people.

There is something very impressive to the imagination in this institution, which gathers under its comprehensive wings the natives of such numerous and distant lands, and sends them back to preach the same faith in so many different tongues. It is the centre of a circle the circumference of which clasps the whole earth. It seems to come, more nearly than any thing since the apostolic age, to the fulfilment of the Saviour's injunction, 'Go ye into all the world and preach the gospel unto every creature.' The faces of the pupils, colored with every shade of hue known to the human family, and shaped in every mould that ethnology has recorded, all wear the same expression of serious and earnest devotion. It looks through the dark mask of the African, the copper skin of the Chinese and Malay, and the blue eyes and blooming complexion of the Scandinavian. The breaking up of a class in one of our colleges is a serious occasion, though it is the first step in the race for the prizes of life ; but with what feelings must these young men take each other by the hand for the last time, when they are about to be scattered and dispersed, like the rain-drops which fall on the water-shed of a continent — to go forth to meet the chances of suffering and persecution, and to see each other's faces no more upon earth ! *

On the 9th of January, 1848, I attended the annual performances, or commencement, of this institution.

* M. Poujoulat, from whom I have before quoted, says, that in 1839 there were seventy pupils. He was informed that no one had ever desired to return to his home before completing his studies, but that this had occasionally become necessary on account of their health, though they had sometimes preferred to die at Rome rather than go back prematurely. He was told that no one recalled their homes with longing, or a desire to return, but those who went back most gladly were the natives of Lebanon, Switzerland, and Scotland ; even religious devotedness not being sufficient to efface the love of home, when that home is among mountains. The rector also said that pupils from Greece and America were peculiarly quick of apprehension, and that the Chinese and the Egyptians, especially the latter, were the reverse.

The apartment in which the exercises were held was of moderate size, furnished with rows of benches, which were closely packed with spectators, and a raised platform at one end, from which the pupils spoke. The places of honor nearest the stage were occupied by half a dozen cardinals, among whom was Cardinal Mezzofanti, whose extraordinary knowledge of languages naturally led him to take a lively interest in so polyglott an institution. As soon as the dignitaries were seated, the performances began with what we should call a salutatory address in Latin, pronounced by a youth whose name was set down in the programme as 'Sig. Enrico Van Buren di Limburgo.' His pronunciation was so unlike that to which my ear had been trained, that his Latin sounded like an unknown tongue. Then followed performances in fifty-one different languages and dialects, including Chinese, Persian, Arabic, Burman, Cingalese, Turkish, Ethiopian, Coptic, Hindostanee, and Syriac. They were generally very short, rarely exceeding five minutes; and as soon as one had concluded he was instantly followed by his successor, so that no time was lost. Several of the exercises in the oriental tongues were concluded by a few strains of singing or chanting, which afforded much amusement to the spectators. The strange countenances and the novel sounds made the whole affair quite entertaining, and many of the youths showed that their religious training had not entirely extinguished the spirit of fun. Many of the oriental languages spoken hardly appeared to be composed of articulate sounds, but to be made up of gutturals, aspirations, and a sort of faint shriek. A young man from Guinea, who was as black as it is possible for a human being to be, recited some Latin hexameters. His manner was excellent, and his hexameters smooth and flowing. The exercise in Portuguese was also by a colored youth, from Rio Janeiro, apparently the youngest of all the performers, looking not more than fifteen years old. He had a clear, ringing voice, and he spoke with great spirit and animation, producing a very general and hearty burst of applause. An English poem was recited by Sig. Eugene Small of Paisley, who spoke with a strong Scotch accent, and very rapidly. His poem, so far as I could follow him, was quite clever. In expressing his hope that Scotland might come back to the fold of the true Church, he used the expression, 'Religion's Bannockburn.' He also recited a poem in the Scotch dialect, in a very animated manner. Two of the performers, John Roddan and John Quin, were from Boston, and were the only representatives from the United States. One of them spoke in Hebrew and in the language of the aborigines of Chili, and the other in that of Paraguay. Of all the languages, the Spanish struck me as the finest in the quality of its sounds.*

* No ladies were admitted upon the floor of the room in which the performances were spoken, but a few of them were present in a sort of upper corridor or gallery, from which they could see and hear only imperfectly. Remembering the vantage-ground enjoyed by the female sex at home on all similar occasions, some of us were disposed to exult a little over those of our fair countrywomen who were present, on account of our temporary superiority. Rome being to so great an extent an ecclesiastical capital, women are often made to feel that they are judged by

THE PROTESTANT BURYING-GROUND.

The Protestant burying-ground is within the walls, near the pyramid of Caius Cestius. The general appearance is pleasing, but not striking; and it has that charm of silence and isolation which seems so appropriate to a cemetery. There are two enclosures, of which one is no longer used, having been filled up with graves. Within this latter are the resting-places of John Bell, the author of an excellent work on Italy, and of the poet Keats. The epitaph upon the monument of the latter is not in good taste, though striking and characteristic; for it is a vehement expression of wounded sensibility, unsuited to a tombstone, which should contain nothing transient or impassioned, but only simple statements and solemn truths. 'The malicious power of his enemies' means nothing more or less than unfavorable reviews by prosaic critics, who wrote with no personal feeling whatever, and were too ignorant of the essential qualities of poety to make their judgments wounding to a healthy sensibility.

The new enclosure is surrounded by a wall, and contains a small chapel. The monuments, which are numerous and mostly of white marble, are columns, obelisks, broken shafts, sarcophagi, or plain slabs, like

a monastic standard. From many places they are absolutely excluded, and the guide-books will make the cool announcement, that this or that spot is so holy that no woman is allowed to approach it. To women fresh from America, where they enjoy the chief seats in the synagogues, the change is somewhat emphatic; but I must do them the justice to say that they submit to their privations very amiably.

those of our own cemeteries. The moderate extent of the enclosure, not more than two or three acres, not only prevents any attempt to produce the effects of landscape gardening, but, for the same reason, the monuments are crowded together and disposed in a somewhat formal and rectangular fashion. But the monuments themselves are generally unpretending and in good taste, and the inscriptions often simple and affecting. The papal government, though it defrayed the expenses of the enclosure, will not permit any allusion to hopes beyond the grave to be carved upon the monument to a heretic; and, for this reason, the inscriptions in this cemetery merely set forth the virtues and graces of the deceased, and say nothing of the resurrection and a future life. Though a grave-yard of strangers, who have died in a foreign land, many of them friendless and alone, and nursed by cold and mercenary hands, is an object to awaken sad thoughts, yet the general aspect of this cemetery is soothing, and even cheerful. Every thing about it is kept with that exquisite neatness which makes it look like a bit of England transplanted to Rome. The turf even in the heart of winter is freshly green, and there is a profusion of flowers, both wild and cultivated. The common monthly rose of our conservatories grows here with great luxuriance, and is always in bloom, hanging its flowers over the monuments and filling the air with a delicate and spiritual fragrance. The sun lies long and warm upon its southern slope, and the hum of insects and the chirp of birds lend to the silence a pulse of life, while over it the blue sky of Rome bends like a benediction.

A very large proportion of the monuments bear the names of natives of England. The most interesting of these is a plain slab, which marks the grave of Shelley; that intense and ethereal spirit who was called away from earth before he had completed his twenty-ninth year — just as his wild visions were yielding to truth and experience, and his fervid mind was working itself clear by its own effervescence — a fact which should always be borne in mind, both in estimating his genius and forming an opinion of his character. A few Germans are also buried here; among others, the son of Goethe.

THE VALLEY OF EGERIA.

About a mile from the Porta San Sebastiano, is a pretty pastoral valley or gorge, as quiet and secluded as if in the heart of the Apennines. On one side is a wooded hill, crowned with the ruins of a temple of Bacchus; and on the other, at some distance, a gentle elevation on which there is a graceful structure which some call a temple, and some a tomb. This is the valley of Egeria — the spot where Numa met his shadowy counsellor. We must draw near to it in the spirit of faith, and let no clouds of doubt darken its tranquil beauty. We look around for the fountain by the side of which the lovers sat and talked, expecting to see something in unison with the simple grace of the tradition; a natural spring of pure water, clasped by a margin of green, overshadowed by a tree, and flowing away with a murmur so low as only to be heard in the pauses of speech. But such is not the fountain of Egeria, as we see it; and, unless he be forewarned, the romantic traveller will experience a slight shock of disappointment. The fountain, so called, is a vaulted grotto, scooped out of the hill-side, lined and floored with brick, with three niches on either side; and a larger one at the extremity, containing a mutilated statue. At this extremity, the water flows through a slender orifice, and is received into a small shell-like basin; from which, falling upon the floor, it glides down into the valley; and, swelled by tributes from the most soil, forms a rivulet, takes the name of the Almo, and finally mingles with the Tiber. The vigorous productiveness of nature has long struggled, and not unsuccessfully, with the intrusive works of man's hand. The walls are overgrown with moss and evergreen and trailing plants; all drawing an exuberant life from the water which oozes and drops around and upon them.

The legend of Numa is one of the most genuine flowers of poetry that ever started from the hard rock of the Roman mind. It is the symbol of a truth which psychology teaches and history confirms, that periods of solitary self-communion are necessary preparations for the claims and duties of active life; and that he who would influence men permanently and for good must draw alike from the depths of his own spirit, and from the inspiration of a power higher than himself, his elements of encouragement and support. The strength that comes from self-contest, and the patience that springs from self-discipline, alone give to the movements of the mind that tranquil power, which is most likely to win success because it is best prepared to encounter failure.

I visited the valley and grotto of Egeria with a party, most of whom were young and some of whom were beautiful. The painter who had wished to embody his visions of the airy nymph need not have wandered from the spot on that occasion; for we could have furnished him with faces which breathed alike the purity and the loveliness of that conception of the rugged heart of old Rome. Thus surrounded, it was not difficult to feel the genius of the place in all its power. But the mood of the hour was drawn rather from youth and hope, than from traditionary memories and the solemn shadows of the past. The silence was broken by playful speech and unromantic laughter; but the deep-souled Numa himself would not have frowned upon the smiles which were the natural language of hearts as innocent as they were gay. A shower that broke upon us as we walked home, was borne with invincible good humor, and such of us as were old enough to speculate could not but draw the moral that such cheerful spirits and such sunny tempers would go far towards making up a domestic Egeria.

END OF VOL. I.